PRAISE FOR
WILHELM LOEHE:

Erika Geiger narrates Pastor Wilhelm Loehe's story with accuracy, sympathy, and vigor. Avoiding hagiographic impulses she paints a picture of Loehe that allows readers to see his humanity in the multiple scenes of his life: a boy saddened by the premature death of his father, a struggling student of theology, a disenchanted pastor wondering if he had a place in the church, a grieving widower, an energetic preacher, a caring shepherd, a determined organizer of missions, and an aging and somewhat broken old man yet living in Christian hope. This first, full length biography of a key player in Lutheran history is accessible to lay audiences and appreciated by scholars.

—Prof. John T. Pless, MDiv
Assistant Professor of Pastoral Ministry & Missions
Concordia Theological Seminary, Fort Wayne
Co-President of the International Loehe Society

Those looking for a model for pastoral ministry with integrity do well to emulate Loehe. Few pastors have mobilized their congregations for mission as he. Steady, patient preaching and teaching, combined with scholarship, zeal for outreach, and all from a "pastor's heart," placed Loehe to move his congregation and ministry to have both a local and an international impact. Loehe's work was guided by a thorough commitment to Jesus Christ and a love for the church—the center of a vibrant service grounded in Scripture and guided by the Confessions—leading to liturgical renewal, social mercy, diaconal ministry, and missional outreach. May this fine translation help shape and inspire a new generation to do ministry in the spirit of Loehe.

—Prof. Mark Mattes, PhD
Professor of Religion and Philosophy
Grand View University, Des Moines, IA

Erika Geiger's masterful biography breathes new life into Wilhelm Loehe and his legacy for the mission of the contemporary church.

Through a splendid use of original source material the reader is immersed in the challenges and affairs confronting Loehe in his time. Moreover, one is able to trace how the commitments of Loehe continue to influence the mission of the church today. The excellent translation by Wolf Knappe makes this compelling book the standard work on Loehe's life in the English language.

—Prof. Craig L. Nessan, ThD
Academic Dean and Professor of Contextual Theology
Wartburg Theological Seminary

While there is precious little in this book about the LCMS, it is a must read for every LCMS Pastor and a strongly recommended read for the LCMS layman. The author is able to capture the essence of the theological formation of Loehe. His catechesis as a Confessional Lutheran had as much to do with the struggles in his life as much as it did with formal training at the University. From his lonely school days to his frustration with raising children as a widower, from his love for the Ministry to the struggles with sinful parishioners, from his love for the Lutheran Confessions to his position that the Confessions were not yet complete, from his care for the hurting and the lack of support for his deaconate; you can walk through his life and see how the "theology of the cross" was his only hope and stay. Loehe clearly was a man who understood the connection between faithful adherence to the Word and God and the Mission of the Church proclaiming the Cross of Christ.

—Pres. Brian Saunders, MDiv
President of Iowa District East of the LCMS

Until now, Loehe has been known to English readers primarily through his *Three Books about the Church*. Now, Erika Geiger's biography adds another important dimension to Loehe's witness to the Gospel of Christ: Loehe's own life as pastor, father, friend and teacher!

—Prof. David Ratke, PhD
Lenoir Rhyne University, Hickory, NC

WILHELM LOEHE (1808–1872)

The Life, Work, and Influence of

Wilhelm Loehe

(1808–1872)

By

Erika Geiger

Translated by

Wolf Dietrich Knappe

Concordia Publishing House • Saint Louis

Peer Reviewed

Published 2010 by Concordia Publishing House
3558 S. Jefferson Ave., St. Louis, MO 63118–3968
1-800-325-3040 · www.cph.org

English translation copyright © 2010 Wolf Dietrich Knappe

All rights reserved. No part of this publication may be reproduced, stored in a retrieval system, or transmitted, in any form or by any means, electronic, mechanical, photocopying, recording, or otherwise, without the prior written permission of Concordia Publishing House.

Originally published as *Wilhelm Löhe 1808–1872, Leben, Werk, Wirkung* © copyright 2003 by Freimund Verlag, Missionsstr. 3, 91564 Neuendettelsau, Germany
www.freimund-verlag.de

Cover artwork: Wilhelm Loehe (around 1850)

Manufactured in the United States of America

Library of Congress Cataloging-in-Publication Data

Geiger, Erika.
[Wilhelm Löhe (1808-1872). English]
The life, work, and influence of Wilhelm Loehe : 1808-1872 / by Erika Geiger ; translated by Wolf Dietrich Knappe.
p. cm.
Includes bibliographical references.
ISBN-13: 978-0-7586-2666-0
ISBN-10: 0-7586-2666-5
1. Löhe, Wilhelm, 1808-1872. 2. Lutheran Church--Clergy--Biography. I. Knappe, Wolf Dietrich. II. Title.
BX8080.L57G4513 2010
284.1092--dc22
[B]

2010042043

---

1 2 3 4 5 6 7 8 9 10 19 18 17 16 15 14 13 12 11 10

Dedicated
to the memory of my father,
Bishop Hermann Dietzfelbinger.
From 1953 to 1955 he was the Spiritual Director
of the Neuendettelsau Deaconess Center,
one of the successors of Wilhelm Loehe
who in many of his thoughts and concerns
felt very closely connected to Loehe.

By
Erika Geiger

TABLE OF CONTENTS

FOREWORD

Wolf Dietrich Knappe's translation of Erika Geiger's *Wilhelm Loehe 1808–1872* comes at just the right time for an English-speaking audience as interest in the Bavarian pastor, theologian, churchman, and missionary leader has been growing in the last decade. Controversial for his protestation against a diluted Lutheranism in the middle years of the nineteenth century, Wilhelm Loehe would become something of an enigma. Some dismissed him as a product of a conservative romanticism unsuitable for ministry in an enlightened world. Others saw him as one who was dangerously flirting with notions that would lead to an abandonment of the evangelical character of Lutheranism and a relapse into the worst of medieval Romanism. Acclaimed a heretic by some, hailed as a hero by others, Wilhelm Loehe played a significant part in the expansion of world Lutheranism including American Lutheranism by way of his support of the fledgling Missouri Synod and the leadership he would eventfully give to the Iowa Synod ultimately to become part of the present Evangelical Lutheran Church in America.

Wilhelm Loehe was a complex figure shaped by the Pietism and the Confessional Awakening of the nineteenth century. Erika Geiger narrates Loehe's story with overall accuracy, sympathy, and vigor. Avoiding hagiographic impulses she paints a picture of Loehe that allows readers to see his humanity in the multiple scenes of his life: a boy saddened by the premature death of his father, a struggling student of theology, a disenchanted pastor wondering if he had a place in the church, a grieving widower, an energetic preacher, a caring shepherd, a determined organizer of missions, and an aging and somewhat broken old man yet not without the lively hope of the heavenly Jerusalem.

The book is well-researched and documented but retains the character of a lively narrative, giving the reader glimpses into Loehe's humanity, his setting in nineteenth century Germany, and essential insights into his theology and pastoral work. Geiger's telling of Loehe's marriage to Helene and the grief he endured at her premature death certainly adds a profound "human interest" touch to the story.

An interesting addition to Geiger's work is to note that Loehe found the Ohio Synod's use of the distribution formula from the Prussian Union liturgy problematic. Here one might see my "Wilhelm Loehe and the Missouri Synod: Forgotten Paternity or Living Legacy?" in *Currents in Theology and Mission* (April 2006), 126–127.

Prior to the appearance of this book, Loehe's story has only been available in piecemeal fashion to American Lutherans in shorter books such as Erich Heintzen's popular treatment, *Love Leaves Home: Wilhelm Loehe* (CPH, 1973) or James Schaaf's introduction to the now out of print, *Three Books About the Church* (Fortress, 1969). Yet interest in Loehe is certainly growing in American Lutheranism as can be witnessed by several theological journals devoting separate issues to him: *Word & World* (Spring 2004), *Currents in Theology and Mission* (April 2006), and *Logia* (Holy Trinity 2008). The formation of the International Loehe Society in 2005 and the publication of David Ratke's *Confession and Mission, Word and Sacrament: The Ecclesial Theology of Wilhelm Löhe* (CPH, 2001) provides further testimony to a scholarly engagement of Loehe in North America.

Concordia Publishing House renders a distinct service to English-speaking Lutheranism through the publication of Wolf Dietrich Knappes's translation of *Wilhelm Loehe: 1808–1872* by Erika Geiger.

Prof. John T. Pless
Concordia Theological Seminary
Fort Wayne, IN
Co-President, International Loehe Society
Easter Tuesday 2010

PUBLISHER'S FOREWORD

We are excited to publish Rev. Dr. Wolf Knappe's translation of Erika Geiger's biography, as commended by the International Loehe Society. Loehe's story is important to share in English since the deaconess movement is growing outside his homeland of Germany. For example, the Concordia Deaconess Conference is experiencing annual growth. A former conference president, Deaconess Pamela Nielsen, notes that the deaconess movement has gained momentum in the burgeoning Lutheran churches of Africa (Kenya, Sudan, Ghana, South Africa), the Far East (India, Malaysia) and South America, as women in these churches seek training as deaconesses.

Loehe also continues to generate interest for his views on mission, ministry, and the doctrine of the Church generally. 2011 marks the 200th anniversary of his younger contemporary, C. F. W. Walther (1811–87), with whom Loehe corresponded and with whom he sometimes sharply disagreed.

Neither Loehe nor Walther sought disagreement. The infant Missouri Synod supported lay leadership against the perceived domineering clergy of the Prussian immigrants in Buffalo and Wisconsin. Some Prussian pastors were expelled from their congregations, which angered J. A. A. Grabau. Some pastors sent by Loehe took issue with this situation and the polity of the Missourians; these pastors may have swayed Loehe against Walther. Although Walther and his colleague, F. C. D. Wyneken, traveled to Germany in 1850–51 to attempt a rapprochement, this did not succeed and by 1855 the Iowa Synod formed. These events continue to generate interest as American churches consider their histories and their relationships to one another.

In sum, we believe this biography will help people understand Loehe as a dynamic servant of Christ, who continues to inspire church leaders, laity, and missionaries from his day to our own.

"Whatever is not intensive is not extensive"

FOREWORD TO THE GERMAN EDITION

"Wilhelm Loehe and Neuendettelsau, oh, of course!" Thus the conversation might run. "His deaconesses—unfortunately there are fewer of them all the time. And missionaries, really, they are pretty much outdated." Is that really so? Or was there something more to it? More than 130 years after his death Wilhelm Loehe (1808 to 1872) is as good as forgotten, except in his Franconian homeland.

Yet some things continue to speak on behalf of this man: How a small school for deaconesses could develop into a diaconal organization that would influence all of Europe, and how from a failed mission to American Indians a world-wide missionary enterprise, based on partnership, could be born. And the "Society for Inner Mission", founded by him in 1849, still exists and is active today. But what formed him spiritually, what he taught and what kind of Church he wanted is hardly of interest any longer. And whoever occupies himself with Loehe usually asks the question: "Was he not a narrow-minded confessionalist? A High Church person who fled from the social problems of his day into the liturgy?"

A collection of his sermons and writings does exist.[1] But the biographies are either outdated or out of print. "Who is Wilhelm Loehe?" Erika Geiger wants to answer this question in this new presentation in a way that is easy to understand. She distinguishes herself by making liberal use of the sources, so that Loehe himself is speaking. Nor does she hide the fact that even while he was alive he often raised people's indignation and that today we at times must ask critically what was important for him.

If you occupy yourself with Loehe you have to be prepared to have him ask you questions also, and that this Lutheran theologian of the nineteenth century questions much of what is being understood as Lutheran in the twenty-first century. Friedrich Wilhelm Kantzenberg discovered "Prodding for the present" in Wilhelm Loehe already 30 years ago. Some of these "scandalizing" jabs could prove to be beneficial. Not all details, but certainly some basic theological insights of Loehe are almost breathtakingly contemporary, if one discovers them. Here are just a few hints:

Today it is taken for granted that the modern Protestant can be a Christian even without a church. Loehe weighs in against this: A Christianity without Church is unthinkable! This says one who has suffered no less under his church leadership than have some today in a territorial church which threatens to be stuck in questions of structure, finances, and power. I need the Church because I am indebted to the Church for the Word of God. I need the Church because in it I can celebrate the presence of the living Christ. I need the Church because in the international character of the Church I experience fellowship with brothers and sisters that goes beyond all borders. In this quality it is more than just an officially organized church (*Amtskirche).* Do we have the courage to speak up for this spiritual vision of the Church against all frustration and disappointment with the (visible) church?

For some years now one could often hear that Protestant Christianity in Germany could do without the specific confessions of the Reformation and could restructure itself into a broadly common Protestant Church. Against this Loehe states: A Church without Confession is unthinkable, and the Lutheran Church does not have to be ashamed of its confessions. Thus, not a "church of confusion" but a "church of confession" (so Loehe). Whoever denounces this as narrow minded overlooks the fact of the degree this man was open to the heritage of the Roman-catholic Church, open even to a "continuing educational growth of Lutheranism" in doctrine (!) and piety, open to a change toward an ecumenical, newly formed, united Church. Do we have the strength to combine a Lutheran profile and ecumenical openness in a constructive way?

Much effort is being invested today in order to keep up the public structure of the State Church in Germany and to guarantee the public subsidies for the education and social work of the Church. Against this Loehe: The future does not belong to the State Church or to a "world-wide Protestant Church," but to a "voluntary Church." To even think about this seriously in our days is considered unethical. Nobody wants to gamble with what has grown over the centuries, even though everybody can see that changes are happening. It is hard to accept the fact that one cannot win majorities with the gospel and that the Church of the future could be a smaller "fellowship of believers" without any firm support from Berlin, Brussels or Strasburg. Do we have the faith to accept the role of a minority?

And finally: Our celebrations of Holy Communion have become more frequent and more joyful, services in which we celebrate our fellowship. That is beautiful, but not necessarily only good and right. Against this Loehe: In the mystery of the Sacrament of the Altar Christians receive the true body and the true blood of Jesus Christ, under the bread and wine. This should be expressed not only in the old communion hymns, but also in the prayers and in the words of institution. Certainly we cannot copy the sacramental piety especially of the old Loehe. But the Lutheran Eucharist should be celebrated even today not just joyfully, but also in humility, not just very informally, but also in a dignified way. It is remarkable that the Council of the Evangelical Church in Germany (EKD) found it necessary now to publish an "orientating help (*Orientierungshilfe)* for the understanding and praxis of Holy Communion in the Evangelical Church"—not only during Church Assemblies!—and that the leadership of the church of Wilhelm Loehe has installed a task force for the same theme. Are we willing to continue celebrating the Eucharist as a communion with the living Jesus Christ and a fellowship with one another?

All these are questions of the country pastor from Middle Franconia to us, questions which can raise indignation. Much in Loehe's thinking and acting shows tendencies based on the Restoration Movement, Romanticism, and Idealism. But he also stood for downright revolutionary ideas and wanted to see God's Word as the only source for service in the Church.

I wish that Erika Geiger's book will find many readers, who let Wilhelm Loehe lead them anew to this source. For "whatever is not intensive is not extensive."

Munich, on the Day of St. Michael 2003
Dr. *honoris causa* Claus-Juergen Roepke
Oberkirchenrat (retired)

TRANSLATOR'S PREFACE

In August of 2008 I attended the second meeting of the International Loehe Society which was held in Neuendettelsau. The Society had been founded three years earlier at Wartburg Seminary in Dubuque, Iowa.

During this meeting Erika Geiger gave a reading from her recent Loehe biography (Geiger, Erika. *Wilhelm Löhe 1808–1872, Leben, Werk, Wirkung*. Neuendettelsau: Freimund Verlag, 2003.). I was fascinated by it and immediately bought the book and read it upon my return home. I was hoping that it would be translated soon so that I could recommend it to my American friends and colleagues. When I found out that no one had undertaken this task so far, I started working on it myself with the encouragement of the author, also of members of the Wartburg Seminary faculty, especially Craig Nessan.

While I tried to be true to the original text, I found that there were a number of words or expressions for which there simply is no English equivalent. Just three examples:

Landeskirche. It is often translated as "State Church," but that has different connotations in English, where it implies that the State governs the Church. In German it simply means the Church in a particular "Land" or State. In Geiger's book it always means the Lutheran Church in Bavaria. I first thought of "territorial Church," but that doesn't sound quite right either. I finally decided to let the German word stand, but put it in italics.

The same goes for many titles and offices, such as "*Oberkonsistorium*." "Upper consistory" does not sound quite right, so I left the German word in italics.

Diakonie is another word that is hard to translate. It is not just the deaconate, which would mean the job of a deacon or a deaconess, but in the book refers to the sum total of all that is done in and through Neuendettelsau. Again, I leave it in italics.

I would like to express my sincere thanks to the people who did the proofreading and offered other valuable suggestions for the translation, especially Margaret Trinklein, Robert Hereth, John Pless and Marcus Baikie.

Many thanks also to Craig Nessan and other members of the Wartburg faculty for their encouragement, also to Albrecht Herzog of the Freimund Verlag, to Benjamin Mayes, Edward Engelbrecht, Amanda Lansche, Sarah Steiner, all of Concordia Publishing House, to Dietrich Blaufuss who tirelessly promoted this project from Germany, and of course to the author, Erika Geiger.

May the book in this new form be an inspiration for many in the English speaking world, as it has been an inspiration for me.

Wolf Dietrich Knappe
Wauwatosa, Wisconsin
May 2010

INTRODUCTION

In September of the year 1855 the young vicar Ernst Lotze was riding in the mail coach on the road from Nuremberg to Ansbach, listening to the cheerful melodies the coachman was playing on his horn. Ernst Lotze was on the way to see the famous Pastor Loehe who had started a school for missions and for deaconesses in Neuendettelsau. In addition Loehe was famous throughout Germany and beyond as the author of many theological publications.

The young traveler came from Thuringia. After passing his finals in theology he had worked in the Stoy educational institute. He was about to start as a pastor in his *Landeskirche*. But he didn't feel mature enough for this office, especially since he read Loehe's writings about the great importance of the ministry and what demands it makes. So he took heart and wrote to Pastor Loehe, whom he had admired from a distance, asking whether he could receive some practical experience under his guidance. Loehe, who happened to need a helper for his growing amount of work, had invited him for an interview.

Three hours by coach from Nuremberg lays the ancient cloister Heilsbronn. Here the vicar had to leave the coach and walk the rest of the way. For a good hour he wandered South, through a pleasant valley, and then up to a plateau. Behind a little forest of firs there was before him "the really unassuming village" Neuendettelsau. Of course, because of Pastor Loehe, it would eventually become so famous that letters from America sent to the old free city of Nuremberg often were addressed to: "Nuremberg, near Neuendettelsau."

The young wanderer walked on a dusty road past small, low houses. On the West end of the village, which is higher, he could recognize the large brick building of the deaconess mother house with a golden cross on its gable. To the right of the church sat the parsonage, a half-timbered building, not especially large, but in considerably better shape than the other houses. Through the low window the visitor could see a number of men and women gathered for a conference. He remained modestly standing before the door until he was noticed from inside and Pastor Loehe came out to greet him in a friendly way. The first impression remained unforgettable for Lotze, as he wrote in his memoirs:

> *Medium height, dressed very simply, but completely befitting, with his pastoral biretta in his hand so that the nobly formed face with the high forehead and penetrating eyes was brightly lit: Thus he stood before me. The deep, resonant voice, the simple, dignified attitude, the quiet harmony of his movements, the deep peace that he emanated—and all this completely natural, so masculine and so true . . .* [1]

The guest was asked to come in, and immediately to participate in the conference. Afterwards he was invited to the parsonage for a simple supper and was given his lodging. The next day Loehe met with him for two hours in order to get to know him. The mission inspector Friedrich Bauer, head of the mission school and long-time friend of Loehe, also took part in the interview. Both gentlemen became convinced that the vicar was the right co-worker for them. He was overjoyed; he wanted to laugh or cry for joy. As he left, Loehe and Bauer accompanied him to the end of the village. Then they separated, hoping for a speedy reunion.

With joyful expectation vicar Lotze started his new job in the beginning of 1856. He soon became Loehe's most important coworker. 1857 he became the co-rector of the deaconess motherhouse. But after 10 years of close cooperation with Loehe, Lotze asked, fairly suddenly, to be released to return to his Thuringian homeland.

What was the reason for this separation? Loehe had already thought of him as his successor. Did he feel pushed to the wall by Loehe's overwhelming personality, which would keep him from developing his own persona?

Loehe was a person about whom the opinions are divided. Many venerate him without reservations; others feel repulsed by him. For some he is a rigid Lutheran; others accuse him of leaning toward the Roman-catholic Church. Some saw in Wilhelm Loehe the best that the Bavarian Lutheran Church had to offer, others petitioned the church leadership to remove him from office. His deaconesses would go through fire for him. He was an inspiring teacher and a pastoral caregiver by the grace of God. People came from all over to

Neuendettelsau to his famous, richly liturgical services. And yet for many this village is a stone of offense.

Who was Wilhelm Loehe?

1

CHILDHOOD

Johann Konrad Wilhelm Loehe was born on February 21, 1808, a Sunday, in the house of a well-to-do burgher of the middle-Franconian city Fuerth. The tall corner house in the lower Koenigs Street had received an addition just before the birth of the child. It was connected with the main building with a wooden corridor. The child was born in one of the rooms of that new addition, where he was also baptized a few days later.

THE FAMILY

The father, Johann Loehe, was a "merchant of spices and salt,"[1] a respected and beloved citizen of the town. He came from a long-time Fuerth family which owned an inn "The Green Tree" in Gustav Street. King Gustavus Adolphus of Sweden lived there for a short time during his campaign against Wallenstein and gave the street its name.

In his younger days Johann Loehe, a strong and "handsome man," left his hometown and worked for several years as a waiter in Heilbronn. He returned, a self-made man "in stately splendor,"[2] as his son proudly reports. Johann Loehe married the oldest daughter of Waltheim, the mayor and a dealer in spices. When she died after a short marriage, he married her younger sister Maria Barbara. They had eleven children. She inherited the spice business from her father which Johann Loehe administered after his marriage.

Wilhelm Loehe's childhood memories reach far back. The well-known parental house; the bridge over the Regnitz where his nurse gossiped with other servants while the child on her arm looked at the river full of wonder; the mother who sang him to sleep as he sat at her feet. He occupied himself with sewing, just like his mother. In fact he wanted to become a tailor in order to be like his mother!

But the "first person in the world" for little Wilhelm was his father, to whom he looked up with great admiration. Johann was not only a city counselor but also captain of the militia. What a picture: Whenever the father in his captain's uniform stepped out of the door, he gave orders with his "lion's voice." There was nothing more satisfying for Wilhelm than to be noticed and praised by his father. Sometimes he was permitted to write something for his father and show how well he already had mastered the art of letters. Listening at the door, he learned how his father spoke appreciatively with his mother about the progress of his son.

At the age of four the child had already begun to read, so his parents arranged for private lessons until he entered school at the age of five. But Wilhelm didn't like it there; he trembled before the strict teachers and was "miserably bashful."[3]

It was much nicer at home where a large circle of siblings surrounded him. There were four older sisters, then Wilhelm, and after him came little brother Max, three years his junior, and finally the youngest little sister Sabine. Three sons and a daughter of his parents had already died as infants.

There were always enough playmates among the renters of the house. Wilhelm liked especially to "play pastor." In the courtyard he would climb on a chopping block that was supposed to be the pulpit, don an apron as a cassock, and preach with great seriousness to the assembled children. His mother watched, touched and thoughtful, and said to her husband: "There will be a pastor lost in him if you do not let him study."[4]

But Johann Loehe didn't want to hear it. It seemed "inappropriate favoritism" to prefer one of his many children by letting him study.

But one time, when the pastors of the deanery were assembled to the Synod in Fuerth's St. Michael's Church, he took little Wilhelm with him to the church and let him look at the "venerable assembly"[5] from the upper balcony. It was a view which made a deep impression on the child.

Grief and Worries

In the home of his parents Wilhelm felt well and safe, but he also shared in the suffering and pain that broke upon the family.

The youngest daughter, Sabine, died at the age of 14 months. With the little girl very sick, his mother sent the seven year-old Wilhelm out of the house. He was given a penny so he could buy a picture poster. He returned happy, only to find the house in mourning: His sister had died. Wilhelm threw himself weeping over the cradle. To his consternation he also saw his father crying, he who had always appeared so big and strong.

"Oh, so many sick ones from my youth on!" Wilhelm Loehe sighed later, looking back to his childhood. The illness of the oldest daughter Anna, who suffered from epilepsy, hovered over the family like a shadow.

Her little brother was filled with horror when he experienced one of her horrible fits for the first time. The parents also suffered under the awful condition of their daughter. One time Wilhelm watched his father walking back and forth in the room, crying, and heard him saying that he "would give his blood"[6] if only he could help.

But gradually Wilhelm learned to deal with the sickness of his sister. At mealtimes he sat next to her. If he noticed that a fit was coming, he took away any dangerous objects. When she was conscious again he marveled at her "heavenly cheerfulness."[7]

Death and Burial of Wilhelm's Father

In 1816 the family was hit hardest by the death of the father. At age 52 Johann died of an inflammation of the brain after a short sickness. On the day of his father's death, eight year-old Wilhelm was fetched from school. At home his mother and sisters were gathered around the deathbed, weeping and praying. His mother put Wilhelm's hand into the hand of the dying father and made him promise that he would not "bring shame over his dear father in the grave." Shortly afterwards the father expired.

Wilhelm basically did not understand what happened and refused to let all that mourning get to him. He seemed so uninvolved that one of his sisters hit him because of his "being so dull."[8]

On the day of the funeral, when the whole city was full of excitement, the child was overcome by the strange up and down of his feelings. In a black tail-coat which he was not used to, short pants and long stockings, he was supposed to carry a wreath behind the casket, together with two cousins. Someone gave Wilhelm a "funeral pretzel" which certainly did not go well with his suit.

All the funeral guests were assembled in the house when the sexton appeared in order to organize the procession to the cemetery. He fulfilled his duty with great solemnity. At other times Wilhelm knew him as a funny guy. In his stressed emotional condition the busyness of the master of ceremonies made him laugh out loud, which earned him disapproving looks. Quickly he reached for the wreath, put his pretzel in his pocket and walked behind the casket of his father to the graveside. There were many speeches in honor of the revered citizen and city counselor, who was "a blessing and a pillar of the city."[9] Suddenly the little son was overcome by wild pain and sorrow. He cried out loud and wanted to go to his father. He had to be restrained from all sides to prevent him from jumping into the grave.

It took a long time before he calmed down somewhat. But when the funeral procession was finally starting on the way back, Wilhelm suddenly was very hungry, pulled the pretzel out of his pocket and wanted to bite into it. The sexton was upset and forbade that unseemly behavior. He and several other participants of the funeral considered Wilhelm's behavior very strange. They did not understand how the child was so inwardly distraught.

For a long time Wilhelm could not get over the death of his father. One evening he was sitting in front of the house, looking down at the bridge over the Regnitz and watching the wonderful spectacle of the sun going down. Suddenly the thought occurred to him that, just as the sun goes down, his mother could also leave him as his father had, and that then he would be all alone. Frightened he ran in to his mother, hugged her with startling ferocity and cried out his terror. Big sister Anna took him by the hand and led him outside again. She showed him the "heavenly splendor," the stars which are already becoming visible, and described to him the "sapphire streets" of heaven on which he "someday will walk."[10]

CHURCH LIFE IN FUERTH

After his death Mother Maria Barbara Loehe took over her husband's business, having been a co-worker with him. Resolutely she pursued her old plan to let the gifted son Wilhelm study theology, "out of love for the ministry and the Church," as her son gratefully testified: "I owe her a thousand thanks. Who knows whether I would have become a Christian if I would not have become a pastor?"[11]

The Walthelm family from which his mother came was considered in Fuerth to be very pious, which was not necessarily a recommendation; for anything "pietistic" was regarded as suspicious by the government, and not appreciated by the Lutheran *Landeskirche.* After the time of the Enlightenment there was a wide-spread spirit of rationalism that read the Bible with the measuring stick of human reason; so there was little left of the Christian faith except some moral teachings. But here and there in the country small "islands of living Christian life"[12] were kept alive since the time of the Old Pietism.

Thus there was in Fuerth a small group of Herrnhuters who met in the house of the watchmaker Huber. They kept in touch with the Herrnhut Community of Brethren, which was founded by Count von Zinzendorf and which endeavored to bring about a renewal of spiritual life in the *Landeskirchen.* The brassfounder Walthelm, a relative of Loehe's mother, belonged to this group. When the government in Ansbach demanded to know whether the Herrnhuters were acting outside of the law, the Lutheran pastor Fronmueller answered in 1812: "They do not act against the Church but are faithful in fulfilling their duties, and they are not a secret society."[13]

Maria Barbara Loehe stayed with the Lutheran Church and regarded the old city pastor, who had confirmed her, with high esteem. She did look into the rationalistic ideas of her time, only to return to the faith of her parents. Besides the Bible, the old devotional books like Arnd's "Little Garden of Paradise" and Starck's "Handbook"[14] formed the foundation of her faith. Thus Wilhelm and his siblings learned a deeper and more convincing piety at home than in the religious instruction in school, which exhausted itself in teaching moral philosophy and ethics.

Many Jewish families were living in the lower Koenigs Street where Loehe's parental house was located. From childhood on he was familiar with their life and customs. The Jewish festivals played a special roll in the city of Fuerth, where almost a fifth of the people were Jews. During the Jewish festival of booths his mother sent little Wilhelm with his older sister Doris down the street: "Go, girl, show Wilhelm the booths!" This festival, during which each family built their own booth, always felt "homey"[15] to Loehe.

The Passover festival was also a part of Loehe's childhood memories, so that in later years he could say:

"I am not a Jew but I grew up among Jews and have seen all these things. From my youth on my mind and eye have been open to them, to all the liturgical glory which today's Jews still have . . . All that has often touched me."[16]

LATIN SCHOOL

Wilhelm's mother was very concerned that he should receive the best possible education. Before he was ten years old, in the fall of 1817, he was sent to the Latin School. He also received private lessons in French, Italian, English, Geometry and drawing. Some years before then he had received violin lessons. Finally there were also private lessons in Greek, so that the days of the twelve year-old were filled from morning to evening with lessons. Of course, that proved to be too much of a good thing for the delicate boy, so that they called him in Fuerth "consumptive Loehe."[17] What impressed most were his penetrating, deep blue eyes in a small face. He did not like sports, perhaps because of his weak condition. He enjoyed only running and jumping and soon gave up gymnastic lessons.

The violin lessons were not crowned with success either, even though Wilhelm tortured himself with them for more than ten years. The best part of these lessons for him was the view from the room of the teacher out on the "bleaching ground" at the river. Otherwise they were "painful hours." Wilhelm was always glad when he could carry his "little violin"[18] home again. He considered himself not musically gifted. But this did not lessen his longing for music and his love for it.

Among his fellow students Wilhelm was pretty isolated. He did not join in their pranks, but tried to prevent them. Sometimes he even told on his comrades to the teachers, "though tremblingly." No wonder that he was very unpopular in his class, and that he was attacked by "whole hordes."[19] It took some time before he learned to defend himself, but then he fought with such wrath that at times he even was victorious.

RATHER A PHARMACIST?

At the beginning of his time at the Latin School Wilhelm apparently was overwhelmed by all the many subjects. He didn't like school and didn't progress as hoped. His mother started to wonder if an academic career was perhaps out of his reach. Across the street there was the

"*Loewenapotheke*" where they liked to see Wilhelm and where he often spent time among medications and jars of salve. Perhaps it would be better for him to become a pharmacist? His mother talked with Wilhelm's teacher, sub-rector Kuechle, who was willing to give special lessons in botany to the boy. So the two of them walked out into nature to botanize. But while the student loved to roam through woods and meadows, he was not in the least interested in individual little plants and their parts. So sub-rector Kuechle discouraged the idea of becoming a pharmacist. Nevertheless he was convinced that Wilhelm was very gifted and affirmed his mother's original plan to let him study.

Without any apparent reason Wilhelm's educational career improved from his eleventh year on, so that he was soon at the head of his class. His splendid final report card, composed in the style of the times by the "royal Bavarian sub-rector Kuechle," certified that Wilhelm Loehe endeavored "with excellent industry in the glory of pure youthful morality to use the talent which Providence has granted him."

The student did not miss a single day during the whole school year, "even though his somewhat tender health wanted to become shaky." However, his teacher recommended "He should try to unfetter himself from his old anxiety when giving a report or an answer."[20]

Confirmation Class

By graduating from Latin School Wilhelm became eligible to enter the *Gymnasium*. But before then, between Easter and Pentecost of the year 1821, confirmation class took place. It lasted three hours every day and was taught by the three pastors of the main church in Fuerth.

Wilhelm looked forward to confirmation class, for Church meant a lot to him. Undeterred by the mockery of his class mates, he attended the service every Sunday. It started at 8 AM with the celebrating of Holy Communion. Only those members of the congregation who wanted to attend communion appeared that early. Most of the congregation came later for the sermon. But Wilhelm was so impressed by the celebration of the sacrament that he was there at 8 AM, even though he was not allowed to commune before he was confirmed. While the celebration took place up front, in the chancel, Wilhelm sat in the back of the nave, in the pew which he inherited from his father. Next to him sat only an old resident of the hospice, who also appeared every Sunday. Both of them listened, deeply stirred, while the old pastor chanted the words of institution. When the cantor started the "holy, holy, holy" they joined in with a loud voice, even though Wilhelm never sang along in school because he was afraid that he might miss the right note. But here, in the church, he felt free to join in. Participation in the sacramental service was for him a "great celebration and a joy."

What was it that attracted the boy in such a magical way, in contrast to his peers, so that he did not want to miss a single celebration of communion? Wilhelm Loehe experienced even at this age the great mystery and wonder that Christ gives Himself to His congregation in the bread and the wine, this meeting with the Holy, Incomprehensible.

Confirmation would allow him to participate in this mystery. Unfortunately confirmation class was a disappointment for him. Like in the religious instruction in school, only morals were taught, God was talked about only in a very general way, no Bible stories about the "acts of salvation of the Lord" were told, no Bible verses or hymns were learned. In spite of this Wilhelm's respect and love for old Pastor Fronmueller was not shaken. As always he impressed him through his "dignified appearance" and his "earnest praying."[21]

Confirmation

Confirmation took place on Exaudi Sunday, a week before first communion on Pentecost. Two hundred confirmands were streaming into the church. But no one had told them what would happen. Shortly before the celebration the sexton came to their benches and explained to them that he would give them a signal when they would respond "Yes." To young Loehe this seemed very inappropriate. With a certain rebellion he shouted out his "yes" even before the pastor had finished all the confirmation questions.

The week after confirmation was dedicated to the preparation for first communion. At home mother and sisters saw to it that the confirmand could find the necessary peace and quietness. It was customary to thank the pastor at the end of confirmation instruction, and to ask his forgiveness. One also had to ask the family for forgiveness.

Saturday before Pentecost the confirmands first went to the parsonage in order to receive, while kneeling, the blessing of the three pastors. Then they went to the church for private confession. As Wilhelm knelt before Pastor Fronmueller, in his excitement he forgot everything he was going to confess. But the gracious old gentleman helped him over this difficulty and dismissed him "richly absolved and blessed again."[22]

At home there were presents waiting for the confirmand: a book, a watch and six silver spoons. On the piano there were candles lit; mother had done everything to make this day of honor as festive as possible for her son. A walk out into nature was also called for. At this time of the year all the trees were blossoming, and there were flowers in the meadow down by the little alder woods near the river. The growing boy was moved to joy. He enjoyed a "festive time," like never before.

Then, on Pentecost, came the great event: first communion. In the morning Wilhelm's mother came to his room and handed him a letter in which she had written down all her thoughts for this day: "To my son Wilhelm, on June 1821, the day of his first communion."[23] Loehe always kept this letter as a precious legacy.

In confirmation class the teachers avoided a detailed explanation of the sacrament and let it go with just a "lukewarm instruction." Therefore Wilhelm did not know if he was going to taste blood from the chalice? But during the celebration of the sacrament all these questions and any anxious deliberations were pushed into the background. The thirteen year-old experienced the presence of God in a way he never knew before. All of his life he would remember this "experienced blessedness."

After the service the family sat around the table for a joyful festive meal. One could see the beaming joy of the confirmand so clearly that his sister Babette exclaimed: "Our Wilhelm will not see a day like this again until he receives his ordination!"

About 30 years later, remembering his first communion, Wilhelm Loehe wrote: "It is truly wonderful that there are such festive occasions as we have in the Christian Church. Praise God that I was born and raised in His Church!"[24]

2

TIME IN THE *GYMNASIUM*

Unfortunately there was no school for higher education in Fuerth, so that after confirmation Wilhelm had to attend "*Progymnasium*" in Nuremberg, the Melanchthon gymnasium. The founding of this old venerable institution at the Egidienberg goes back to the reformer Philipp Melanchthon. A few weeks before the end of the school year, in the summer of 1821, subrector Kuechle personally escorted his hopeful student to Nuremberg, where he was admitted to the lowest class of the *progymnasium*.

FUERTH AND NUREMBERG

In Nuremberg Wilhelm could stay with a relative of his mother, who received him warmly. Nevertheless leaving his family, and especially his beloved hometown Fuerth, which he loved with all his being, was difficult for him.

He knew its history, the legend that Fuerth had to thank Emperor Charlemagne for its origin. At the confluence of the river Rednitz with the Pegnitz, which comes from Nuremberg, the emperor tried to cross and was nearly swept away by the strong current. After a fortunate rescue by the ferryman, Charlemagne donated a little church at the Rednitz, which was dedicated to St. Martin of Tours. The village and later city of Fuerth was founded by this event.

For a long time, until the end of the 18th century, the place was a "bone of contention"[1] between three dominions: that of the Markgrave of Ansbach-Bayreuth, the Cathedral Priory of Bamberg and the Free City of Nuremberg. The three-leaf clover in the city's coat of arms refers to this conflict. In order to improve Fuerth in the rivalry with his famous neighboring city of Nuremberg, the

Markgrave of Ansbach ordered the erection of factories, which caused a tremendous influx of workers. Around 1800 about 13,000 people lived in the crowded space. Often more than 20 people lived in one house.

When Napoleon started to extend his conquests across Europe, all the ancient principalities were destroyed, and new ones were created. In 1806 Nuremberg and Fuerth fell to the newly founded kingdom of Bavaria, but the old rivalry between the two neighboring cities continued. Young romantic poets like Eichendorff, Clemens Brentano and Ludwig Tieck, had re-discovered the Middle Ages, and they were delighted with the picturesque city of Nuremberg with its ancient fortress, its city wall fortified with towers, and the beautiful gothic vaulted ceilings of the Sebaldus and Laurence churches. In contrast the "factory city" Fuerth appeared modern and ugly, therefore "American"[2] and was scornfully skipped by romantic tourists.

HOMESICK FOR FUERTH

Wilhelm Loehe felt completely the opposite. During his time in school in Nuremberg he could hardly wait for the weekend when he could go home, together with other gymnasium students from Fuerth. He wrote about this in his childhood memoirs:

> Every time home was greeted with great love, as if we had not seen it for half a life-time. In Fuerth everything was beautiful; Nuremberg was nothing by comparison. Truly, I will never again experience such happy, joyful walks in good company like the ones from Nuremberg to Fuerth, nor any more sad than the ones from Fuerth to Nuremberg.[3]

Home and family occupied a place of great importance in Wilhelm's life. Shortly after he started school in Nuremberg, he received the news of the death of his oldest sister Anna, who at the age of 30 succumbed to her grave illness. Her epileptic fits had worsened during the preceding weeks, so that one could hardly restrain her. "The whole house was often on their knees,"[4] Loehe reported later. He was praying for her delivery.

On August 6, 1821 Wilhelm again was walking the one and a half hours to Nuremberg. He was deeply in thought about his sister, until toward evening he suddenly felt the certainty that she has been delivered from her suffering. The next morning his presentiment was confirmed by a notice from his mother. Wilhelm wrote back: "My best mother! I felt more joy than pain when I received your letter . . . And why should I mourn? . . . If there is such a thing as a presentiment, I felt the hour of her death . . . "[5]

SCHOOL

The student Wilhelm Loehe was no more excited by the instructions at the Nuremberg gymnasium than he was by the city of Nuremberg. Even though he was always the first among his fellow students and completed all the work conscientiously, his heart was never in it. The main focus of instruction was the ancient languages, Latin and Greek. One read the classics, Virgil, Horace, and Homer and translated the works of the poets Sophocles and Euripides into Latin. Later Loehe opined that he was "much too immature"[6] to appreciate the beauty and the value of the classics. Instruction was mainly limited to the linguistic side, so that the contents of what was read often remained unintelligible to the student. Some things also seemed very offensive to him, especially the stories about the "dissolute living" of the gods in Greek mythology. Thus Loehe criticized that the teachers should have clearly expressed their opinion from "a Christian viewpoint," for "in the right light one can look at everything; but only few teachers can give that light."

RECTOR ROTH

To Wilhelm's great fortune such a teacher came to the Melanchthon gymnasium in the fall of 1821: Rector Karl Ludwig Roth proved to be a person of great importance for the growing young man.

He started out with "exceeding strictness, just the way one imagines a school rector," so that the "trembling and shy boy" withdrew anxiously. But the wise teacher had quickly noticed this special student. He respected and encouraged individuality in each person entrusted to his care. He appreciated Wilhelm's great diligence but warned against studying all night. He admonished him to take care of his body and not ignore sickness and weakness.

Rector Roth also succeeded in making the ancient authors come alive for his students. His enthusiasm for Tacitus was infectious and awoke in Wilhelm an interest in history. He was not the only one that was impressed by the humanity of this teacher, who was not in the least opposed to "modest contradiction" from the students. And if he believed that he did someone an injustice, he came down from his desk, shook hands with him and asked his forgiveness. The students did not consider this a weakness, but respected him all the more, because they felt that his heart "with all his strictness is mild and good."

For Wilhelm Loehe this teacher became his great model, especially when in the upper class, the so-called lyceum class, he became his home-room teacher. Without bashfulness Rector Roth confessed before his students his "decisive religiosity." With this he won Loehe's heart completely. With deep veneration the boy looked up to him. Loehe ordered every book and every magazine which the teacher recommended, "trusting in the goodness of his mother"[7] to come up with the money.

On the other hand Rector Roth often looked at the student Loehe with concerned sympathy. He asked himself why this highly gifted young man was so bashful and lonely and why his fellow students rejected and mistrusted him. With all his good qualities Loehe should have been a better influence on the class!

One day, before the beginning of instruction, the rector heard wild noises coming from the classroom and yanked the door open. Inside there was a riot with much shouting. Only Loehe and the boy next to him did not participate. The rector walked up to the two and reprimanded them because of the noise. When they indignantly assured him that they had taken no part in the ruckus, the teacher replied: "That's exactly what I criticize. You prefer a better behavior for yourselves and let your fellow students rage without making use of your reputation."[8]

But in spite of all the efforts of his teacher, Wilhelm Loehe could not be enticed to come out of his reserve. The rector did not get through to the real cause of his oppressed and withdrawn personality. The growing young man suffered under the restrictions of the school. His exceptional mental gifts were hampered, frustrated by the monotony of the school's daily routine. Later he expressed the opinion that "had he been treated more freely according to his special gifts, this would certainly have helped him to a more harmonious development."[9] In spite of his reverence for Rector Roth, school in the long run became an unbearable prison.

The fact that the Rector thought very highly of Loehe but at the same time was worried about him, because of his suspected lack of social contact, can be plainly seen in the evaluation in Loehe's final report card in the fall of 1826:

> He is a young man of great endurance in all his work and is animated by a completely honest and firm will for the Good. Because of this he has developed his many gifts in an excellent way and has achieved great success in all subjects, with the exception of mathematics where he received the grade "good." He leaves the institution with the praise due to a totally blameless and exemplary student. It only seems necessary to warn him that in his strict isolation he should beware of becoming an indoor scholar in the most narrow sense of the word.[10]

THE "*STUBENBURSCHEN*"

(BOYS THAT SHARE A LITTLE ROOM OR CHAMBER)

But outside of school Loehe by no means led the life of a hermit. Two families of friends in Fuerth, whose sons also went to the gymnasium in Nuremberg, expressed an interest in having Loehe, who was a few years older than their sons, take them under his wings and supervise their studying. His conscientious way of living and his excellent academic accomplishments made him seem to be a very appropriate "tutor." So Loehe moved out of the room with his relatives and lived, beginning in April 1823, with his *Stubenburschen* (chamber boys, or room-mates),[11] as he called them. Together they rented a room from the widow of a professor. One of Loehe's protégés was Gustav Ritter, who showed great love and affection for his older friend.

Even during vacation, which, of course, was spent at home in Fuerth, Loehe worked with his young friends with grammar and reading of the ancient authors. Besides that he continued his own studies. During the fall vacations of 1825 he kept an exact diary of the texts they worked through. At the beginning of the new school year he showed it to Rector Roth, who was impressed and wrote at the bottom: *Optimam viam non discendi modo, set etiam vivendi te invenisse puto*. ("I believe you have found not only a very good way to learn, but also to live.")[12]

But of course during vacation and on weekends at home one did not only study. Loehe visited his comrades and friends in the neighborhood, or they gathered at his place. At such times one would hardly recognize the serious and silent gymnasium student. In this circle he came out of himself and took a leadership role. His happy temper and his high spirits came to light.

There were excursions, for instance, to the estate of a manor house. "Bring along your umbrellas," Loehe ordered the day before the trip, and the friends appeared with gigantic umbrellas, made of white linen, that were the fashion in those days. "In an emergency a whole family can find protection under them."[13] The monsters were opened in any kind of weather, and the group marched across the market place through the city, and out into the country, attracting great attention. Out there, on the estate, they bought fresh milk from an old peasant woman, to enjoy with the sandwiches they brought along.

For a while Loehe also visited the theater regularly with his friends. However, during his later school years this kind of entertainment seemed "too vain" for him. Instead he suggested romantic evening walks and showed a special preference for walking in the cemetery from where one could see "the flickering lights of the city and the flickering stars in the sky." Not all his friends would come along on such spooky excursions. One night Loehe dragged one of his friends who seemed especially afraid "by his neck to the grave of his father," in spite of his howling and screaming.

Such stories gave the young Loehe in his home town the reputation of being a "crazy guy."[14] This did not displease him. As was befitting his age, he wanted to distance himself from the self-content citizens. While they walked the streets in well-fitting, tight dress, according to the prevailing fashion, he intentionally ran around in wide loose-fitting garments. Based on his strict religious convictions he believed he was right to walk past people whom he considered unbelievers without greeting them, even if they were well-known to him and belonged to respected honorable circles.

HIS POSITION IN THE FAMILY

His mother tolerated these puberty-related attempts at rebellion by her son and let him be. Why should she chide him when his teachers were always full of praise for him and he always brought home first prizes? And also when apparently he was determined to enter the ministry, thus fulfilling her most ardent wish? Nor could she criticize the fact that he had a heart for the poor and indigent, even though she sometimes moaned when Wilhelm gave away clothes and linen, or when he gave away his Christmas cookies to the poor.

Besides that, at home he enjoyed a very esteemed position as the oldest male family member. His sister Lisette was eleven years older than he. For her wedding to the merchant Hoeppl from Fuerth Wilhelm wrote a letter with good wishes and admonitions and closed with these words: "My sister! Your father is long dead. I, as the oldest son bring you his blessing in addition to that of your mother."[15]

His other two sisters also married during Wilhelm's time at the gymnasium, so that only the two sons remained at home with their mother.

In 1825 Wilhelm's sister Barbara Conradina, called "Babette" married the son of the old city pastor Fronmueller, to the great joy of her mother. Babette was the liveliest and most social among the Loehe daughters. As a young girl she had many girl-friends from the best families of the city. With them she visited "places of entertainment" and dancing festivals, something that was not commonly done in the Loehe family. This inclination toward worldly joys awoke the sarcasm of her younger brother Wilhelm who tried repeatedly to spoil her fun, "to destroy her beautiful hairdo, ridicule and perhaps even spoil her ball-gown, to tease her to the core..."[16] But he had to admit that Babette was in no way superficial but had many intellectual interests and occupied herself with belletristic and spiritual literature. After her wedding she moved with her husband into the city parsonage, where she not only kept house but also took care of her aging father-in-law.

The youngest sister, Dorothea, closest in age to her brother, was born four years before him. Since their childhood he was "very close"[17] to her and this closeness would last a lifetime. She also married in 1825, Eberhard Schroeder from Fuerth, a maker of eye-glasses, widower of a girlfriend who died at an early age.

So all three sisters started their households in their hometown. They kept in contact with their mother, and Wilhelm visited them as often as he could whenever he was in Fuerth.

Traveling to Pommersfelden and Bamberg

In September 1825 Wilhelm Loehe undertook a 5 day journey by foot, together with friends, from Fuerth via the famous Baroque castle Pommersfelden to Bamberg. It is the first time that he left his home to see strange places. An exact diary of his journey preserves his impressions. Joyfully the friends wandered via Eltersdorf to Erlangen. Then a heavy rain came down, the wanderers got lost in a forest, and finally, completely drenched and exhausted, they reached the town of Dechsendorf. There they rested a while. They arrived in Pommersfelden late in the evening. The young traveler was not very impressed by the scenery they came through during the rain: "I have seen nothing in this entire region which I had not seen better, or at least equally beautiful back home."[18] However, he chided himself that this attitude was very "narrow." In Pommersfelden, viewing the gorgeous "palace"—he meant the castle Weissenstein, built by Dientzenhofer—he had to admit: "I have never seen a more beautiful building."[19] He described in detail the famous staircase and the splendid collection of paintings.

The friends stayed a day in Pommersfelden and then continued wandering to Bamberg. Here it was difficult to find a place to stay. Finally the "White Lamb," the third of the inns they looked at, had the right rooms for the friends and "cheap food."[20]

In the evening and on the following day they toured the cathedral city. For the young people who came from protestant surroundings, their first encounter with Catholicism felt strange and repugnant. On the road Loehe already took offense at the crosses and figures of saints by the wayside. He called them "caricatures." When he entered the cathedral, he found the interior beautiful "without the tasteless decorations of the Catholics." But "everything has been decorated with nonsensical pictures." The votive gifts, "fingers, legs, hearts etc made of wax" are disgusting to him. "My Lord and God, how is Your religion mocked by these orthodox believers!"[21]

Conscientiously the three friends also visited all the other attractions of Bamberg. Loehe gave his greatest praise to the "hospital for the sick": "You citizens of my hometown, learn to have some public spirit. Such a house is excellent. The cleanliness that prevails in all the corridors, halls and rooms is extraordinary."[22]

Before the return trip the friends decided to visit a high mass in the cathedral. Loehe was impressed by the sermon, but not by the high mass of the canons in their rich vestments, which seemed to him "rather a stage-play than a worship."[23]

They walked back to Fuerth via Forchheim and Erlangen. Loehe concluded his notes: "I am happy to finally finish this travelogue and to come back home. No one reading this short description could guess how much joy I feel over coming home again! I do not have anyone whom I could trust with the quiet blessedness within my breast, with my suffering and all my feelings . . . My soul is related to You, O God. Give me strength to lift myself up to You, because I have not found a single soul that is striving upward, whose friendship I would not have to reject."[24]

The diary shows in part a still very youthful, immature world view, with judgments that are abrupt and one-sided, fitting his age. In the last sentences there is a new sound, a sound of great longing to be understood, longing for true friendship which the young man apparently does not find with his friends whose "empty talks" on the way often bored him.

Spirit of Romanticism

This longing increased during the following months. From April to August 1826 young Loehe again kept a diary in which he tried to give expression to his feelings and perceptions. He lived in a time that was incredibly fruitful in literature: The romantic poets were marketing their books, but Goethe's later works were received by the public with enthusiasm.

Loehe read whatever he could get his hands on, from Goethe's "Iphigenie" to the "glorious Egmont"[25] and many others. But he felt especially attracted to Jean Paul: "With veneration and love I daily approach the reading of my favorite authors, but to none of them with such sacred awe as Jean Paul Friedrich Richter. This true poet, to whom a fiery ray from above has opened the world on the other side, is truly a priest . . . "[26]

Loehe formulated his longings very much in the style of Jean Paul:

> The evening comes and my longing increases. What do you really demand, O ardent longing in the quiet breast? Bring about the dusk, O evening; night, spread out your mantle over the resplendent earth . . . O that I am still glued to the earth . . . Carry me, carry me, imagination on soft wings to the graves of my hometown. There I want to sit and cry because among all people I have found not a single man, not a single woman that could love my soul unreservedly![27]

Closeness to nature, friendship, love—the great emotions of romanticism fill the heart of the young man. He is looking for a soul mate to whom he can dedicate and open himself completely.

Gustav Ritter and His Family

Could it be that Gustav Ritter would be such a friend? For years he had solicited the friendship of Loehe, who was his senior. Loehe would have loved to believe it. In his diary he dedicated exuberant passages to Gustav: "But you . . . do not forget that in your breast is the only heart that Wilhelm can lie down on . . . our hands are joined together until they will only wilt and fall apart in death!"[28]

But when Gustav transferred to the gymnasium in Ansbach in the fall of 1826, Loehe knew that the younger man could offer him the friendship he longed for. In Loehe's judgment Gustav was a faithful soul, "not a great intellectual light, but in his character a very valuable young man."[29] For his farewell Wilhelm wrote to him that he would always love him, "as a brother loves his younger brother, but he would not and could not feel the same way, live the same way, think the same way that Gustav does." He still felt alone with his "heart full of holy, flaming feelings," his "thinking and meditating" always seeking a person with whom his "spirit finds an echo."[30]

True, Loehe did not want to give up the friendship with Gustav—there continued a busy correspondence between the two of them. But he counseled the younger one to find a friend of his own age and gave him advice for his life.

Wilhelm, the mentor of their son, was a highly respected guest and warmly welcomed in Gustav Ritter's family in Fuerth. He looked at the three sisters of his friend with interested and searching eyes when he thought of a "future wife" and came to this conclusion: "All three of them stand before a severely judging male eye in the pure light of feminine dignity."[31] Very thoroughly he went over their good and bad sides. Johanna, the youngest, finally was his "last hope."[32]

In May of 1826 Johanna was about to be confirmed. Wilhelm felt himself moved back five years to the time when he himself was "looking forward to confirmation and first communion." Was Johanna going to experience a similar blessedness as he did?

"O my beloved girl whom I will not let out of my sight, if only you would receive a permanent impression on your heart, so that the vanities of this life will not touch you, or at least will not pull you away!"[33]

But the festival, to which he had looked forward with "holy joy," brought him bitter disappointment. The confirmands showed a silly behavior. "These children, a bad bunch" came "laughing" to the church. "Johanna also did not come up to expectations. She was spoiled for me during the celebration and afterwards . . . " Deeply sobered Wilhelm decided to withdraw from Johanna. What remained for him was his faith, his trust in God. He encouraged himself: "May love be your blessing, now and in all eternity: the love of God, and once you are mature the love of a friend, or spouse. Do not let Johanna out of your sight and your heart either. Watch her and have the courage to throw away your love for her if she does not earn your respect."[34]

SEARCHING FOR GOD

Where is God, and how can you find Him? For the 18 year- old Loehe this was the most important question and it occupied him constantly.

"My God . . . let me find You in nature, on earth and in the starry skies, in people and in the worm . . . let me move freely in the fields of knowledge, found my faith on reason and on conviction . . . Who would despise me if I am that way, who dare to chide me to my face if I carry such virtue in my bosom?"[35]

Loehe showed himself here as a child of rationalism; he wanted to understand and recognize God through reason and wanted to come to Him by way of a virtuous life. He would like to hold in his hand the "scale of reason" and the "scale of virtue." The "blessed Spirit"[36] should enlighten him and he implored the "eternal Being" for "clarity, rescue from the uncertain floating of inclinations and ambitions."[37]

The "holy religion" was "strength and comfort" for him: "O, whenever there is a mystical twilight in my soul and I raise myself to the great thought of God and immortality, all ecstasy (*Schwaermerei*) leaves me and I am filled with the Spirit of God!"[38]

Surprisingly the name Jesus Christ appeared very little in these notes. Christ was "pattern and example"[39] for this young man who was striving for virtue and perfection but had not yet become of utmost significance for him. Loehe fought a hard battle for the "sanctification of his soul." He did recognize very well that his life was "filled with mistakes and sins and lack of many things and pride." He saw his "deep rooted vanity, the weakness in his faith."[40] Crushed, he stated: "I wanted to lift my life out of base vulgarity, and I am still very dissatisfied with myself!—God, God! I have a foreboding of severe testing from Your hand!"[41]

Many years later Loehe would read these diaries again and be confounded as he wrote: "There stand the sins of my youth. What a visionary I was, and how I hid my sin, yet I lived in it. But the Lord did not give up on me even then . . . "[42]

GRADUATION

On September 6, 1826 Loehe passes his finals—the *Abitur*—the day that he had anticipated for a long time. Finally he could leave the "hateful city" Nuremberg which had surrounded him with its "tormenting walls" for five years. Finally he was free from the "snare of the fowler" and could rise "to the heights where dwells pure joy!"[43]

Before beginning his studies he once more took a short trip, this time by himself, to Frankfurt and the Rhine River. This "pilgrimage"[44] was made especially to see the poet Goethe in Frankfurt. But to Loehe's disappointment Goethe was not at home and therefore the traveler soon left. He went on to Mainz, then upriver toward the South via Worms, Mannheim, Heidelberg, and home again.

3

STUDY OF THEOLOGY

With great hopes and expectations Wilhelm Loehe began his theological studies in the nearby university city of Erlangen on November 5, 1826. The fact that he wanted to study theology was taken for granted. It had been his goal from his early youth, and he knew that would fulfill a deep-felt wish of his mother. After the restrictions of his time in school he hoped that this would be the beginning of a new, free life. But this freedom in no way meant that he would enjoy his life like his fellow students and take part in excursions and drinking bouts.

His teacher Rector Roth, who knew that Loehe tended to be a loner, had urged him to join a fraternity. So Loehe joined the "*Bubenreuther*,"[1] albeit with inner reluctance. At his first visit to the fraternity house the arrogant behavior of the Senior repulsed him. During the course of the following months he so seldom appeared at the fraternity that after half a year, to his great relief, he was excluded from the society.

"I don't belong there," Loehe opined. "I only followed the advice of Rector Roth against my inner voice. So it's alright that I was kicked out from the place where I should never have gone."[2]

Academic freedom meant something totally different for this goal-oriented young man thirsting for knowledge: Finally he could use all of his time, select the lectures and seminars according to his own inclinations and interests, and pursue his own studies. This resulted in a minute-by-minute planned schedule for the week. Every lecture-free hour was dedicated to prepare for the classes, to follow up afterwards, and to continue studying the ancient and modern languages. During mealtime Loehe usually read some travelogues.

THE PROFESSORS

Of the numerous Erlangen professors Rector Roth recommended especially Professor Christian Krafft to his students—to the astonishment of Wilhelm, who was just a beginner. Krafft was known as a "mystic"—not a complimentary description at the time of rationalism. In spite of this Loehe obeyed his old teacher and visited Krafft's lectures on the Letter to the Hebrews and on History of Missions five times a week. He did this even though these lectures were really meant for students in the upper classes, not for beginners. Krafft, "a very pleasant and exceptionally pious man"[3] had the greatest influence on Loehe. He became for him "a permanent blessing, a leaven which should permeate my life more and more,"[4] as Loehe gratefully confessed later on.

For Loehe had to endure difficult inner struggles during this first phase of his studies. They dealt with the question of faith, and whether he was worthy and called as a preacher to proclaim the gospel of Jesus Christ and His work of redemption. Depressed, he wrote to Gustav Ritter: "Oh, I can by no means confess that I am truly hungry and thirsty for the forgiveness of my sins, as you seem to believe! That exactly is my misery! But the Lord does listen to me eventually and I know . . . He will let me become a true preacher of the faith . . . If only I would be accepted! I will go, even if He sends me to the heathen!"[5]

Professor Krafft became his spiritual guide during this inner conflict. He was also pastor of the Reformed congregation in Erlangen, and by the grace of God he truly cared for the souls of his people.

Loehe, deeply moved, reported to his sister Dorothea how the professor started a lecture with the petition of the Lord's Prayer: "Hallowed be Thy Name!" Then, moved to tears, the professor spoke of the importance of that lecture for himself as well as for the students. The listeners felt that he was totally committed to the great task of "picturing for them the foundation of faith in a scientific lecture." He had asked the students to "permit him, as a friend, to talk about himself." Loehe concluded his letter:

> But now these tears, and under tears the most humble confessions of how he was led, outwardly and inwardly to his personal convictions, which are mocked by so many. He

> described how he was estranged from the true life in God and in Christ, his struggle to believe, which no one is spared, his blessedness now, and the peace which no one knows until he has received it . . . After such a struggle and such experiences one must teach dogmatics. These other faithless professors—I have no idea any more, how they can still teach dogmatics. I want to listen to a person who has been led in such a way, who speaks from his own experience and thus knows it for certain.[6]

Christian Krafft, who could speak so openly to the students about his experiences with God, belonged to the Erlangen circle of the so-called "Revival movement,"[7] which at this time was starting in many places in Germany to counter the wide-spread rationalism. From this came Krafft's reputation as a "mystic" and the hostility of many of his colleagues.

Another academic teacher who became important for the young Loehe was Karl von Raumer (1783–1865), professor of mineralogy and natural history, who was called to Erlangen in the spring of 1827. He also had experienced a religious revival and joined the circle around Krafft in Erlangen.

Karl von Raumer had an open house and heart for his students. Loehe soon belonged to those who met frequently at his house. He always revered Karl von Raumer as a fatherly friend, and even after his graduation remained closely connected and frequently corresponded with him.

Loehe noted carefully that Professor Krafft and Professor von Raumer confessed their Christian faith not only with words but also in deeds. Before his time in Erlangen, Raumer had founded an educational institute for poor and neglected boys in Nuremberg, the oldest "rescue house" in Bavaria. In Erlangen he joined the Mission Society for the support of the Basel Mission, which Christian Krafft had founded.

Such an active Christianity, these diaconal-missionary activities, immediately made sense to the young Loehe. He was attracted to the work of Pastor Johann Friedrich Oberlin who had died in 1826. Oberlin not only gave spiritual care to the impoverished peasants in the isolated Steintal in the Vosges Mountains for 59 years, he also watched over their bitter existence and helped them decisively in many practical ways. He urged them to build roads and bridges, advanced agriculture through new methods of planting, founded a school for infants and for knitting, and sought to improve the education of the older children. Loehe was greatly interested in this man who recognized his task and went at it with determination in the place where he had been called. In 1827 the Erlangen Professor Gotthilf Heinrich Schubert, who also belonged to the Revival movement, published a book about Oberlin with the title: "Trends from the life of Johann Friedrich Oberlin." After reading it Loehe wrote enthusiastically to Gustav Ritter: "Oberlin is a precious mirror for us. May the Lord make us into such capable tools in His hand."[8]

He immediately ordered six copies of the book to pass on to others.

THE MISSION SOCIETY

Wilhelm was eager to do something of his own as well. In Fuerth, where he spent every weekend, he started a "reading society" among his relatives and acquaintances. Newly published Christian writings and tracts were to be read and discussed there. In order to be continually provided with new literature, Loehe got in touch with Pastor Heinrich Brandt in Roth, who was the leader of a society for the distribution of Christian literature and the editor of the "Homiletical and Liturgical Correspondence Journal." Loehe also joined the "North German Society for the Distribution of Christian Literature."

In that same year, in the fall of 1827, a second group under Loehe's leadership started meeting in the home of his sister Dorothea Schroeder. Inspired by the example of Professor Krafft, Loehe started a "Mission Society" for the support of the Basel Mission. The participants were almost the same as those of the "reading society": Loehe's brother, sister, and a few friends. It was almost a "family missionary circle." Stockings were knit and baskets were woven. When they were sold, the money was given to the mission. The society also collected donations in order to purchase missionary tracts, which were read and then passed on.

The nineteen year-old student was sensible enough to realize that the mission institute would not be able to support a missionary with the income of the society. But perhaps others could be inspired to start a similar "little circle!" A practical person by nature Loehe knew how important small beginnings are. This can be clearly seen in the "mottos" which he gave to the mission society:

> "Even if we do little, we do it out of a good heart!
>
> Even if we do not do much, we do something!
>
> If we do something small, its blessing can make it into something big!
>
> Even if we do little for others, it can serve for our own awakening!
>
> Even if we are only few, nevertheless He is in our midst! Amen! Amen!"[9]

Missions would not be the only beneficiaries of the society's support. The members themselves, Loehe opined, will have the greatest benefits, because through their activities, they will progress in their spiritual life. Loehe also foresaw that people would upbraid him and his circles as "Pietists": "But that can't be avoided. We are looking forward to it, for what will happen to us will only be what happened to Him in His earthly existence."[10]

What was young Loehe's relationship to the Pietists, the pious ones who were so maligned in his *Landeskirche*? He also wanted to be pious and, like his family, be counted among the "pious ones." But in his opinion piety should not so much be based on feelings, as he once wrote to his friend Gustav Ritter who "was by nature exceptionally emotional." "This can easily degenerate into an impure, hypocritical state when it is applied to religious matters."[11] The right measuring stick for piety should always be the Bible: "Even in its language it gives the right guidance." The language (of pietism) should remain free of "sugar-coated expressions"[12] and should rather take its orientation from the old church hymns, for instance from the verses written by Paul Gerhardt.

In Berlin

All his intensive study of theology and his work in the mission society did not deceive the student Wilhelm Loehe. When he was honest with himself, he knew that he had yet to find the certainty of faith, the "peace in Christ" in spite of his "overflowing longing."[13] Most of his fellow students, except a few faithful friends, considered him "a hard, strict, envious, hostile person who spoils his own youth."[14] The impression derived from the fact that Loehe was attempting to come nearer to God through a strict conduct of his life beyond reproach. And yet he realized "that, the way I am, I will never be fit to be a servant of God." Was he still tied too firmly to his family, his home town, his home? Did he cling too much to that "which is not God?"

Realizing that it was high time to separate himself from his mother and his siblings, Loehe decided "to go into the wilderness for a while," to leave everything that he "loved and did until now" in order to totally give himself to his "dear Master."[15]

The "wilderness" for him was the city and the University of Berlin where he decided to study for two semesters, together with a friend. He wrote to a Berlin acquaintance and asked him to find a "modest little room"[16] for the two of them. On April 7, 1828 the two friends started out on foot. They walked via Bayreuth and Hof to Ebersdorf in Thuringia. There they found a congregation of the Herrnhut Brethren. The two friends inspected their institution, the prayer chapel, and the cemetery with interest. Then they continued via Gera to Leipzig, where they looked for the grave of Christian Fuerchtegott Gellert in the cemetery of St. John's church. They walked on via Bitterfeld, Treuenbrietzen and Potsdam until finally, on April 18, they arrived in Berlin.

With his usual passion Loehe immediately threw himself into studying at the university. One can find famous names among the professors, like Hegel, Schleiermacher, Hengstenberg, Neander and Gerhard Friedrich Strauss who at that time enhanced the reputation of the University of Berlin. However, philosophy was not Loehe's strong suit. After attending a lecture by the famous philosopher Friedrich Hegel, he wrote perplexed into his diary: "nothing understood, or nothing to understand."[17]

He visited the theological classes of Hengstenberg, Strauss and Neander much more diligently. The lectures of Schleiermacher he only audited now and then. One day he sat way up front, staring attentively at the teacher. There was something so inquisitive and penetrating in Loehe's look that the professor got irritated and turned away.

The professors of theology not only gave their lectures, they also preached on Sundays in the various Berlin churches, so that an ambitious student like Loehe could sometimes listen to three or four sermons in one day. Schleiermacher's way of preaching at first seemed strange, but then he learned to appreciate him. But he was most deeply impressed by the practical theologian and cathedral preacher Gerhard Friedrich Strauss. He wrote to his sister:

> This afternoon I was in church with the genuinely pious, evangelical Strauss. For an hour and a half he only preached. The sermon was precious. Only now do I perceive what a real pastor is, from what he has to say about religion." Hopefully Loehe continued: "I come ever closer to my redemption: I am redeemed, but my faith is still a baby in diapers.[18]

Strauss's lecture "Pastoral Catechetics" also helped him to clear his thinking about "things pietistic." Strauss had "enlightened" him about the "right differentiation between mystics and pietism on the one hand, and that which is evangelical on the other hand." Therefore he wishes that in the mission circle in Fuerth, to which he corresponded regularly, "Lutheran simplicity" should rule. That means that he does not want these meetings to become "hours of private edification." Edification belongs to the Church. In the mission circle and the reading society Luther's writings should be read. The young theologian occupied himself with them intensively at this time and recommended to the people in Fuerth: "I advise you all repeatedly (to read) Luther's wonderful, spirit-filled writings."[19]

One should also read mission reports and historical writings as well as the Bible, "but without any explanations." So Loehe learned to see the difference between "edification" and "Christian entertainment."[20] What was always held against the pietistic circles was the separation from the Church into small groups that had their own interpretation of the Bible and their own edification. They easily fell under the suspicion of separatism and came into conflict with State agencies, which forbade "secret meetings."

In Berlin also, Loehe was interested in diaconal enterprises. He became acquainted with the "institution for voluntary employment of the poor" of Baron von Kottwitz, who was in contact with the Herrnhut pietism. Kottwitz had provided occupations and income to hundreds of the poor and unemployed. In a former military barrack he put at their disposal material and implements for spinning flax and for weaving. Living quarters, a dining room and a hospital also were included in this institution which had won the approval of the Prussian king and was supported by him. Every evening there was a devotion. Loehe was once asked to take over an "hour of devotion," which he gladly agreed to do.[21]

BACK IN ERLANGEN

Loehe had planned to study in Berlin for a whole year, two semesters, but his mother called him back after just half a year. Loehe was torn between regrets about leaving Berlin, where his studying had brought him "undeniable benefit,"[22] and the realization that his stay in Berlin was a heavy burden on the family treasury. On the other hand there was the joy of returning to his beloved homeland sooner than expected.

In the fall of 1828 he took up his studies in Erlangen again. Now thoughts concerning his professional future came into the foreground. Looking back on his semester in Berlin he recognized the fact that he was not made for an academic career. Apparently for a while that had seemed enticing to him, but his "mental gifts" did not seem sufficient to him. He had to give up "the former dream of a learned life," At the same time he realized that the call of a Lutheran pastor is "the most difficult profession, sometimes a curse and sometimes a blessing."[23] Loehe declared: "This office is my call and my science!" The remaining time of study he now wanted to use primarily for the direct preparation for this future life.

"For most of my life I have lived without a love for my calling, just like a wooden saint, not like one whom Jesus purchased with His precious blood and wants to sanctify with the Spirit! How necessary it is now to use the short time of two years very carefully for serious preparation!"[24]

According to the new rules of the church authorities, Loehe could have passed his examination for candidacy as early as the fall of 1829 but he didn't feel in the least prepared for this: "I cannot pass an examination at this time just yet."[25] When it turned out that he was also lacking the practical seminars necessary to complete his university studies, he was not unhappy. He still had a whole year for his own studies and the preparation for the examinations. He could live at home in Fuerth during this year and attend the seminars in Erlangen from there. As always, he enjoyed being with his family and did not long for outside invitations and amusements in any way. He wrote to a friend:

> Please excuse me from that meeting to which you have invited me in such a friendly way, dear brother. I am like a monk; my family is my order . . . We often went through suffering together; therefore we also like to be joyful together. Often we sit together for hours without talking. But then, when we part, we have been exceedingly happy.[26]

Now and then the student was asked to preach. This gave him sobering insights into the average day of the individual pastor. He reported angrily about Pastor Beck in Burgfarrnbach, for whom he preached on a Sunday: "It would have been better if he would have become a *Beck* (a baker) than a pastor. Beer, bread, food, enjoyable parties is all he talked about."[27]

Loehe was strict and uncompromising—with himself and with others. He denied himself everything that could somehow look "worldly" and would keep him away from God. As an example, he wanted to sell the (books) of formerly so beloved poets, like Goethe's "Faust" and "Iphigenie."

But how were things with his faith, with the certainty of salvation which he had longed for? Why was it that, in spite of his virtuous life, he still felt so lost?

He complained about his "arrogance," he knew that even into his "prayers vanity flows," and often he could not feel any love for his neighbors:

> There is just no good will toward others within me, only envy and hatred—selfishness above and below, also in the middle. That's because I still have no faith and no love for Christ. Without the love of Christ, it is impossible to love the brothers . . . This proud heart is just never satisfied. Where there are weaker people, I lead the discussion; where there are stronger ones, I keep silent so as not to betray my innermost thoughts. And if anyone speaks a reasonable Christian word, I hate him.

That mercilessly Loehe characterized himself in his diary. Arrogance, pride, envy—those are the leading faults which the highly gifted young man, full of despair, found within himself and could not overcome. Gradually he came to the conclusion:

> Thus I become ever more convinced through my own experience that by my own strength I cannot fulfill the divine will. The Lord promises to dwell within us only by faith. That is a divine certainty and cannot be confirmed through any human feeling . . . We should never believe that we could possibly please our Savior by decorating ourselves, so to speak, with a little repentance and good works . . . [28]

Just how much his pride and vain glory stood in the way of his seeking Christ he repeated clearly in a letter to a friend:

> To be "saved by grace" is often hard for me. To be saved through repentance would be easier and more comfortable for my heart that seems to thrive on misfortune. But I thank my God who has taught me these days—something which my proud head imagined to know all along—that one has to be and remain a sinner and be saved by grace. "Here comes a poor sinner who would like to be saved just for the ransom." It is the greatest miracle in heaven and on earth that one has to be born anew . . . [29]

Thus Loehe wrote this in November of 1829. His letter reveals that he had found the long sought-for peace in Christ, the "ability to rest in the wounds of Christ."[30] He did not experience a sudden conversion; rather a prolonged process of suffering and struggling brought him to the certainty of redemption by grace alone. Of course he would not be spared countless struggles and temptations in the future. Yet, once he had this experience of faith it would never be lost again. He was not looking for a "sweet feeling," as he wrote to Gustav Ritter, but for the peace of God which "passes all understanding, all feelings, all efforts of the will."[31]

At this time Loehe felt very close to Luther in his inner life and read much in his writings. To Luther also, this "saved by grace" brought the peace of God. For Christmas 1829, Loehe received Luther's works in eight large volumes as a Christmas present from his mother and his brother.

The Finals

Loehe was newly relaxed as he looked forward to the final examinations. "I don't care about a wonderful report card." But now he felt called to proclaim the Gospel. His "only wish" was to "start out as a vicar."[32] He was willing to take any position; he would even be ready to go to the German congregations in the Caucasus. But the closer he came to the examinations, which he was supposed to take in Ansbach before the consistory, the more doubtful he became. Some wild rumors were circulating that many of the candidates would fail the examinations. One who "fell through" reported that in Ansbach there are some "crazy benches." Loehe comforted himself with the thought: "If I fall through, I am going to the heathen."[33]

His concern about not passing the examinations was totally unfounded. Loehe noticed that the written requirements were easy for him and that he could write them in half of the prescribed time. The examiners praised his "deep knowledge" and graded him with a II with the remarkable addition: "Very good, nearing excellent."[34] Only the sample sermon which he had to furnish for the examinations invoked a suspicious protest from the consistorial examiner in charge. For three quarters of an hour he went over the sermon critically with Loehe. He called him "the leader of these mystics" and claimed that he was "worse than the worst Herrnhuter."[35]

What kind of reproach was this? The text of the sermon was 1 John 1:8: "If we say we have no sin, we deceive ourselves and the truth is not in us." The thoughts in Loehe's sermon were founded totally on the Lutheran doctrine of the justification of the sinner by grace alone. Even revived and born-again Christians are still dependent on grace and must not consider themselves as sinless. One can feel here the young preacher's personal experiences with pride and self-righteousness when he emphatically admonishes all to have insight into their own sinfulness.

What would the consistory of the Lutheran *Landeskirche* have to criticize in this sermon? For those who adhered to the rationalistic orientation of the Church the doctrine of the redemption of the sinner through Jesus' death on the cross had been completely pushed into the background, since it did not agree with reason. Sermons of the Enlightenment were rather occupied with everyday problems, appeals to morality, and questions of education or of the economy. Pastors were "publicly hired teachers of virtue,"[36] so to speak. Someone like Loehe, who spoke of the supernatural reality of God, was immediately stamped as a "mystic," one who speculates about other-worldly things. And since the Herrnhuter were suspected of the same thing, anyone who espoused this viewpoint was immediately thrown into the same pot with them. Many friends of Loehe read this sermon after the examinations and judged it totally differently than the strict examiner. Karl von Raumer, for instance, opined that he would hire Loehe immediately if he were the patron of a congregation.

4

YEARS OF WANDERING AS A VICAR

So Loehe passed the examinations with honor and was given this recommendation: "Qualified for higher office in the Church."[1] But at the same time he got the reputation of being a "mystic and a pietist" because of that sermon he prepared for the examinations. This would be a great hindrance for his future career as a pastor.

As a candidate of the Bavarian *Landeskirche* and as a Fuerth resident he was referred to the Ansbach consistory. Since the so-called "*Protestantenedikt*" of 1818 there were three such consistories in Bavaria. This edict put down new rules for the relationship between church and state. Besides Ansbach there was Bayreuth, and also Speyer for the Rhenish Palatinate which belonged to Bavaria. These consistories were subject to the *Oberkonsistorium* in Munich. The president of the *Oberkonsistorium* was the legal expert Friedrich von Roth, the brother of Loehe's rector at the gymnasium in Nuremberg. This *Oberkonsistorium* in turn was subject to the ministry for the interior and therefore also to the catholic king of Bavaria who valued the fact that he was to be considered the "supreme bishop" of all Protestants also; for ever since Luther's days the German princes were also the supreme bishops of their *Landeskirche*.

For the candidates that were examined in Ansbach in 1830 there were no positions available. They had to expect a long waiting period. True, Dr. Fronmueller, the old pastor who had confirmed him, would have loved to take him on as his vicar. But some of the Fuerth dignitaries—Loehe calls them the "Fuerth big-shots"[2]—prevented this by petitioning the *Oberkonsistorium*. The consistory listened to them and denied the request of the city pastor: As a newly graduated candidate he lacked experience. Besides that, his examination sermon was too mystical. As a consequence many pastors were suspicious of him, so that they didn't trust him with pulpit supply.

"This is my greatest cross," Loehe complained in a letter, "that I have to remain silent . . . For no pastor in the area lets me preach; they immediately refuse me. When the bells are ringing, my heart cries out because I am not allowed to preach . . . "[3]

A few other opportunities for employment also proved to be futile. Loehe tried to be patient and to bow under the will of God and to use the time for theological studies.

UNTERLEINLEITER, AUFSESS, FUERTH

Early in 1831 a ray of hope appeared on the horizon. Leonhard Kuendinger, pastor in Streitberg in beautiful "Franconian Switzerland," advised his friend Loehe in a letter that the congregation Unterleinleiter had just become vacant. Until a new pastor is called, an interim pastor was needed and Loehe should apply immediately. Right away he hastened to Streitberg and to the consistory in Bayreuth, where he received permission to work a few weeks in Unterleitner until a decision concerning an interim pastor had been reached. Happy and eager Loehe started preparing his sermons. He also took over teaching in the school, since the teacher had died shortly before then.

The congregation was very pleased with the new preacher. Representatives of the congregation asked him to sign a petition to the consistory, requesting him to be the interim pastor. Loehe reported to his sister:

> Among the Leinleiters I am one of the smaller people. It looks amusing when four such big, smart and handsome men of these mountain people stand next to your beloved, skinny little brother. Today two of those four have walked at the crack of dawn through the snow and across hills and valleys to Bamberg in order to personally deliver the petition. You can see, not only do I love these people, they return my love, even though I preached pretty sternly.[4]

The dean of Bamberg invited the famous candidate to preach in Bamberg. He approved of what he heard and promised the congregation that among the four applicants for the position of interim pastor he would give a special recommendation to Loehe. Unfortunately the consistory in Bayreuth was of the opinion that a candidate who had just passed the examinations should not be an independent vicar. An additional attempt by the congregation in Loehe's favor, applying directly to the *Oberkonsistorium* in Munich, was also without success. In mid-February Loehe was back in Fuerth and again forced to put out feelers in all directions.

During the Easter season he helped out a friend who was pastor in Aufsess, not far from Unterleiter. There he got to know the lord of the manor Hans von Aufsess and they became good friends. Baron von Aufsess wanted to start a new congregation in nearby Wuestenstein. As a *patron* he had the right to do so. Until then Loehe should gain more practical experience under the supervision of an older pastor. His friends told him he should ask the older and sickly pastor Ebert in Fuerth for this kind of help.

In a very polite letter Loehe offered his services as a helper to the old gentleman, not as a "complete vicar," but only in cases where "age and sickness make it difficult for you to carry the burden of your office."[5] After thinking about it for a while—as mentioned before, Loehe did not have a good reputation in his home town—Pastor Ebert accepted this application. He had many admonitions for the young candidate to guard against "mysticism." Loehe in turn accepted the admonitions very humbly. He promised to show his sermons to the pastor for his approval before every service, but as to his faith, he would not deny it.

Ordination

There was not much opportunity to work effectively and independently under Pastor Ebert in Fuerth, but at least working there gave the candidate the chance to be considered for ordination. His mentor wrote a petition on his behalf. As a result Loehe received the invitation to come to Ansbach on July 25, 1831 to be ordained there. This admission to the sacred office had an overwhelming significance for him. From then on he would celebrate the day of his ordination every year, just like a spiritual birthday.

Like everybody who was ordained before him Loehe signed the book of the ordinands. With great firmness he declared the Augsburg

Confession and the confessional writings of the Evangelical Lutheran Church to be the basis of his faith. Then he continued:

> With the help of God I will preach the true doctrine and not be silent until the Lord Himself will receive me, His peace-loving soldier, from the church militant to the sacred silence of the church triumphant! I also will seriously endeavor to let my life be like my faith, lest while preaching to others I myself would be disqualified. (1 Corinthians 9:27)[6]

On the day of his ordination Loehe had a special experience which he reported many years later. While reading his Bible in the morning, he prayed for a special word from God for himself on this important day. As was the custom in pietistic circles at such an occasion, he opened his Bible and without looking put his finger on a certain verse. It happened to be Isaiah 6:8–10:

> Then I heard the voice of the Lord saying, "Whom shall I send and who will go for us?" And I said, "Here am I; send me!" And he said, "Go and say to this people: Keep listening, but do not comprehend; keep looking, but do not understand. Make the mind of this people dull, and stop their ears, and shut their eyes, so that they may not look with their eyes, and listen with their ears, and comprehend with their minds and turn and be healed."

Loehe was irritated and thought: "This is not a fitting text. I don't like it, I must have another one."

He tried it a second time and came up with Acts 28:25–27, exactly where these verses from Isaiah are being quoted. Now the young man was shocked, but in his "stupidity," as he called it later, he thought: "Now I don't like the text for sure. I have to have another one." He dared a third attempt and found John 12:38–41, where for the third time, he read the same passage from Isaiah. Loehe concluded his report: "At that I felt that this was a solemn moment, especially since the John passage continues: 'Isaiah said this because he saw His glory, the glory of Jesus.' Now I had enough and I said: 'Here I am, Lord, send me!' "[7]

Loehe's mother and two of his siblings were present at the ordination service which took place in the St. Gumbertus Church in Ansbach. Also present was a friend and fellow pastor, Leonhard

Kuendinger, whom he urged especially to come since he knew "how one feels"[8] at such an occasion. The ordination with the laying on of hands was performed by Pastor Fuchs, a member of the consistory. He was assisted by two other pastors. Loehe returned to Fuerth deeply impressed by this sacred act and the grace of God which he had felt and experienced as a confirmation of his faith.

Being a vicar under Pastor Ebert was not very pleasant. The old gentleman was jealous and watched out that the young vicar would not gain too much influence in the congregation. He was permitted to preach during the early Sunday service, to bury some of the poor, and to teach confirmation class to a woman who was converting. But that's all he was allowed to do. No wonder he felt dissatisfied. Often he was called to a sick-bed. It became known in Fuerth that he always came immediately when a sick person asked for him, and that he was able to comfort and assist, even when death approached. Once, when the relatives of a dying person remarked that his visit was meaningless, since the patient no longer was in his right mind, Loehe answered: "But my mind is still intact. I can still learn something from this patient."[9]

He had learned how much of a blessing for himself he could gain during these visits. But he noticed that Pastor Ebert was not happy with these activities and considered them interference with his own pastoral rights. It eventually became clear to Loehe that he could not stay for any length of time in this "awkward situation."[10]

KIRCHENLAMITZ

This business of Wuestenstein seemed to drag along. But one day Loehe was asked to become the vicar in Kirchenlamitz in the Fichtel Mountains. Rev. Sommer, the Dean of that district, was also an older and sickly gentleman. He wanted to have a "vicar of the old faith" and promised him "plenty of work."[11] Someone recommended Loehe to him.

Loehe really felt good about the fact that he did not have to apply for the job but was called and asked. He was only too happy to accept the offer. His future boss wrote to him about what was expected of him: "You are going to be a biblical preacher, and, of course, I like that. That is our real calling . . . I hope that you are going to be my substitute and that you do not sit in the roadhouse for five or six hours a day; that you do not gamble or go to balls. That is the last place where you may find a woman that you would want to marry . . . "[12]

Loehe, with his pure morals, was exactly the right vicar for a man of such principles. He arrived at Kirchenlamitz on October 20, 1831. From the last hill he could see the white houses down in the valley. He wrote in his first letter to his mother about his new place of work: " . . . and above (these houses) the moon, shining bright and quietly into this corner of the world—a great joy. This is my field where I can be the sower . . . I like this place, even at night: I saw beautiful houses and streets that were wide and long."[13]

Arriving at the parsonage the new vicar was greeted heartily by the woman of the house. The Dean shook hands with him from his sickbed. Loehe was treated to a good meal and then shown into his "nice, simple room." The next day the Dean introduced him to his duties. He was a "tall, tall man with a benevolent face."[14] He did not give many orders, but basically let him have a free hand. The woman of the house cared for the young man in a motherly way. She cooked wonderful meals and had his room heated, not sparing the wood.

The two old people were happy to have the young helper. At night he had to sit with them and converse, which was not a simple matter, since the old gentleman was very hard of hearing.

But at such times Loehe was able to familiarize himself with his new field of work. He was told that Kirchenlamitz was almost completely destroyed by fire the previous year. Even the main church and the parsonage fell victims to the fire, so that the services now had to be held in the old cemetery chapel. The parsonage and many other buildings had been rebuilt with the help of the State and insurance money. Even king Ludwig I gave 2,000 *gulden*. That's why there were those beautiful buildings and the wide streets which so impressed Loehe when he arrived.

But appearances are deceiving. There was much poverty and need among the people. There was a knitting mill and flax was harvested in the area, so that many people worked as weavers; but often they did not earn enough to feed a family.

For the young preacher there was plenty of work, which was very welcome after his unsatisfactory occupation in Fuerth. According to his contract with Dean Sommer he had to take over all preaching on Sundays and special holidays, funerals, baptisms, weddings, even confirmation instruction and all parish administration. Besides that, as a representative of the local pastor, he has the oversight over the schools in Kirchenlamitz and the surrounding villages.

The Schools

In the first week of his office Loehe promptly visited the schools and was very upset by the conditions he found there, especially in the small villages and hamlets. There were classrooms which looked worse than a cow-barn and teachers who were simple trades-people without any pedagogical training. One was a shepherd, and on nice days he preferred tending his flock rather than teaching the children. Loehe wrote in his diary: "I found a school that was unbearably hot and just crawling with young children. Some of the boys have to sit on the floor, because there is no table. The handwriting of the teacher is bad, and so the children also have bad handwriting . . . "[15]

In other places there was no school at all, so the teacher had to go from house to house with his "itinerant school."

The Vicar did everything in his power to help. Once or twice a week he visited the country schools. Many of the Kirchenlamitzer children came to his house in order to be tutored in reading and writing. "These little people give me much joy," Loehe wrote to Karl von Raumer, whom he asked for advice and help, since he was an experienced pedagogue. There was, for instance, the case of a deaf-mute girl and Loehe asked how he could best deal with her. For the sake of the children Loehe even attempted to learn to play the piano. He sang with the children in spite of his lack of musical talent, according to the old Franconian saying that his mother often quoted: "Help what may, if you can't sing you have to shout!"[16]

He ordered medication against scabies for the school children from his brother Max in Fuerth. He knew that he also had to care for their health.

Since there was such a lack of teacher training, Loehe wanted to improve this situation also. Every Wednesday he gathered eight village teachers in his house and "instructed them in the word of God and other subjects, both by lecturing and in mutual discussion."[17] Most of the teachers were grateful for this continuing education, though some were offended by these efforts by the young vicar and were hostile towards him.

WORKING WITH YOUTH

Another worry for Loehe was the incredible demoralization of the young people growing up in the country. "You won't believe," he wrote to his sister, "what kind of people are here—what coarse vices they have." He was upset especially over the shamelessness of the girls. He heard "stories of whoring and adultery" and of "the horrible custom of men keeping girls for weeks in their own house before marrying them, in order to find out whether they would like them. If not, the girls were sent home again."[18]

Even his very young girls and boys in the schools went to public dances. Sunday dances and markets on Sundays, according to Loehe, are opening the gates for lewdness and debaucheries. There were a high number of illegitimate births with the sad consequence of poverty and social stigma for the single mothers.

Loehe understood that poverty was the source of many social problems. But in his opinion the main cause for the moral decay lay in the fact that people were looking for their salvation not in the faith in Christ but in worldly amusements.

What could the pastor, the one that cared for their souls, do against this? The first thing Loehe did was to start a "Bible society" in order to "enter every house with the Word of God."[19] Some important men in the congregation, including the mayor, joined this Bible society, so that Loehe felt strong support for this enterprise from the congregation. In the first year a hundred Bibles were distributed. Those who were able paid a small price for them. Poor families received a Bible without cost. Everybody was to know God's Word and through it become awakened to the Christian faith.

Two years later, in order to involve especially the young people in this activity, Loehe started "auxiliaries," separately for boys and girls. They visited in homes and among the sick and distributed Bibles and tracts.

In 1833 he published a tract "Dina. Against the youthful lusts,"[20] which at first appeared anonymously. But soon it became known that the vicar of Kirchenlamitz was the author. He wanted to show the horrible consequences of unchastity by using the example of Jacob's daughter Dina and her story (Genesis 34). With flaming words and prophetic zeal he warned the young people about this pernicious way and pointed to the faith in Christ which gives power to lead a holy life.

In spite of his sharp preaching of repentance and his obvious efforts to keep the young people away from worldly pleasures, Loehe nevertheless was very popular with the Youth. They came "in droves"[21] to him, because they felt that he was genuinely concerned about the salvation of their souls.

However, this popularity could also have strange results. One day a peasant girl came to him. "She wanted to visit the vicar." Loehe thought that she had a spiritual problem and asked if he could help her. Bashfully she giggled and answered: "I just don't know." She mumbled some things, but after he kept on asking, she blurted out: "I just think all the time that you are my sweetheart."

Obviously she had come to the wrong conclusion. Loehe gave her some "stern lectures"[22] and admonished her to think more of spiritual things. She finally left, bawling.

SERMONS

Sermons were Loehe's "greatest joy and greatest misery," as he wrote to his friend Gustav Ritter, who in the meantime also had become a theologian:

> O how I moan from Monday to Sunday. Then, when the bells are ringing, how I work—how I have birth-pangs—with the sermon. I am sure that no one understands me—I always feel that I know nothing. Is that not misery? And yet I feel a quiet joy. A spirit—hopefully God's Spirit—pulls me along so that I am not myself when I preach. It is truly my greatest joy!

And yet, after every sermon he felt that he did not speak the required truth with clarity. He asked God's "forgiveness and life coming from Christ, for myself and for the congregation. And so it becomes a comforting and joyful misery!"[23]

Whenever Loehe preached, the little church was full to capacity, even though he did not spare the congregation. When he preached repentance he became so loud in the pulpit that he had to admonish himself: "You are acting like a bear!" But afterwards he felt that his words were not "without a blessing"[24] and had an effect.

Loehe could preach about very concrete problems such as the crime of smuggling. Because of the proximity to the Czech border this was a thriving business in Kirchenlamitz. He called the smugglers and those who profited from their trade thieves and rascals, and he directed these words even toward respected members of the congregation who grew rich from smuggling. Even Dean Sommer must have felt accused, since he often had bought smuggled goods, but Loehe did not spare anyone. He once wrote after a service that his severe lecture "came crushing down; I was very severe and rough."

After this service some well meaning friends advised the young vicar he should no longer walk alone in the dark, for he had riled up the smugglers against himself.

Thus Loehe became the "feared boogeyman of the entire area," as he himself said. But he was also "much loved." There were "almost as many strangers in my church as members of the congregation. They often had a four hour walk to the church."[25]

Society for the Poor

The initiative for the founding of a society for the poor came from the wife of the pharmacist Reinsch. Loehe immediately supported her project. About ten women and girls of the congregation met once a week to sew dresses for the poor. While they did this, someone read from the Bible or some devotional book. The women also made visits to the poor families, and if the mother was sick, took care of the children. It was important for Loehe that they not only bring material help, but also keep an eye open for the spiritual well being of the poor "so that in this way the kingdom of God may spread among the poor."[26]

The young vicar had brought life and progress to the congregation. It was like a revival for many. Even a colleague of Loehe, Pastor Georg, who loved horses and dogs and at first was hostile to him, had now become his friend. Loehe described him as "not exactly a beer guzzler, only a little rough, but very good-natured."[27] The two of them discussed religion for hours. While there were disagreements between them, the older one was infected with the spiritual passion of the younger one.

Loehe would have loved to start a mission society in Kirchenlamitz, but there was a paragraph in the Bavarian constitution which forbade "all secret meetings under the pretext of domestic worship."[28] This included meetings to promote missions. Loehe tried to get around this paragraph by conducting mission prayer hours in individual homes. During these meetings reports from mission fields were read. The girls from Sunday School knitted things for the mission and donations were collected.

After a year and a half in Kirchenlamitz, Loehe could thankfully say: "God blessed almost everything which I start with determination. The little flock of believers is increasing. Especially among the young people there is much blessing."

But he did not want to praise himself; for he considered pride, vanity and love of self his worst faults. He knew that he owed every success to the grace of God: "To say it briefly: I am one of the luckiest vicars—I do not wish for or desire any more. I expect every day that God will cut down a special switch to use on me."[29]

Recalled from Kirchenlamitz

He didn't have to wait long for that "special switch." True, because of all his hard work many members of the congregation were on his side, but he also had made a number of enemies. And since some of his enterprises had been pushed to the limit of what was permitted, he gave his enemies ample opportunities to attack him.

In January 1832, only three months after starting his call, the circuit judge Beck had sent a complaint to the District in Wunsiedel that the sermons of the vicar were too judgmental. This earned him the first reprimand. He was admonished to "use a more moderate style in his sermons according to the loving spirit of our gentle Christ-religion."[30] The next reprimand came from the consistory in Bayreuth which had received a complaint that he conducted small group meetings. Such "secret gatherings" were forbidden. The consistory saw Loehe as "a young man, convinced of his own worth, but lacking basic knowledge of the world and of people." Dean Sommer was charged in a letter to keep a watchful eye on his "private vicar."

Loehe received this "nasty blow from the consistory" with equanimity. Being self-critical, he recognized that "there is some truth to it, and I have to take notice of it."[31] In the following days he was a little more careful and sympathetic in his labors without neglecting his spiritual and pastoral tasks. He also tried to come to an understanding with his worst enemy, circuit judge Beck, whose daughters attended his youth group. For a while he proceeded with his work without interference while unexpected storm clouds gathered.

The day after Christmas 1833 Loehe received a summons from the county court with a report of the local police "regarding secret meetings of a new religious sect." A cop on the beat reported that in "Kirchenlamitz there are secret meetings in several homes" and that young men get together in the apartment of vicar Loehe several times a week, "and what they are doing is praying and singing."[32]

Loehe was asked to defend himself against this strange accusation, which was not difficult for him; but gradually it became evident that the church authorities disliked the "pietistic activities of private vicar Loehe"[33] and were endeavoring to have him removed from Kirchenlamitz. First he was ordered to appear at the district office in Wunsiedel. There he was accused of a "wide-reaching and harmful mysticism" and of "exaggerated zeal." He "causes a disturbance of public order." Also he was accused of spreading "harmful tracts and writings" and of condemning "every sensuous amusement, even the smallest innocent entertainment."

So the complaints were not just about "secret meetings" but about Loehe's whole personality which confronted people and pushed them toward a decision. This disturbed the peace of the citizens who were quite comfortable in their rationalistic Christianity.

Nothing he offered in his defense[34] could change the attitude of the district and the consistory in Bayreuth. Even though Dean Sommer bravely spoke up for his vicar, and a majority of the congregation was on his side, Loehe's call in Kirchenlamitz was terminated as of March 1. He wrote to his friend Kuendinger:

"Next Wednesday I will leave, maligned and blasphemed by the world, loved and bemoaned by the congregation, hated by some in their midst. I leave my vineyard in order to find rest at home, as long as God wills it. I am going to stop by in Streitberg on my way . . . "[35]

On February 26, 1834 Loehe left the place of his first independent activity. He was given an honorable escort by "three carriages with people from the local government."[36] Via Streitberg he returned home to his mother in Fuerth.

The hateful attacks and the dishonorable discharge deeply troubled the young vicar. Toward the end of his time in Kirchenlamitz his health was not too good either. He had to undergo a difficult surgery because of a sinus infection.

More painful was the hurt in his soul. On the one hand he knew that he had been treated unjustly: "I have preached repentance and the gospel without regard of any person. That is my crime."

On the other hand Loehe was self-critical enough to recognize that his harshness and his ethical demands without compromise were partly to blame for his unfortunate situation: "That's how things are with me—and will be. I am a knife, and who likes to be cut? I do have balm, but only for wounds, not to give perfume to the people."[37]

Did he ask too much of his congregation with his "superfluous strictness?"[38] He knew that his high-handed character often pushed people away and thus stood in the way of the "greater blessing" of his office. By now he no longer liked the tract "Dina. Against the youthful lusts." It was not evangelical enough, but contained too much Law.

He wanted to learn "repentance and humility"[39] from these experiences. But at the same time he asked the Lord that from now on his heart should "no longer cling so closely to a congregation or any kind of creature . . . "[40]

President Friedrich von Roth

The Consistory in Bayreuth sent mountainous files concerning Loehe to the *Oberkonsistorium* in Munich, convinced that justice had been done by removing this troublemaker. But in the meantime Loehe had also turned to this governing body and presented his side of the matter. His friends urged him to do so. Among them were the professors Krafft and Raumer in Erlangen, and especially Rector Roth in Nuremberg whose brother was the president of the *Oberkonsistorium.*

In March of 1834 Loehe was invited to come to Munich and was given the opportunity to personally defend himself before the gentlemen of the *Oberkonsistorium.* President von Roth was favorably impressed by the young pastor who knew how to present his cause well and clearly.

A sharp rebuke was sent to the consistory in Bayreuth for the way they had treated the young theologian. President Roth especially attacked the unclear accusation of mysticism: "Every religion that proclaims mysteries contains mysticism. Mysticism is to be criticized only when it mixes emotions and faith through the influence of an exaggerated fantasy."[41] But such was not the case with Loehe. He clearly confessed the teaching of the evangelical-Lutheran Church. The accusation of Loehe being a sectarian was pure nonsense.

Thus Loehe was completely rehabilitated. However his recall from Kirchenlamitz was not going to be set aside because of his difficult relationship with the circuit judge. He spent some time at home. For a few weeks he supplied the pulpit of the reformed Pastor of St. Martha's Church in Nuremberg, and then he received "in a very honorable way"[42] the call to be interim assistant pastor of the Egidien Church, also in Nuremberg.

NUREMBERG

Loehe returned to very familiar surroundings, for the Egidien Church stood at the Egidien Hill next to the Melanchthon gymnasium where Loehe went to school. In contrast to his time in school, he was now very happy in the old imperial city. He lived in the house of vinegar producer Volk at the Webersplatz, where he was given a "pretty room with wood paneling, polished and ancient"[43] in the tower. The family Helferich lived one floor above him and they also became good friends with Loehe. He socialized often with old and new acquaintances. In Nuremberg he was often in the house of his revered Rector Roth and met there Johannes Merkel, who later on would become the mayor of Nuremberg.

In Merkel's house Loehe found a circle that was closely related to the "German Christian Society." This was one of those movements that worked for spiritual renewal of the Church. For many years it had a solid center in Nuremberg. The Basel Mission originated from this Christian Mission Society and was eagerly supported by the Nuremberg circle. Loehe's Fuerth mission circle also sent its gifts there.

Loehe spent less than a year in Nuremberg, from June 1834 to April 1835. It was a happy time, filled with rich, creative activity. The workload at first didn't seem to be too great: every two weeks a sermon on Sunday afternoon; in between a weekday sermon and some pastoral and catechetical tasks. But Loehe knew how to quickly expand his area of activities. Rector Roth turned over to him the religious instruction in two classes of the gymnasium. Loehe also taught in a school for boys, had an adult class, gave lectures in Volk's house and conducted a well-attended Bible study in the chapel of the Egidien church on Sunday mornings at 6 AM.

Very quickly Loehe gained a certain fame as a preacher in Nuremberg. His powerful voice filled the church on Sunday afternoons to the last pew. He could talk for hours without getting tired. His listeners paid rapt attention until it got dark, and the sexton had to bring a light to the pulpit. The preacher then had to first speak the words of the closing hymn for his congregation, since it was too dark to read the hymnbook. The people left the church very impressed. An apprentice, moved by the pastor exclaimed: "Is that ever a guy!"[44]

Loehe very openly attacked anything that seemed offensive to him: "You mothers are bringing your daughters to the ball decorated like whores!"[45] he thundered from the pulpit. He considered public dances and balls, as always, the cause of much evil. His tract "The Daughter of Herodias"[46] deals with such social amusements.

His sermons were talked about everywhere in Nuremberg. They had an "electrical" effect on many other pastors. But a "Loehe opposition party" that had nothing good to say about him also formed. They saw in him a "representative of the coarsest mysticism." At this time of rationalism, when the faith of the average church-goers had become very superficial, many felt attacked by Loehe's frank language which they were "not used to," while "this same language filled others with enthusiasm."[47] This was the way the Nuremberg Dean Seidel defended the young preacher's effect on the congregation. He and the Ansbach consistory took Loehe's side when the magistrate of the city wanted him to be recalled because his sermons caused so much unrest.[48]

1834 "Seven Sermons" of Loehe were printed. A year later he published his "Sermons on the Lord's Prayer."[49] However, in Nuremberg he also published the tract "Concerning the divine Word, a light that leads us to peace"[50] which clearly reveals that Loehe was beginning to distance himself from the revival movement. "Revival" and "conversion" were important ideas for him in Kirchenlamitz. Since then he had become convinced that the uplifting and sweet feeling associated with these experiences are often confused with faith. They "are not what is permanent and great in this matter." Only the "promises of the Word of God" and the sacraments as the visible Word are unchangeable. "Faith can be small or great; God's Word is always the same." A person can be saved only "based on the Word." "So from now on do not trust in institutions, not in praying and waking, certainly not in our running and efforts." Trust only in "God's Word and promise . . . In this way we get a fixed point outside of the world. From this point we can lift the world off its hinges and its sorrow will be changed to pure thoughts of peace . . ."[51]

Loehe studied Luther's doctrine of justification during this time, that "points a person away from his feelings and toward the divine Word."[52]

According to Loehe feelings play too much of a role in the revival movement. This "sentimentality" easily can cause a person to try to work out his own salvation, which can only lead to works righteousness. On the other hand, "Luther's opposite nature (*Wesen*)" which trusts only in the divine Word, is a "great gain": "One still has feelings, but they are quiet and great!"[53]

Helene Andreae

In January of 1835, while visiting a family named Helferich, Loehe met their relation from Frankfurt, Frau Lisette Andreae and her 16 year-old daughter Helene. A younger daughter Caroline had already been living with the Helferichs, and Frau Andreae desired to stay with them for a longer time. Her marriage to the well-to-do merchant Ferdinand Andreae was not a happy one. She suffered from depression and often lived for months away from her husband. Helene came with her mother, with whom she was very close.

Later Loehe remembered his first meeting with Helene Andreae: "When I went upstairs in my robe to visit the Helferichs, I saw a girl, standing in the door next to Caroline. She was quite tall, with a child-like countenance, but also with a determined expression. That was Helene."[54]

A few days later mother and daughter approached the vicar in his room. Frau Andreae requested that he give confirmation instruction to her daughter. Helene had started confirmation class in Frankfurt, but because of the trip her lessons were interrupted.

In the following months Helene came almost daily for her lessons. Loehe was eleven years older, and with his strong faith and his power to convince he had a great influence on the young girl. She trusted him completely as her spiritual guide. Loehe also had many pastoral talks with her mother and stood by her during the dark hours of her depression.

There was not enough time to complete Helene's confirmation instructions in the Egidien church, because on March 31, 1835 Loehe's interim in Nuremberg came to an end. However, he had an opportunity to stay in the city and substitute for a sick pastor in Behringersdorf, near Nuremberg. There, in the church in Behringersdorf, Helene Andreae was confirmed by Vicar Loehe on June 8, 1835. Later he would write about this day and about his confirmand: "She literally blossomed in the love and desire for God and God's Word . . . I still saw her in the evening in Helferich's garden—and was sad that I no longer would be her teacher. I never had a student like her."

Confirmation meant saying good-bye to mother and daughter. Shortly after that event they returned to Frankfurt. It was not easy for Loehe to be parted from them: "My heart is aching from saying good-bye to my people . . . "[55]

And what about Loehe's feelings for Helene? Certainly she was someone who mattered to him. But in the letters which he wrote to her in the months following he was almost too careful, writing only about pastoral subjects, and signing: "With my complete paternal blessing, your teacher W. Loehe."[56]

But Helene needed his continuing advice and his help. Her father was upset, because she seemed to reject all the joys of this world, apparently under the influence of this Nuremberg vicar. No social gatherings, no dancing, and on Sundays she wanted to go to church twice! Loehe was in a difficult situation. On the one hand he wanted to affirm her practices. He knew that in Frankfurt the "Christian faith is pretty superficial." On the other hand he had to admonish her to be obedient to her father, as long as that did not interfere with her conscience: "Be humble and gentle in dealing with others; but do not move away from the pure doctrine and a pure conduct."[57]

At the beginning of 1836 the merchant Andreae stopped the correspondence between Loehe and his former confirmand. He sent a stern letter to Loehe, forbidding further letters from the interim pastor to his daughter, since "they affirmed her decision to withdraw completely from all worldly amusements." The interim pastor could come and find out for himself that "neither Frankfurt, nor his house are hellish places."[58]

Now it was Loehe's turn to show obedience toward the father's authority which he had so often recommended to Helene. In his answering letter to Helene's father he promised not to write to Helene or her mother again. He regretted that Mr. Andreae did not come to Nuremberg for Helene's confirmation. A personal acquaintance perhaps might have convinced Andreae that he, Loehe, "truly clings with his heart and his conduct to the faith of the fathers," but his "behavior and character are not that dark or grim."[59]

Loehe conscientiously kept his promise—for a year. In the meantime he passed his second and final theological examination in Ansbach. This was required for pastors in Bavaria who had completed five years as vicars. Again his final mark was "very good, close to excellent."

ALTDORF

But the fact that he had passed these finals did not mean that his years of wandering had ended. For two weeks he could supply the pulpit in Lauf, then he was called to Altdorf for half a year. In this former university city, there was a teacher's college where all protestant teachers in Bavaria were trained. Loehe became the interim second pastor and also inspector of the schools.

One of his problems was how to keep house in the large parsonage. Until now he always lived with other people, receiving room and board from them. He decided to take in two boys from Kirchenlamitz who later planned to attend the teacher's college. In exchange for room and board they were to do the cooking and cleaning. Loehe in turn would instruct and prepare them for college. However, housekeeping was more than these young employees could handle. A guest from Nuremberg spoke unkindly about the meals in the parsonage. Loehe, in a conciliatory mood, remarked: "The Kirchenlamitz dumplings may be a little hard, but they are pure and made from un-cooked potatoes."[60] What was worse: Loehe, who was so particular about order and cleanliness, had to assume those chores himself, which was very time consuming. After a few weeks he ended this arrangement and hired an elderly maid for his household.

In the congregation Loehe recognized a great desire for pastoral care. He spent much of his time visiting and in individual conversation. He found great acceptance during his weekly prayer services.

About a dozen of the 120 Altdorf college students established close relationships with Loehe, visited him at home, and considered him their "spiritual father." These "Loehe followers"[61] were looked at askance by the other students and ridiculed because of their piety. But they remained faithful to their mentor until April 1836 when Loehe had to move again. He became interim pastor in Bertholdsdorf in the district of Windsbach.

Bertholdsdorf

He wrote an enthusiastic letter about his new place of labor to his sister Dorothea:

> This is the most beautiful spot I have ever lived in. In the valley of the Aurach there is a low chain of hills which divides the already narrow valley into two even narrower ones. Where the hills start, there rests . . . Berthelsdorf. The village main street rises slightly. Then there are some 12 or 15 steps up to the cemetery, and that's where the little church is...From the cemetery there is a paved path to the beautiful large parsonage courtyard. The parsonage with its two gardens is like a stunning little mansion. In one of the gardens there are hundreds of roses, and, even more gorgeous, a multitude of white shining lilies . . . I feel very well, and the country air is so good for me that my clothes are getting too tight.[62]

The question of who would keep house for him in Bertholdsdorf found the best possible solution: his mother was willing to move into the parsonage with him for the duration of his stay there.

Loehe showered her with great love and thankfulness. He hoped that he could offer her "a little rest and relaxation"[63] in the rural environment, in spite of all the work she is did in the house. But this good intention was not easily realized; the young interim pastor, rejoicing over the beautiful parsonage and the wonderful rural surroundings, invited everybody to come to Bertholsdorf. At Pentecost some 30 people occupied the parsonage—all of them friends and relatives. No wonder that Loehe's mother felt overburdened with so many guests.

Bertholdsdorf was by no means such an idyllic little town as it appeared at first glance. Behind the doors there was often bitter misery, as Loehe soon learned when he visited the homes: "God have mercy on the poor Bertholsdorf, which both in physical and spiritual regard should really be called *Bettelsdorf* (beggars' town)!"[64]

Moral conditions were terrible here, as everywhere in rural areas where "poverty was the greatest curse." In a paper concerning church discipline, which he wrote a year later, Loehe described how in some families "there is only one bed for six to seven people, father, mother and children of both sexes. They sleep all huddled together." Often several families shared just one room, both for living and sleeping. "Since they are used to living that close together and there is the necessity to do everything in front of everybody, feelings of shame and modesty are forgotten."[65] Loehe was horrified to discover that even small children "are whoring together"[66], and that in the Bertholdsdorf congregation there were more than 40 single mothers with a total of 56 children. This was also the result of poverty for the issuance of a marriage license depended on "your bank account and your possessions,"[67] so it was practically impossible for the poor to marry.

One experience particularly gave him pause. While on a hike, he was surprised by a thunderstorm and fled into a house where he found a single mother with four children. When she told him her story with tears, he felt ashamed and thought: "What injustice exists if a Pharisee would look down on someone like that!"[68]

Loehe recognized quite clearly the connection between poverty and vice. As a pastor he considered it his first duty to preach "repentance and the gospel," but beyond that he felt that "faith and love" had to be revived in the congregations so that one could create "welfare institutions"[69] which help the poor.

Another problem was the many mental patients in the country, the "possessed," as they were called. Loehe was asked by his colleagues in the Windsbach district to research how the possessed were treated with liturgies and prayers in the ancient church. One day a couple brought their mentally ill son to him. He had been treated without success by many Catholic priests and by doctors. They were convinced that he was "possessed" and therefore a case for spiritual exorcism. Loehe devoted himself intensively to this 25 year-old man and asked him to tell him about his life. Through Loehe's influence and his talking with him the man improved somewhat, so that he went home with his parents "a little happier."

Loehe wanted to document this case and sent it to several doctors in order to ask them for their opinion.[70]

THE "HOMILETICAL LITURGICAL CORRESPONDENCE PAPER"

All these experiences emphasized for him the importance of practical theology. He wrote about it in the "Homiletical-Liturgical Correspondence Paper" which had already published several of his articles. Since he started working in the Windsbach district, the editor of the paper, Heinrich Bandt, also Dean in Windsbach, had engaged him even more frequently as coworker.

Since its beginning in 1824 the "Homiletical Liturgical Correspondence Paper" had developed into a "fighting paper of the revival movement" against Rationalism.[71]

Loehe wanted to give it a new direction, as he wrote in the introduction for the year 1836: "Regarding the goals which the Homiletical Liturgical Correspondence Paper should adopt for 1836,"[72] there should be less polemic from now on. The paper should "support the brothers under God's blessing, strengthen and establish them."[73] That meant that the subjects to be dealt with would be pastoral-theological. Within this framework Loehe wrote a series of papers the following years, starting with the article: "To my fellow pastors. Pastoral considerations of a shepherd who, feeling the honor and the burden of his office, has chosen the Word of God as his lamp."[74]

MERKENDORF

In the meantime his service in Bertholdsdorf was coming to an end. As of November 1836 Loehe was to become interim pastor in Merkendorf, again for just half a year. Merkendorf also belonged to the Windsbach district and was only a two hour walk from Bertholdsdorf. A little embittered Loehe wrote to his friend Kuendinger: "I really achieve a lot, don't you think? I wander toward my 12th position. I want to see whether a dozen is enough, or whether after Merkendorf I might find a place where I can stay, where I can teach intensively for a long time under God's blessing. Perhaps, perhaps not!"[75]

Here in Merkendorf Loehe's spiritual career almost came to an end. Bound by his conscience, he refused to marry a divorced inhabitant of that town a second time. The first marriage of that man had lasted only half a year, and the divorce was granted for insignificant reasons and had caused a lot of resentment in the congregation. Loehe based his refusal on Matthew 19:9, where only adultery is given as a valid reason for divorce. Therefore, bound by his conscience, he could not possibly remarry that man, the baker Reinfelder. However, the man had a legal marriage license. Because of the close alliance between Church and State, a pastor was also a sworn servant of the State and a State official. It was one of his duties to perform a marriage which the State had authorized—there were no civil marriages.

The bridegroom who had been refused submitted a complaint to the assize court. The case was sent to the consistory in Ansbach. While the consistory did bemoan the lax practice of the State regarding divorces, it nevertheless ordered the interim pastor of Merkendorf to "conduct the church wedding necessary for the beginning of a second marriage."[76] If he could not do it for reasons of conscience he had to be dismissed from his office. This was a difficult conflict for the young preacher who had found the "most precious thing" of his life "in the sacred office!" Again he turned for help to the *Oberkonsistorium* in Munich and asked that "his conscience may be spared." He also cited the fact that Catholic priests refuse to remarry divorced persons. He asked for the same "regard for his conscience"[77] in his case.

The *Oberkonsistorium* was basically of the opinion that Loehe acted against the duties of his office and warned him strictly against "continued refusal"[78] in similar cases, but in this special case, which had been thoroughly investigated, it ordered another pastor, one less scrupulous, to perform the wedding.

So Loehe got off once more, but he made a negative impression on the governing authorities, and at the time when he had finally completed his time as a vicar and was eligible to apply for a congregation of his own. Was this why his greatest wish, to serve in a city church, was never fulfilled? His friends among the professors in Erlangen tried to get him a position in that university city. For credentials he could show outstanding marks in the examinations and several tracts and articles in periodicals which he had published. While he was in Merkendorf he published "A Little Book about Confession and Communion for Lutheran Christians." His Nuremberg sermons also appeared in print. His name was "known like the pestilence,"[79] as he said at one time. So why would the church authorities not grant him a field of endeavor commensurate with his gifts? Were they afraid that Wilhelm Loehe, this "uncut diamond"[80] as one of the examiners called him, might continue to act inappropriately and cause unrest? Is that why some would not want to see him in a very public position, but rather away in the country where he would not be noticed so much?

5

NEUENDETTELSAU: WEDDING, MARRIAGE, FAMILY

Neuendettelsau—the first time Loehe visited this place was on a trip from nearby Bertholdsdorf. The two villages were only an hour and a half apart. He wanted to introduce himself to the senior of the Chapter there, a Pastor Weigel. In contrast to the picturesque Bertholdsdorf, Neuendettelsau is situated on a flat plateau. It appeared to the young visitor to be very sad and neglected: "I would not even want to be buried in that nest,"[1] he said to himself, shuddering.

But it was exactly from this Neuendettelsau that shortly afterwards a delegation of farmers and village leaders came to ask Loehe to apply for their church, since Pastor Weigel was applying for another position. If he would agree, they would go down on their knees before their patron, the Baron von Eyb, to have Loehe as their pastor. Loehe's enthusiasm about this proposition was limited, since he was hoping for a city church. On the other hand he was pleased by the "good opinion of the Neuendettelsauer people"[2] and did not want to be abrupt with them. So he made them this promise: "If your church becomes vacant and is offered to me before I receive a call from Erlangen or another place, I will apply in God's name."[3]

CALLED TO NEUENDETTELSAU

Late in the fall of 1836 Pastor Weigel was transferred to Leutershausen and the church in Neuendettelsau was vacant. A messenger arrived at Loehe's in Merkendorf with a letter from Dean Brandt who reminded him of the promise he gave the Neuendettelsauer farmers.

The Dean was very interested in Loehe's applying for this position. He wanted to keep him within the Windsbach district.

At this time Loehe realized that the hoped for position in Erlangen would go to another applicant, according to the will of the *Oberkonsistorium*. Also the Dean of Windsbach let him know that the proper consistory in Ansbach had no intention of offering him a more influential position. What else could he do but to apply for Neuendettelsau? He wrote a lack-luster private letter to the Patron, Baron von Eyb in which he indicated his interest in the Neuendettelsau parish. He had to send the letter through the official channel to Dean Brandt, who forwarded it with a "powerful recommendation" to the Patron. In mid-December Loehe received a very gracious letter from the Baron in which he promised "the highly esteemed interim pastor"[4] the position, much to the latter's "almost unwilling surprise."[5] Thus Loehe became pastor of Neuendettelsau, even though it was not what he wanted. What kind of feelings did he experience?

"After I thought about it I no longer make a sour face and the thought of staying in that congregation to my end no longer scares me . . ."[6]

Gradually it dawned on him that it wasn't all that bad. What he wrote in his letters sounded more positive all the time:

> Neuendettelsau is about an hour from the Heilsbronn Cloister and the same distance from Windsbach . . . It lies on a plain, is a large, nice village three times the size of Bertholdsdorf, has a pretty little church, a mansion with surrounding park, and a patrimonial legal system. The church pays from 800 to 900 florins. Many a pastor who has served for 10 years would be happy if he could have this congregation. I am much envied, especially by other applicants . . .[7]

ONCE MORE IN KIRCHENLAMITZ

According to the rules of the church, a congregation had to be vacant for at least half a year and be under an interim pastor. The interim pastor who was installed there and was to remain in Neuendettelsau until the end of July 1837 was Loehe's friend Wilhelm Tretzel. Loehe watched his activities with some concern. Under Tretzel's influence there was an awakening in the village, similar to the spiritual movement that Loehe had sparked when he was interim pastor in Kirchenlamitz. But precisely that experience in Kirchenlamitz made him thoughtful. Many who had changed their lives had fallen back to their old ways once he had left. Loehe had written many imploring letters to Kirchenlamitz in recent years. Now, in July 1837, he visited his former congregation once more. His friends—among them Dean Sommer, Pastor Georg and the pharmacist Reinsch—greeted him most heartily, but Loehe also found out that there were many "lost sheep."[8] As for his enemies, they had not forgotten their old spite. They immediately protested to the assize court when it became known that Loehe wanted to give a Sunday sermon. Vicar Loehe had been removed from Kirchenlamitz because of "spreading pietism." It was known that he "disturbs everywhere;"[9] therefore he should be prevented from preaching to avoid further fighting within the congregation.

Under these circumstances Loehe gave up preaching in Kirchenlamitz and traveled home again on Sunday morning.

Why was such a revival as Loehe experienced as interim pastor in Kirchenlamitz so brief and, in the long run, failed to bring about a turn-around in the life for many of the people? What did that mean in regard to Neuendettelsau, where his friend Tretzel now experienced a similar spiritual awakening? It would be up to him, the new pastor, to pick up these beginnings and steer them in a permanent direction: "Tretzel is going to separate the Neuendettelsau people from the world. May God grant that I can gather them into His holy Church."[10]

COURTING

So this was his spiritual program for Neuendettelsau. But first he had to think of his own future. He was being admonished from all sides, from friends and relatives all with good intentions, to get married, since now he had a good position and a parsonage. There were practical reasons that cogently spoke in favor of marriage: Loehe's mother, who had kept house for him during his last two interims became "daily more anxious and upset" and was "never happy"[11] with her son during the disagreements over his ministry in Merkendorf. Behind her back Loehe asked his brother to call her back to Fuerth under some pretext.

But who was going to keep house in the Neuendettelsau parsonage? According to the well-meaning advice-givers the best solution would be if he could start his ministry on August 1 already married. A single pastor would be a great attraction for young women that were willing to marry and their potential mothers-in-law. Loehe had not been spared such propositions in the past, but he always turned them away roughly.

What did he think of marriage in general? During the restless and uncertain years as vicar, he banished the thought of marriage: "I have no love-affair and do not desire one,"[12] he wrote 1832 to Gustav Ritter who had suggested his sister Karoline as a potential bride. At that time he wished to take a vow of celibacy, never to marry at all. But even at that time he believed that it would be better for a pastor to marry and that this would be "in conformity with the principals of the Reformers." Now that he would have his own congregation the time had come to put into practice his theoretical deliberations on that topic. He was ready to "enter a sacred marriage. Doing this I will honor God's Word more, have more pain and enter a more serious school than if I would remain single."[13]

Loehe, whom his friends accused of having a "monkish inclination,"[14] considered marriage an exercise of duty which he had to take upon himself in obedience to the order of creation and to the "principles of the Reformers."

One also must note that at the beginning of 1837 he had not decided on any particular woman. He did keep thinking of Helene Andreae, even though he had not seen her for a long time. Also, obeying the order of her father, he had not written to her.

In the meantime he had met Pauline von Roth, the daughter of the president of the *Oberkonsistorium.* For a while he considered a marriage with her. On the one hand it would be tempting to become a member of the Roth family. On the other hand his modesty held him back. As far as Pauline was concerned, while he appreciated her beauty, he was bothered by the fact that she had a limp. Even worse: "he suspects she has a bossy character."[15] In his mind there was a clear hierarchy where the man had to be the "master in the house."[16] Otherwise "not only is he no man, but also no Christian." A bossy woman—that would have been a frightful specter for Loehe!

How different was "soft Helene!" She came "closer to his heart"[17] than he himself believed, as he now realized. But she was a very sheltered child in a big city—how would she manage a household in a country parsonage?

Loehe wavered between these two women. Then he met the sister of his friend Tretzel. He liked her very much. But when he found out that she was already engaged, the image of Helen loomed larger in his thoughts again.

Easter Monday, March 27, Loehe preached his last sermon in Merkendorf and left the same day for Fuerth where he wanted to spend the time until the beginning of his ministry in Neuendettelsau. Immediately a meeting of the family council was called to discuss the burning question of his marriage. Loehe's sister Dorothea had remained in touch with Helene Andreae and her mother during the two years that the young vicar had been forbidden to write. Through her Loehe was informed that mother Andreae would ardently approve of a union between him and Helene. She let him know that Helene herself, who has already turned down two suitors, would not say "No" to him.

The family council unanimously agreed that Loehe should ask for Helene's hand in marriage. Resistance from the grim father Ferdinand Andreae was to be expected. He was tremendously prejudiced against this suitor. In spite of this, Loehe took courage and in a letter asked Ferdinand Andreae for the hand of his daughter in marriage.

The merchant Andreae took his time with an answer. First he made some inquiries concerning Loehe's financial affairs. He found out that the young pastor came from a solid Fuerth family of merchants and had very well-to-do relatives. Based on this information, a family council was also called together in Frankfurt. One aunt remarked realistically that Helene, with her strict principles, could never hope to find another husband. She might as well marry the pastor.

This wise counsel decided the issue. Loehe received the gracious approval of the parents. It was now up to him to turn to Helene herself. Of course the father was still suspicious. He set the condition that the daughter herself must administer her dowry, not, as would have been customary, the son-in-law.

Having received the approval of her parents, Loehe wrote to Helene on April 25, 1837 and asked her to become his wife: "I have asked for your hand, because, before God, I would not know of anyone that would be more pleasing to my soul. I pray to the Lord, my God and your God, that our union will be blessed. May the Lord grant that in the stillness of your soul you can write Yes and Amen to me . . ."[18]

Only a day later Helene held his letter in her hands. Immediately, that same day, she wrote her answer, in part using his own words: "In the stillness of my soul I can write to you my Yes and Amen. . . . The Lord . . . knows that I love you more than all other men and that I very much look forward to becoming your Helene."

For her there was not a moment of hesitation or doubt: "I didn't have to ask God first for the understanding of His will. I could only thank Him that . . . He leads me on His way so full of grace and love." The young pastor who confirmed her had remained unforgettably in her heart: "You have taught me to love the Lord. I thank Him that His grace has not been in vain for me." She was quite certain in this case: The Lord "gave into my heart joy and love for the calling of a pastor's wife, a rural pastor's wife. May the Lord give to me, His weak tool, power and strength so that I may be a true helpmate for you . . ."[19]

Loehe was extremely happy when he got this letter, written just the way he would have written. He would keep it for the rest of his life as a precious keepsake. Loehe's mother likewise shed tears of joy when she got to read the letter and she thanked God for this daughter-in-law.

Loehe was planning a visit to Frankfurt the week after Pentecost. The wedding was planned for the end of July, before the start of his ministry in Neuendettelsau. How was the bridegroom feeling?

"For me the sun, the moon and the stars do not shine any differently than before—my life has found its center a long time ago,"[20] he wrote in a letter. He was very careful not to let himself be so caught up in romantic feelings of love that he would be pulled away from the "center," the service of his Lord. He observed how many colleagues became lax in their calling after they married, but he wanted to prove that there is another way. He wanted to demonstrate his "faith in his ministry and in his home" and "from now on have four arms and four legs for the benefit of the congregation."[21]

Therefore, before starting out for the visit to Frankfurt, he asked God that he "would preserve his soul from the passions of a bridegroom." With a definitely reserved attitude he met his bride, whom he had not seen for two years. Helene had turned into a "slender young woman with a rosy face which she complements with the natural grace of a calm, silent, serious simplicity."[22] Her reticence was perhaps even greater than his. She barely shook hands with him and remained so extraordinarily quiet that her mother finally admonished her to be a little more open. But precisely through this quiet, friendly behavior she won the heart of the bridegroom. "For again and again it was apparent that she was certain of her way and happy in her situation." When Loehe took his leave after a week and asked her: "Will you come along as far as the post office?" she shook hands with him in a friendly way and said: "No, but when you come back I will go with you all the way." Later Loehe would say about this farewell: "The bride rose very high in my eyes."[23]

After this reunion the tone of Loehe's letters became much warmer and more loving. He reported about the wedding of a friend where the "many young ladies" including the bride could not impress him: " . . . for I have chosen you. I hold your hand, you are my most beloved!" When there was some table talk about the duties of a pastor's wife, Loehe expressed the thought that Helene would be a faithful helpmate in his ministry, not a "flatterer," but one who would "encourage him in his ministry." "You shall help me pull my net—and one day, on the day of harvest, thank the Lord with me!"[24]

In the Neuendettelsau Parsonage

Before the wedding Loehe had the run-down parsonage in Neuendettelsau restored at his own expense and the parsonage garden prepared. Furniture, stoves, and curtains were ordered from Frankfurt. Almost to the last day before the wedding Loehe had to wait for permission to be "married abroad"[25]—for Frankfurt is outside of Bavaria! On July 1837 Wilhelm Loehe and Helene Andreae were married in St. Katherine's Church in Frankfurt. On the way home the young couple stayed for a few days in Fuerth, in Loehe's father's house, and on August 1 they moved into the Neuendettelsau parsonage.

What did Neuendettelsau look like at this time? The low thatched houses with their dirty window panes, the "disorderly manure piles"[26] in front of every house were not an inspiring sight. Only the baronial mansion, the parsonage, the inn and the homes of wealthy farmers were roofed with expensive tiles. If it rained, one had to wade through the mud of the unpaved village streets, otherwise through dust. Loehe, who was so fussy about cleanliness, could not walk the short way from the parsonage to the church without having his robe splattered with dirt. Therefore he had this way paved during the first year of his ministry—the first paved street in Neuendettelsau.

In spite of its tiled roof the parsonage was hardly different from the houses of the farmers, even though Loehe tried to beautify the interior. It looked more like a "pastor's hut" with small and narrow rooms. In front of the parsonage there was one of the four village ponds. Its muddied bank was a welcome gathering place for geese and chickens.

These poor rural conditions did not upset the young pastor's wife, Helene Loehe. She brought a joyful, life-affirming spirit to the parsonage. She was determined to quickly learn all the skills of a rural pastor's wife, which really meant skills of a farmer's wife. She had a very winning way in dealing with people. She asked an old peasant woman to teach her how to use a spinning wheel. She asked another to teach her how to bake bread. A baker taught her how to make soap. All of her husband's worries that she might not be able to cope with a rural household soon dissolved. Happily he watched his "farm wife" work—full of ambition and without much ado—both in the house and in the garden. Delighted, he wrote to his mother-in-law who had been worried about her daughter:

> Your daughter Helene looks like life itself. . . . Last week she learned from the midwife how to hackle flax, although her fingers at times got in the way: But she does it splendidly. . . . From M. I bought 300 heads of cabbage, nice big ones, and tomorrow J.A. comes to help cut them. They threw a load of straw on the entrance to the cellar of the barn, so that it would be warm in the winter . . . and what a pleasant domicile that is for the fat hen and the other scratch-feet animals that belong to the lady of the house. The geese which Helene plucked all by herself last week are really famous. I have to buy ticking several times, because so much is needed for pillows and feather beds. We keep so many geese out of love for the Frankfurt guests. Those lousy cackling things know very well that I am not a real Frankfurter. One of them found my leg with her beak, in spite of the fact that I was wearing my gown, since I was coming home from evening services . . .[27]

Loehe was a changed man. He had never written such happy letters before this. He became infected by the happiness of his young wife, who was absolutely blossoming in her marriage. She was no longer the quiet, shy girl; "her happy temper, free from any meanness and worries lets her be so happy that she becomes downright playful." Could Loehe's claim be true, that she was "really made for marriage," because she "can be happy only with her husband?"[28] Anyway, he was happy about her "playfulness" when she came to his desk and "grabs the quill with her mouth and holds it with her teeth"[29] until the page he was writing on was dry.

Who would have thought that this strict, inflexible man would turn into such an enthusiastic spouse? All the scruples that made him think that marriage could interfere with the duties of his office disappeared in the face of the joyful experience of a growing love. During the first weeks of their marriage he did worry in his diary whether he had "flirted too much"[30] with Helene before getting out of bed. But increasingly he understood that in contrast to all his fears she had become a great asset for the congregation as well. Enthusiastically he wrote to a friend:

> Instead of bragging a lot about her, I will say briefly: She helps me from morning to night to pull my cart, and the verse of the Scripture is being fulfilled: 'Her husband will praise her.' No wonder that my wife becomes dearer to me from day to day. In the beginning there was only a little love, at least in comparison to what is now living and growing.[31]

A little later he wrote in a letter to Helene's mother: "We learn every day that married life is more beautiful than just being engaged. However, both engagement and marriage are like a piece of sugar cane which is soon chewed down, unless a love which is not of this world sanctifies the marriage and makes it into a sacred union."[32]

Work in the Congregation

As Loehe had feared, the work in the Neuendettelsau congregation was not easy at first. His predecessor and friend, interim pastor Tretzel, had started a small circle for revived Christians. They met privately for times of devotion. Of course there were also people in the village who were against such pious circles. These antagonists were not exactly the nicer people of the village. They looked to the new pastor to oppose such pietistic tendencies.

This put Loehe in an awkward situation, and he could now appreciate what kind of problems he had left for his successors when he himself was a revival preacher. In the meantime he had come to the conviction that people who have experienced such a spiritual awakening cannot be left to themselves. They have to be incorporated into the life of the church.

He was wise enough to permit these private meetings to continue for the time being, and to participate in them. But he moved them into the parsonage and into the church. He conducted an hour of devotion about biblical topics in the church one evening a week for a group of men and women, young men and girls.

Helene Loehe, who had a beautiful voice, gathered the young people to sing in the parsonage. Almost every evening she had a group of girls or of boys in her room, as many as 60 children, which she knew to "rule" very well, as Loehe stated admiringly. In fact, she was "the darling of the congregation."[33] Loehe wisely refrained from singing, but in between the hymns he told stories of "Zinzendorf's life, so rich in love."[34]

Even though Loehe moved these hours of devotion into the church, the meetings raised the suspicion of the local police, and they were soon forbidden. Loehe was not unhappy about this, for in the meantime he considered the public proclamation of the Word via sermon, catechizing and liturgy to be more important. They are the only means of pastoral care, except "private pastoral care," namely conversations with individuals.

Thus the Sunday service was to be the center of congregational life. Loehe tried everything to awaken understanding and interest for the various parts of the service within his congregation. Already in 1836 he had been elected to the "committee for liturgy" of the district. It was to examine the first draft for a new Bavarian order for the service. He had studied many old Lutheran and old church orders of service. Now he tried to carefully introduce to the congregation some old forms that had become dear and important to him. That was not easy with these Franconian peasants. They clung to old habits. One old man already considered it an imposition that the congregation should join the pastors in saying the "Amen" after the prayer. He didn't think he should "do the work of the pastor." But Loehe was able to prove to him that the "Amen" is the responsibility of the congregation.

There was also resistance when Loehe wanted the congregation to kneel during the Lord's Supper. He announced this new custom during the service and explained the deeper meaning of it, but then added dryly: "Unmannerly people are allowed to remain standing."[35] All the members of the congregation knelt down.

During "*Christenlehre*" (religious instruction) on Wednesdays and Fridays, Loehe taught the catechism. Even grownups took part and were sometimes questioned by the pastor, just like the children. During these hours he wanted to acquaint the congregation with the old-church responsive prayers, the "Te Deum," and the "Litany." Patiently he practiced the unknown words with the people. He considered these prayers that are spoken again and again very important and educational and he did not fear the accusation that this would be mere "lip service."

"If all our singing and praying in church is effective only if it is the expression of an existing inner life, there would have to be deep silence. . . . I recognize more and more that liturgical institutions will be of value only if they are no longer new. Newness is disturbing; what is familiar is uplifting."[36]

Loehe spent as much time and effort as possible in preparing his sermons. He was a very gifted orator, but for these peasants he had to speak very simply and down to earth. He also saw here an opportunity and the necessity to speak against many evils. In one sermon he pointed out the terrible condition of the small bedrooms where parents and children sleep together in dirty and miserable beds, and where old and sick people are shunted off to dark corners. Afterwards the talk in the congregation was: "We are not going to listen to such a 'bed-sermon' again."[37] Loehe heard this and in the future avoided language that was too concrete, and to coarse. There was also a woman who listened very attentively to his sermons and occasionally criticized them. After one particular sermon she very openly remarked: "Everything was pretty mixed up."[38]

Because Loehe considered the Sunday service the heart of congregational life, he wanted to see the whole congregation participating in it, including the mothers of small children. Therefore he engaged two peasant girls to watch the children in the parsonage during the service. From these beginnings, Helene Loehe started a pre-school for little children. Soon a group of some ten children came every afternoon so that the mothers were free to work in the fields or at home. The children learned songs and Bible verses and she told them Bible stories. There were also some toys and "learning aids."[39] Unfortunately this pre-school had to be closed after two years for financial and other reasons, even though it was very popular with the parents.

THE LOEHE CHILDREN

On July 19, 1838 Helene Loehe gave birth to a son in the parsonage. In baptism he received the name of her father, Johann Ferdinand. The birth was difficult because the child was unusually big. Loehe reported in a letter to Karl von Raumer, who was supposed to be sponsor to the child, that, according to the opinion of the doctor, Helene would not be able to give birth "with her own strength, in spite of vehement birth pangs:" "So we built a kind of throne for my sweetheart with cushions on a table. I sat at the wall behind her, held her firmly in my arms, two people held her legs—and thus my son was finally pulled into daylight with great effort. After an unforgettably bitter quarter of an hour our sadness was turned into joy."[40]

Loehe was very much touched by the experience of this difficult birth. He needed time to get used to his role as a father. At first he did not know how he should look at this son with "the eyes of a father."[41] He felt like a stranger to him. But soon he could write happy letters to his mother-in-law about her "*Herzblatt*" (dearest): "He lies at his mother's breast and guzzles…Sometimes he is very friendly and loving. Then I feel that he is my son. But sometimes, when he wants to exert his will, I am glad that there is a hazelnut bush in my garden. A switch cut from this bush will do him good some day . . . "[42]

In great detail Loehe described Christmas of 1838 in the Neuendettelsau parsonage. It was celebrated with the family, the servants and many guests.

> We celebrated a beautiful Christmas. The morning of December 24 was spent in writing my sermon. After dinner I let Helene have the joy of opening the things from Frankfurt. . . . Ferdinand was still a little unhappy on Christmas Eve. The greatest attraction for him was the rooster.

> In his excitement he broke it the same day he received it. Now he likes it even better: Apparently, for him a rooster without legs is more wonderful than one with legs . . .

Loehe reported further that he was able to select his own Christmas tree in the forest:

> I loved the walk—over the crunchy snow, under the beautiful evening sky with the mysterious clouds and a wonderfully, holy view of the quiet *Dettels-Aue* (Dettels-meadow). We went and searched and searched. Finally we found a gorgeous little tree, which was like a beautiful lamp in the shape of a pyramid. We cut it down . . . then home and forward! . . . When everything was arranged, we sat down at two tables that were set, very cheerfully. After dinner we trimmed the tree . . . wonderful oranges, bright red apples, shiny lemons, golden eggs, pretty nets with golden potatoes among the branches, and new beautiful birds, sitting on the branches and singing a song for me about the new creation in Christ Jesus. Finally we were tired and went to bed. But the little boy didn't let us rest very much. He slept much during the day; therefore he helped the angels sing during the night . . . [43]

With just as much detail Loehe described the first day of Christmas with two services and the distribution of gifts in the parsonage.

But Loehe also reported other events in Neuendettelsau. In the village there was frequently talk about ghosts in the parsonage. One night Loehe and his wife indeed could hear with horror the so-called "*Klagmutter*" (moaning mother):

> She is also heard by the peasants who are doing their threshing that night. Mrs. Zeitlinger (a friend of ours) and I hear the locked doors downstairs slamming, and I feel as if the upper and the lower landing and the stairs were lit up. Since then the house is quiet. But also since then the parsonage and the pastor are subjects of the strangest rumors. It's assumed that the pastor is fighting with the devil. In the community they say that the devil wants to get the pastor . . . People look at me with fear and awe. It is so bad that even the police take notice. The brigadier visits me and expresses his desire to catch the devil.—Look, what a life we have in Dettelsau! How amusing

> things are in the possessed but now cleansed parsonage! Now the devil, who is no longer in the house, apparently went into the people and their tongues, like he went into the pigs . . . [44]

That's what life was like in Dettelsau. Loehe and Helene were blessed with three more children at eighteen month intervals: a daughter Marianne and two sons Gottfried and Philipp. In just a few years Helene had become a mother with many children. Screaming and loudly rejoicing children filled the parsonage. Loehe enjoyed the domestic good fortune of his children. He educated them in a very strict manner, but he also enjoyed being with them: "This is certain for me," he once wrote, "that to play with the children for one hour is as beneficial for me as if I had studied for an hour."[45]

Even more than his children he loved his wife. This became very clear to him when she visited her parents in Frankfurt for four weeks in the spring of 1840. He wrote her many letters and reported the "Neuendettelsau News" from house and garden: "In your garden the lilies of the valley and some gorgeous auriculas are in bloom. If I wouldn't be such a bear, I would put some of them into this letter. But that really would not be befitting a person like me. . . . "[46]

Another letter he closed with a farewell to his "*Frau Landconfect*" (Mrs. Country Sugar), whom he "loves eternally, unspeakably, namelessly." Helene wrote back to her "dearest Wilhelm": "I honor and love you. I am your happy wife and am looking forward to (seeing) my dearest husband."[47]

By this time, Loehe had six years of a happy marriage and a fulfilled family life. The couple often wandered together to the neighboring village of Wernsbach, where Loehe had a service every two weeks. They had good relations with Pastor Leonhard Kuendinger who was installed in the neighboring village of Petersaurach in 1839. His ambitious wife made a big impression on Helene Loehe when they visited there. Just before the installation, Loehe offered his help as a neighbor and wrote: "Ever since we visited you and your spouse, who is such a wonderful housekeeper, my beloved thinks of cows. If you would like, she could send you some fat geese in time for the installation. I am to tell you this and also give you her best regards."[48]

Loehe also started writing again. Based on his experiences in the congregation he wrote for his members. In 1840 two little books were printed: "Seed Kernels of Prayer; A Little Book for Lutheran Christians" and a "Guide for Sick and Dying Lutheran Christians." Often he dictated his manuscripts to Helene and talked with her about his ideas.

Unfortunately there were many "sick and dying" in his congregation. Loehe was constantly making sick-calls, together with his wife. There were especially many childhood diseases in the area which no one knew how to treat. In 1841 Loehe wrote in a letter: "Since the day before yesterday I have spent most of my time with sick children. One was in terrible pain with diphtheria and died today during the ringing of the vesper bell. Another one is nearing death because of scarlet fever—a beautiful nine year old girl."[49]

Sickness and Death of Helene

At the beginning of 1843 another wave of sickness went through the village. Loehe had nine funerals in two weeks and had almost become himself "a living funeral sermon." He said: "Scarlet fever, whooping cough and pneumonia are raging here."[50]

On January 20, 1843 his fourth child, Philipp, was born in the parsonage. Helene's mother had come from Frankfurt to Neuendettelsau for a long stay. Her depression went away when she was with her daughter and surrounded by happy grandchildren. But in March she also fell sick and died after just a few days. She was buried in the cemetery in Neuendettelsau which Loehe had ordered to be built outside of the village a few years previously. He and Helene had bought a field and given it to the congregation to have a cemetery there, along with the gates and a part of the wall. According to Loehe's wish the cemetery should be "a quiet paradise."[51] Now he had a tomb built there where the casket of his mother-in-law was deposed.

Helene, who loved her mother very much, was in mourning. But "her friendly and happy disposition was not dampened in the least," as Loehe remembered later. She had recuperated from childbirth, seemed younger "in good shape and brave."[52] In May her happy husband wrote to Karl von Raumer: "We have a beautiful life. We couldn't wish for a better one."[53]

And yet, Loehe said later, in the summer of 1843 he had some dark premonitions. When he saw how rapidly Helene "walked toward her *Vollendung* (completion, perfection, fulfillment)"[54] he was filled with great anxiety.

On November 1 the two Loehes walked hand in hand to a neighboring village to visit a pastor-friend. They were talking about the "Church triumphant," a favorite subject of Loehe which he had spoken about that morning in a prayer meeting. He compared the Church to a long train of pilgrims. "The first in line are already in Zion while the others are still walking in this world." On the way home Helene talked a lot about herself, she "recapitulated her life," Loehe remembered later: "I considered myself so rich as she returned with me to our peaceful house and went to her beloved children."[55]

Shortly afterwards Loehe got sick with a violent influenza. He was hardly restored to health when Helene, who had nursed him, did not feel well. The doctor discovered an infection of "chest and abdomen." She had several attacks of high fever and finally developed typhus.

For several days her worried husband was suspended between fear and then hope, when the fever had somewhat abated. Until the end Loehe did not want to believe that the worst loss would happen to him. On November 24 he realized that the end was near. Between two vehement attacks of fever Helene once more recognized her husband and implored him: "Oh, hold me! Oh, mother! Oh, Wilhelm!" Then she lost consciousness and could only whimper, "Lord, help me!" Loehe wrote about this hardest hour of his life: "I poured my heart full of pain into prayers, which I do not remember. Only this I know that I could not release her to anyone, anyone, except to Him, our Lord Jesus . . . "

Friends who had come to visit someone on the mend, now stood at her death-bed and prayed with the husband and the people in the house. Helene Loehe, when she drew her last breath, was 24 years old.

Loehe concluded his report about her death: "I thanked her for her countless deeds of charity, for her sacrificial love—I became the most miserable person under the sun, while she inherited eternal riches."[56]

Two days later the funeral procession went from the parsonage out to the new cemetery. As Loehe wrote, he had to "put his fortune into the ground."[57] Many friends had come, including Loehe's sister Dorothea Schroeder and her daughter. Loehe himself conducted the funeral. Helene's casket was carried into the tomb and put next to that of her mother.

Until further decisions could be made, the four orphaned children were sent to Fuerth.

The death of Helene was the hardest blow that could have hit Loehe. It was incomprehensible to him that he had to give up his "most beloved" so soon. He did not understand God's counsel; his faith suffered "severe blows:" "This must have been the reason why for six years the Lord let me grow together with a holy innocent soul and become one with her: He had to find a place where He could really hurt me and shake me up, away from the dream of this life."[58]

The relatives, the friends, the entire village were mourning with him. They all had taken the charming, modest pastor's wife into their hearts. An old friend of Loehe, Friedrich Hommel, whom he knew from his youth, including his days at the university, a lawyer in nearby Heilsbronn, visited Loehe often during these difficult days. He had been a frequent visitor in the parsonage while Helene was still living, and in his diary he praised her "pure, noble, childlike, pious soul" and her "outward appearance" which was "strictly lovely:" "To watch those two spouses live together in such a beautiful, rare and intimate way always made a visit especially pleasant and cordial . . . This woman seemed necessary on this earth in order to make her husband and her family happy . . . "[59]

AFTER HELENE'S DEATH

The most pressing problem was the care of the children and the large household. Relatives and friends offered to take the children, but Loehe refused: "Just because the beautiful top of the tree has been cut off, they want to make things easy for it by taking off the branches as well . . . "[60]

So Loehe wanted to keep the children, but he was "dismayed to find out how much a mother's heart and eye means for little children—what a loss my poor uneducated and ill mannered children have suffered."[61] Loehe's mother came to help, and to oversee the maids. His niece Mina, the daughter of Dorothea Schroeder, also came to help. But the household was not running as smoothly as it should. Grandmother was indulgent with the children. She could hardly manage the older ones. Father stood by helplessly and thought: "Oh God! Oh, Helene!" If Grandmother didn't know what to do any more, she threatened the children with "the aunt in Frankfurt."

Loehe knew very well what his mother was thinking, without her saying a word. A widower with four little children had no choice; He had to marry again as soon as possible. Did she not take the place of her early departed sister, and became the second wife of her brother-in-law when she was only 19? Thus Loehe's mother was thinking of Helene's sister as wife for her son. Loehe could not entirely reject this idea. He knew his sister-in-law would be the "best step-mother," because she was willing on her own "to be of help without ever wanting to replace Helene."[62] And yet everything within him resisted the thought of a second marriage.

Many other people thought and spoke like Loehe's mother, and he was sensitive to this speculation, but he saw a mountain of problems, and "she is no longer here who would always provide a happy end and a friendly solution to my earthly questions."[63]

As time went on it became ever clearer "that there no longer is a Helene in the world."[64] He rejected the plan to marry Helene's sister. A year after Helene's death he wrote to his mother:

> Please don't talk to me about marriage any more. It won't happen. I cannot do that which scares me, just because of the children. I will not venture again into all the changes which marriage would bring. I confess to you that since the death of my beloved Helene, I simply could not imagine ever loving another woman in marriage. Please leave me alone in this matter.[65]

The sorrow for Helene and the pain of separation continually dominated his thinking and feeling. "Oh the sweet habit of living with her!" he complained in his diary. He longed to at least have a picture of her, but the portrait which his father-in-law sent him from Frankfurt didn't turn out well and was a disappointment. "That's not her. It's hard that I cannot even have a picture of her. Oh, God!"[66]

For Helene's birthday on June 27, 1844, as a reminder for friends Loehe composed a booklet with the title: "Life of a Holy Maid of God in a Parsonage." It became a "manuscript for just a few people" in which he described Helene's life, especially her last days. Here already her image was beginning to be transfigured. In the following years he made her more and more into an ideal woman. "In the light of her transfiguration she appears even more beautiful and lovely than I experienced her soul here."[67] He praised her "rare originality of behavior, her being without falsehood, her simplicity." All this had been "transfigured into an ideal"[68] for him. Three years after her death he wrote in his diary: "In my life I was never lucky until I found Helene. Since her death I die daily. May God have mercy on me and my poor orphans!"[69]

What wifely virtues in Helene did Loehe lift up? "I never saw a wife more modest, less demanding, more humble than her,"[70] he emphasized in her biography. She was much younger than he, she had been his student, and her spiritual and religious life was to a large extent formed by him. To be subject to the authority of her husband was unquestioned by her, as well as the readiness to serve in the house and the congregation. In the Neuendettelsau parsonage he was the "head," she was the "heart."[71]

At the same time Helene had a benign influence on her husband, preventing him from being too stiff. Influenced by her youthful temper and her exuberant cheerfulness, he changed a great deal.

"My marriage with Helene turned me into a cheerful man," he wrote shortly after her death. "Because of the overabundance of cheerfulness and friendliness of my beloved, I was more lighthearted with others. Perhaps now I will sink back into my old melancholy again."[72]

Loehe would never again marry. He would prefer to soon follow his beloved Helene into eternity. Only his children were holding him back. Every year he observed the day of her death with painful memories. Four years after her death he wrote a long poem in his diary. Here are just a few verses:

"I want to go look for you,
The one I missed so long.
I cannot stand still
Since you went away . . .

Yet I already know the Gate
Of the house where you are.
There you will be waiting for me
With sweet talk.

I am coming soon,
Then I knock at your door.

You will open for me
As you always did.

With your gracious love
Lead me to your King
And also to the mansions
Where I am so blessed.

If I imagined all this
Too much in an earthly way:
Let me find it more beautiful
In unimagined splendor.

In the meantime I carry within me
A bloody, red wound.
I will look in vain for healing
Until I die."[73]

6

Mission in North America

It was hard for Loehe to overcome his deep sadness and do his daily chores again. He felt paralyzed and was overcome with a longing for death, but there was an incredible amount of work waiting for him: In the house he had to take care of the children and direct the domestic personnel. The congregation demanded all his energy. Also he had started mission work in North America a few years earlier. During the six short and happy years of his marriage, Loehe, from his little village, had laid the cornerstone for an activity abroad which caught everyone's attention.

A short review of this development follows.

Review of Loehe's Missionary Activity

Even in his younger years Loehe was very interested in missions, and this interest continued undiminished. In Loehe's understanding Church and Mission, the spreading of the kingdom of God, belonged closely knit together, a unity. During his student years he had the mission circle in Fuerth. Then there were the mission hours in Kirchenlamitz. In many other places where he worked Loehe always tried to make the congregations aware of the importance of mission work and often collected donations. These donations were sent to the Basel Mission Society. This work was always threatened or forbidden by the State. As a young vicar Loehe was indignant that the church consistories did not demand the "freedom of missions" as a "right of ownership of the Church:" "I think it is shameful that the protestant church in Bavaria does not openly stand up for the commandment of Jesus Christ 'Go into all the world' etc, and does not find peaceful ways to achieve the freedom to do so."[1]

Loehe was not the only one in Bavaria with a passion for missions. While he was studying, a missionary society existed in Erlangen, with professors Krafft, Schubert and von Raumer as members. There was also one in Nuremberg, where it was forbidden in 1822. The friends of missions in Nuremberg tried several times to receive permission to start a new society. In 1834 another attempt was made to "ask his Majesty most humbly for permission"[2] to start a Bavarian society for missions. It was Loehe, the young interim pastor of St. Egidien, who composed the petition. But in spite of the support of the *Oberkonsistorium*, King Ludwig I rejected the petition.

After this Loehe, together with some Nuremberg friends, planned to send out one or two missionaries with private support. Johann Merkel was playing a leading role among them. "Private enterprises" were not forbidden by His Majesty. Loehe's group was thinking of Asia Minor or Syria as possible mission fields. Loehe was to take an exploratory trip to Palestine and Syria, together with Professor Schubert, and was already busy making preparations. But when Schubert invited him in a very friendly and heartfelt letter to come along, he also mentioned that the trip would cost around 1,000 *gulden*. With a heavy heart Loehe had to give up the idea since he could not raise that much money.

"Zealous for Lutheranism"

The plan to send out missionaries privately did not work out for several reasons, primarily because Loehe became increasingly convinced that mission work should not be the task of individual societies but of the whole Church. However the only true Church for him was the Lutheran Church, therefore only Lutheran missionaries should be sent out. Not all his friends shared this strict confessional standpoint, so there were differences of opinion and ill feelings. Besides, no qualified people could be found that could be sent out.

How did Loehe arrive at such an unbending attitude, so that he was called a "zealot for Lutheranism"[3] as early as 1835?

Loehe came out of the Revival Movement that did not consider confessional membership as important as the experience of having fellowship with God in Jesus Christ, and the personal decision to follow Him. "At that time all were one and the same," wrote an enthusiastic witness of that time, "Herrnhuter, Pietisms, Lutherans, Reformed, Catholics—they were all together in one accord . . . "[4]

As an example, two teachers and friends of Loehe, the professors Krafft and von Raumer were very important for his spiritual life. But they belonged to the Reformed Church in Erlangen, not to the Lutheran congregation. This did not bother the student Loehe in the least. Later, in May of 1834, he supplied the pulpit in the reformed St. Martha Church in Nuremberg without any prejudice.

About mid-1835 Loehe took a step beyond the Revival Movement. He studied Luther's doctrine of justification intensively and came to this realization: Faith cannot rely on feelings but on the Word of God, the redemption through Christ which happened "outside of us" and is not conditioned "by our moods and feelings." Decisive is the "total faith without feelings"—that means faith that is not dependant on feelings—"which clings only to the Word."[5]

This faith experience Loehe found affirmed in the Confessions of the Lutheran Church, especially the three Old-Church confessions or "symbols," namely the Apostolic, the Nicene and the Athanasian Creeds, also the Augsburg Confession, Luther's Small and Large Catechism and the Formula of Concord of 1577, which permanently defined the teaching of the Lutheran Church and distinguished it from the other denominations. From this time on, the Evangelical-Lutheran Church and its confession became more and more important for Loehe. In comparison to other denominations, the Roman Catholic and the Reformed Church, the Lutheran Church seemed to him to be the "unifying middle of the confessions,"[6] a "fountain of truth," because it "keeps Word and Sacrament in its pure confession."[7]

Several friends of Loehe among the Erlangen professors followed a similar path from the Revival Movement to confessional Lutheranism, especially Karl von Raumer who changed his membership from the Reformed to the Lutheran Church. The same was true of Adolf von Harless, a friend of Loehe's from the days of his youth. Soon the concept of "Neo-Lutheranism" made the rounds in Erlangen.

"Three Books about the Church"

How can Loehe talk about the Lutheran Church as the "middle of the Confessions?" For instance, consider the Lord's Supper, which is of central importance for Loehe. The Lutheran Church teaches that "body and blood of Christ are truly and essentially present and are truly distributed and received with the bread and the wine."[8] According to the teaching of transubstantiation of the Roman-Catholic Church, bread and wine lose their substance and are changed "into the body and blood of Christ" when the priest says the words of institution. The reformed teaching of Calvin finally emphasizes that "bread and wine are received with the mouth, but the body of Christ is received only spiritually through faith."[9]

For Loehe, it became clear that "in the Lord's Supper of the Romans the heavenly good displaces the element" (the bread and wine). "In the Lord's Supper of the Reformed the element displaces the heavenly good. But in the Lord's Supper of the true Church both appear in beautiful union, as Christ has instituted it."[10]

Loehe put down his thoughts about the Church in the important work "Three Books about the Church" which appeared in 1845.[11]

"Man has been created for fellowship," Loehe explained, "but the fellowship which has been determined by God"[12] is the communion of saints. It is "the Lord's most beautiful and loving thought."[13] This fellowship is not limited to this world. Once more Loehe used the picture of an uninterrupted procession of pilgrims that moves toward Mount Zion. On its summit shines the heavenly city Jerusalem. Here on earth is the church of pilgrims, the church militant. There in eternity is the church triumphant: "Therefore there exists one eternal Church—partly here and partly there."[14]

> The Church is one, gathered from all nations . . . the universal, truly Catholic Church—it is the great concept that is still being fulfilled . . . the concept which must permeate all mission, or it does not know what it is and what it should do. For Mission is nothing but the one Church of God in its movement . . . the realization of a universal catholic Church.[15]

Thus the task of missions is to gather the one Church out of all nations.

One Church—and yet there are many "particular churches," each one having its own "jewel." They are different in their understanding of the Word and in the administering of the sacraments, and therefore in their Confession.

Which church possesses "the greatest truth?" The criterion has to be whether its "Confession is according to the Scripture."[16] And here Loehe wanted to "present the laurel wreath"[17] without reservation to the Lutheran Church. The only thing that bothered him was the name "Lutheran," because it is not appropriate to describe the "great work of the Church" with the name of a human being. In reality it is the old Christian Church of the apostles. Luther had restored its pure confession against the "innovations and misuses" of the Roman Church. Therefore the Church would have to be called "Christian, Catholic, or Apostolic," were it not for the fact that other *Partikularkirchen* (individual churches) have usurped those names for themselves.

"The true Church calls itself Lutheran for the time being until it is given a better name. But in heaven it has always carried the better names and still carries them."[18]

What do all these insights mean for the work of missions? If the Lutheran Church possesses the "true teaching which flows out of the Confession" it must carry "the torch of truth to all nations" by itself and has to begin mission work among the heathen. But that does not mean that it should exclude others: "We will never interfere with or destroy the good deeds of other confessions among the heathen. But we will do our part, as much as possible, to see to it that the purest doctrine will demonstrate and prove its power to save."[19]

THE PRUSSIAN UNION

This turn inwards toward a decisive Lutheranism was confirmed and strengthened for Loehe by outward events. In Silesia there were some fierce inter-church debates in connection with the so-called Prussian Union. In 1817 the Prussian king, Friedrich Wilhelm III had called for a union of the Reformed and the Lutheran Church in his country, because both confessions seemed separated only by outward differences. Originally this call had been received with great enthusiasm in Prussia and the Bavarian Palatinate, also, the union had been completed with great enthusiasm. But when a few years later the Prussian king ordered the acceptance of a new agenda, which he himself had written, firm resistance arose, especially in Silesia. In 1834 several "old Lutheran" congregations and their pastors wanted to separate themselves from the State Church. The State moved against them with the police. In the congregation of Hoenigern the pastor was arrested, and the church door was broken open by the soldiers because the congregation would not turn over the key.

Loehe followed these events from a distance with great interest and some anxiety. He was in contact with one of the Silesian Lutherans in Breslau, Professor Eduard Huschke, and asked him for more exact information. Loehe himself was against any polemic and "personal ambition"[20] in these confessional disputes: "Oh, what misery, until the borders of the confessions which have been moved, are reestablished; how beautifully people could shake hands across the fences—shone upon by the sun of grace in both gardens!"[21]

But the resistance against the Union made it clearer for Loehe that the differences between the Reformed and the Lutheran Confession had greater significancc than hc had assumed. In Bavaria East of the Rhine these differences had been "softened" to a large degree, because according to Loehe, "people were very Lutheran in the Reformed Church."[22] In fact there were only a few Reformed churches, and like the Evangelical-Lutheran church they were subject to the *Oberkonsistorium*.

Confessional Disputes in Bavaria

In the years leading up to 1837 militant fronts were forming between Catholics and Protestants in Bavaria. At that time "Protestants" included all non-Catholics. Up until then the different denominations in the Kingdom of Bavaria practiced peaceful co-existence. Accepting borders that existed before Napoleon, there were exclusively Lutheran counties and free cities in Franconia and exclusively Catholic areas south of the Danube. The first king of Bavaria, Max I. Joseph, was Catholic, but his wife, Karoline von Baden, was Lutheran. To the court in Munich that had been exclusively Catholic, Karoline brought with her several Lutheran ladies in waiting, court officials, and a Lutheran court preacher. King Ludwig I., son and successor of Max Joseph, built splendid classical buildings, wide streets and squares making Munich a cultural center. In 1833 the Lutheran congregation in Munich received its own church, St. Matthew.*

*(Translator's note: At the dedication of St. Matthew in 1833 three vicars were ordained. One of them was my great-grandfather, Wilhelm Knappe).

But during subsequent years the King fell more and more under the influence of very conservative Catholic circles. In 1837 when Karl von Abel, a dedicated and strict catholic, became minister of the Interior, a time of severe oppression began for the *Oberkonsistorium*, which fell under his authority, and for the entire Lutheran Church in Bavaria. Attempts were made to suppress Protestantism in the Catholic schools. There were efforts made to convert Lutheran children. Stories spread about young girls who were brought to cloisters and kept there against their will.

The Protestants were outraged. No one expected such treatment after the Enlightenment, when reason and tolerance would supposedly have reigned.

The great gulf between the king and his Lutheran subjects became obvious in the so-called "knee-bending conflict" which caused a great stir throughout all of Germany.

The "Knee-bending Conflict"

King Ludwig had read a report about the dedication of a church in Algeria. The French troops present at a field mass all went down on their knees when they were ordered to do so. What an impressive show! It really pleased the king and he remembered that in Old Catholic Bavaria kneeling had also been customary. Should he not re-introduce this custom? Forgetting that now there were great numbers of Lutherans in the kingdom of Bavaria, the king ordered in the summer of 1838 that during Catholic military services everybody should kneel "during the words of institution and during the benediction." The same was to apply during the Corpus Christi procession "when the Most Holy was carried by." When the command "on your knees!" was given, all soldiers were to kneel down, including the non-Catholics.

But this kneeling down was a confessional question for the Protestants; for according to their understanding of the Lord's Supper, the blessed host that was carried in the Corpus Christi procession was not the true body of Christ that had to be venerated on one's knees. So some Lutheran soldiers did not obey the order "on your knees!" but remained standing. On the *Lechfeld* (a parade ground) two generals refused to kneel during a Corpus Christi procession. In Ingolstadt a master bookbinder remained standing, even though the captain was yelling: "Bookbinder, get down!" The defiant answer was: "This bookbinder does not get down!"[23]

The King would not accept such refusals of his order. For him it became a matter of prestige: "A King does not give in!"[24] The dispute lasted seven years, with more and more complaints and petitions coming from the Protestant side. Even the *Oberkonsistorium* finally spoke up for the Lutheran soldiers, although in a very humble way. Protests by a group of delegates to the provincial diet were clearer and angrier. The Erlangen professor of theology Adolf von Harless spoke for this group. Individuals, like the Count Karl von Giech* and Wilhelm Redenbacher, a Lutheran pastor and friend of Loehe, also spoke out.

*(Translators note: Franz Friedrich Karl von Giech, born Oct. 29, 1795, died Feb. 2, 1863, was my maternal great-grandfather.)

In 1843 Redenbacher published a report "Truth and Love"[25] in which he called the act of kneeling before the All Holy "idolatry." He called on the Lutheran soldiers to refuse to obey such commands, whereupon he was arrested and sentenced to incarceration in a fortress for one year. The King commuted his sentence, but Redenbacher had to give up his office and live with his large family in great financial distress in Nuremberg until the King of Prussia called him to a church in Thuringia.

LOEHE'S POSITION

Where did Loehe stand while all this was happening? Of course he belonged to those who were fighting against the "Romanists."[26] He was angry with the representatives of the *Oberkonsistorium* who were oppressed by the Catholic ministry of the Interior, and were called upon by the Lutheran pastors to resist. But all they would do was to "bow humbly toward those above and kick those below."[27] On the other hand Loehe could not go along with his friend Redenbacher who led the harshest attack. He considered this an "unwise mistake."[28] In spite of that, he assured his friend in a letter that he stood by him: "I would gladly stand by you when you are called upon to defend yourself, or have to suffer, so that you would not be alone . . . But so far I do not feel that the Lord has called me to do so, and no one should presume to fight on his own . . . "[29]

So he did not feel called to expose himself in this fight, especially since he wrote this letter in the spring of 1844, a few months after the death of his wife when he was burdened with other cares.

The pastors of the Windsbach District, including Loehe, already belonged to the resisters and were therefore in danger of losing their offices. Loehe wrote about this with some sarcasm to his sister: “We are fighting our fight and your brother is not the last. Nothing more pleasant could happen to me than to be relieved of the office of a Bavarian pastor. It’s a pain to serve under such weak-minded and cowardly superiors.”[30]

Fortunately there was no suspension of the obstreperous pastors. The resistance against the knee bending order finally became so strong among the Lutheran population that the King in 1845, after a seven-year long struggle, had to lift it. Likewise, the power of Interior Minister Abel was limited and a special ministry for cultural affairs was created. From now on the *Oberkonsistorium* was subject to that latter ministry.

As for Pastor Redenbacher, Loehe was very disappointed that he accepted a position in a United Church in Prussia, even though Lutheran congregations were open to him as well. According to Loehe, the Prussian Union had created nothing but “confusion”: Next to the Reformed and the Lutheran confessions there now existed a third one, the Union Church. God must have His own plans for the Church, Loehe wrote: “The Lord is not going to unite churches, but He will unite His children into a Church.”[31]

THE DRESDEN MISSION

Through all this inward and outward turmoil Loehe became sensitized to the importance of confessional questions. He was repelled when fellow pastors, according to his opinion, were carefree and unconcerned about differences between the confessions.

This “churchly indifference” bothered him in regard to the Basel mission which he had supported for decades. They considered themselves a “free society” and believed that a missionary who worked among the heathen should not be obligated to follow a certain confession. One should be able to ignore the differences between Reformed, Lutheran, and United confessions on the mission field and only pass on the "basics of the common faith of the evangelical Church."[32]

Loehe had a different opinion. A mission with a common confession would make sense only "if the missions had no other purpose than to bring the heathen to the beginning of Christianity. But they want to and should do more than just revive individuals or groups. Souls should be led on further; congregations should be gathered and led."[33]

Loehe distrusted any revival. It was often only a momentary eruption of feelings: "There is no condition among Christians more ambiguous than that of revival, this small beginning of a new life."[34] It is more important that this beginning be strengthened, and a congregation be formed. This can only happen when connected with a church, and therefore with a distinct confession. Therefore mission must be a task of the Church, not of a free society which does not want to be obligated to a certain confession.

For that reason Loehe withdrew his support of the Basel Mission for a while, and in 1842 he permanently separated himself from it. But how was he going to continue the work of missions which was so dear to his heart? As far as the Bavarian *Landeskirche* (the official State Church) was concerned, there was no telling when any missionary activity would be permitted by the King. But in Dresden the "Evangelical Lutheran Mission Society of Saxony" was founded in 1836 and all Lutheran friends of missions were invited to join. The Nuremberg group authorized Loehe in 1838 to take part in the Dresden Mission festival as an "eye witness,"[35] so that he would have a clear idea of what the mission institute was like. Loehe spent five days in Dresden, had conversations with the leader of the institute, Johann Georg Wermelskirch, and took part in the meetings. His main concern was the training of future missionaries. He was invited to take part in the final examinations of the students and was allowed to ask them questions concerning dogmatics. Loehe was very disappointed over their lack of knowledge. Sometimes they knew less than "well trained confirmands."[36] Loehe made no secret of this opinion and as a result became rather unpopular with the leadership.

So he had conflicting impressions of the Dresden Mission. On the one hand it was a Lutheran society, but on the other hand it did not seem capable of producing well trained missionaries. His relationship with Dresden was not without tensions during the following years.

Loehe did continue to support the mission society with donations but only half-heartedly: "If only I knew," he wrote in 1839, "where I should send my mission-loving people with their hard-earned money, I would want to warn them about Dresden. They should not support an institution whose products are not expected to bring honor to our Church."[37]

HELP FOR GERMAN EMIGRANTS

A year later, there was suddenly a new perspective on missions. When Loehe visited his friend Karl von Raumer in Erlangen on December 8th, 1840, he was shown an appeal from a society in Stade. They were concerned with the fate of German emigrants to North America. In this appeal the German-American pastor Wynecken described in moving words the needs of countless people who no longer could find work in Germany because of the beginning industrialization and therefore emigrated to America. Many of them were members of the Evangelical-Lutheran Church who found themselves in the New World, in widely separated areas, without any church connections and without any possibility for a religious education for their children. The 1,200 Lutheran congregations in North America had only 400 pastors. Pastor Wynecken emphasized very dramatically that help from Germany was absolutely necessary:

> Thousands of families who share your faith…are hungry for the strengthening food of the Gospel. They implore you with loud cries: Help us! Give us preachers that can strengthen us with the Bread of Life, build us up through the Word of the Lord, and instruct our children in the saving teachings of Jesus![38]

Loehe immediately felt that this cry for help concerned him. Many Lutheran Christians from his province of Franconia were part of this wave of emigrants. They were waiting for spiritual help from the home country. The need was pressing. At the same time Loehe saw the possibility of immediately and personally becoming involved, without having to wait for the initiative of missionary societies.

On December 12, Loehe submitted for publication an article to his friend, Pastor Johann Friedrich Walcheren in Noerdlingen, publisher of the "Noerdlingen Sunday Paper." The article, entitled "Lutheran

Emigrants in North America" appeared in the January 1841 edition and was an urgent appeal to the readers of the Sunday weekly. Loehe quoted from Pastor Wynecken and pleaded urgently with the readers to listen to the cry for help so as not to leave the Lutheran congregations over there to the sectarians: "Should we only support the foreign missions of our Church and allow the existing congregations of our Church perish? . . . We should do the one thing and not let go of the other! Come, brothers, let us help as much as we can!"[39]

Upon this appeal, donations began to come in, in fact the considerable sum of 2,000 *gulden.* Shortly afterwards a shoemaker, Adam Ernst of Oettingen, a former student of Wucherer, showed up. He had read Loehe's appeal in Bohemia where he was working, and he felt called to go to North America as a preacher.

But where was he going to receive training and by whom? Since he didn't want to be a missionary among the heathen, but wanted to work among German emigrants he was not a candidate for a mission institute. Loehe had predicted this problem when he wrote his appeal and had written to Wucherer: "Let us both step into the breach and do this thing. It is in vain to put our hope in others."[40]

The two friends were determined to take matters into their own hands. In the course of the year 1841 another candidate showed up, Georg Burger, a weaver.

These both were artisans, but was not the need in North America for trained pastors? Loehe thought about this: "We cannot find theologians, so I believe that we should send out teachers who can also be catechists and are able to conduct reading services."[41]

Didn't the Count von Zinzendorf also send out two artisans from his little Herrnhut congregation a hundred years ago? It was perfectly clear to Loehe that a beginning had to be made in North America with these two as soon as possible. There was no time to train preachers, but these artisans should be able to acquire the necessary knowledge to teach school in just a few months. So Loehe found quarters for the two "pupils" in Neuendettelsau. It was in 1841. Helene Loehe was taking care of a large household, but she instantly agreed to have the two as guests at their table in the parsonage. Loehe himself taught them history, geography, dogmatic, German and English. He also trained them in pastoral care by taking them with him when he visited members of the congregation and by sending them to visit the sick.

Others who could help with the instruction were found in nearby Windsbach. Dean Heinrich Brandt started an "institution for orphaned sons of pastors" in that town in 1837. Loehe had taken an active part in the development of this school. He knew the teachers and educators well. One of them was willing to instruct the pupils in playing piano and in singing.

In the spring of 1842 Oettingen and Burger passed an examination, and in July they started out from Neuendettelsau for North America.

THE COLUMBUS SEMINARY

Four months later Loehe received the first letter from the two "emergency helpers," as he called them. The crossing of the Atlantic had taken seven and a half weeks. Even on board the ship they had started instructing children of emigrants. Arriving in New York they went to a German pastor who lived there. Professor Winkler, who happened to be his guest at that time, was in charge of a seminary for the training of pastors in Columbus, Ohio. He immediately suggested to the two young men that he could take them along to Columbus where they could be trained as preachers in a year and a half. However, their home church would have to pay for their expenses.

Loehe immediately had a hunch that here a "door for considerable effective work in North America"[42] had been opened. He got in touch with Professor Winkler and the Ohio Synod, which began in a merger of the Lutheran congregations in that area. The Synod was very impressed by the two young artisans and expressed an urgent request for another fifty pupils with as good an education as Ernst and Burger had received. What a rich possibility for cooperation! But for Loehe, his inquiry whether the Ohio Synod stood "firmly on the ground of all the symbolic books of the Evangelical Lutheran Church"[43] was a "question of life and death" and he would ask for a pledge to that effect from their ordinands.

After this question had been cleared to Loehe's satisfaction a close cooperation developed. Burger entered the seminary in Columbus, while Ernst chose to go a different way for the time being. In a very short time he started a school for 90 children in three classes while earning his own livelihood as a shoemaker in great demand. Loehe was very happy about this, for he considered the work with the children of emigrants as most important: "We are going to be very pleased," he wrote to Adam Ernst, "if you start one school after another and thereby prepare the way for the brothers that are going to follow you."[44]

And how were things with these "following brothers?" In 1843 a young teacher Baumgart traveled to America. He had converted from Judaism to Christianity and had been baptized by Loehe in Windsbach in 1836. This baptism had stirred up great excitement in quiet Windsbach at that time. Loehe, who preached a stirring sermon to a "crammed full church,"[45] reported afterwards that "things got pretty tumultuous," but Baumgart did "not lose his composure."[46] The young man, who in baptism received the name "Paul Israel" was very close to Loehe and saw him as his "spiritual father."[47] In 1844 three other young men followed him to North America. Like Baumgart they had spent several months in Neuendettelsau and were well-prepared for their task.

In the meantime, Loehe and Wucherer met with the friends of mission in Nuremberg and Erlangen. They would have liked to include them in their work in North America. Many, especially the professors, wanted to send only trained Lutheran theologians to America, but so far no such people had been found. However, there were others who had not studied at a university. Should these ready messengers be rejected; and should one wait for theologians and by waiting perhaps miss "the footsteps of God?"[48] Loehe was thinking very realistically and practically: If right now it was possible to send students to the Columbus seminary, where they could be trained in and for that foreign land, then this would be the faster and more effective way of helping. The German emigrants needed "people who could be both pastors and teachers."[49] Loehe was convinced that one ought to follow the example of the first Herrnhut missionaries and train "emergency helpers" able to handle the special situations and special problems of the emigrants.

Loehe was able to put his idea into practice, and it proved to be very successful. A few years later he could report with pride: "We may dare to assure you that the accomplishments of our emergency helpers are in no way any less than those of the young men who were university trained."[50]

TRAINING OF THE "EMERGENCY HELPERS"

But with this "emergency helper concept" the Neuendettelsau pastor also faced the task of organizing the preparation of the future Columbus seminarians. Many applied for the job: Artisans, teachers, merchants. Not all were fit for the task. Loehe had to be very strict in his selections and had to refuse many. In the summer of 1843 six applicants were housed in Neuendettelsau. They took their meals in the inn. For their lessons, Loehe again found help among the Windsbach teachers.

In order to further support the Columbus seminary Loehe collected urgently needed books and lesson material for the schools. Twelve hundred pounds of books were sent to America in 1843.

Where was he to find the means to send the books, train the emergency helpers, and pay for their passage? Loehe gratefully accepted any kind of help. A Ladies Aid society in Hannover offered to take care of equipping the young people. Loehe wrote that for two of the travelers he needed 18 shirts, 18 pairs of wool socks, 12 *chemisettes* (undershirts?), 18 handkerchiefs, and 24 neckbands: "For the shirts the people over there desire fine cotton, since everybody wears those." If the "mild hands"[51] of the ladies would also provide towels and bed linen, this would be most appreciated.

Official collections were not allowed. Loehe had to think of something else. One idea for financing the work in North America was the founding of a periodical, "Church News From and About North America," which Wucherer edited in 1843, but Loehe wrote most of the articles. Many people bought the paper in order to support Loehe's work. Soon it had 7,000 to 8,000 readers and an annual profit of 7,000 *gulden*. Even without any official collections there were donations from all over Franconia and also from Hannover and Mecklenburg.

But was this effort for emigrants really "mission" work, since it was done for Christians, not for heathen? Again and again friends of mission confronted Loehe with this question. That is why he made good use of the term "Inner Mission" which the Goettingen professor Friedrich Luecke had coined. For Loehe Inner Mission meant work among baptized Christians who are in danger of losing their faith. They are living at the "border between Christianity and paganism." The Lutheran Church's road to the heathen leads through these "lukewarm flocks of Christianity" according to Loehe's conviction: "Inner Mission leads to Outer Mission!"[52]

7

BETWEEN WORK IN THE CONGREGATION AND AMONG EMIGRANTS

All the hopeful beginnings of the work in North America were crowned with success. But then Loehe was suddenly plunged into a deep personal crisis by the death of Helene. Forever more he would consider the day when his wife died, November 24, 1843 as that deep chasm of his life. His energetic walk had suddenly ceased. Even though he resumed his work, in spite of the pain, it was not the same kind of walk. He was tired and looked so bad that he wrote that "many a peasant would start crying"[1] when he saw him.

"AGENDA" AND "BOOK FOR THE HOME"

During this time of mourning, Loehe's "source of rich comfort"[2] was the work on the "Agenda for Christian Congregations of the Lutheran confession" which appeared in 1844.

As he wrote, Loehe had in mind his own congregation as well as the congregations in North America. He dedicated this book to Pastor Friedrich Wynecken, who had provided the impetus for the help for the emigrants. Loehe researched more than 200 older church orders for this agenda and picked out the best for a new order of service for the "brothers across the sea."

He had already introduced many parts of the liturgy in Neuendettelsau, most recently the order for private confession in 1843. He had purposely waited a long time and had only used the common confession during the main service in order not to demand too much from his parishioners. But whenever possible he had lifted up the blessing of private confession and absolution.

But one Sunday he offered private confession, announcing from the pulpit: "I know very well how things are with you. Some of you will desire private confession; others will not like it. In order to do justice to both parties, I am going to be in church this coming Saturday at 12 noon in order to hear private confession. Afterwards we are going to have the vesper service with a common confession."[3]

At the given hour, Loehe asked someone to check whether anyone had come only to learn that the church was full of people who wanted to go to private confession. From then on private confession was more and more accepted in Neuendettelsau. But Loehe wanted to lead his people away from memorized formulas and he encouraged them to "confess freely from the heart." For some of them this was difficult because they did not know how to express themselves in high German and "foolishly were ashamed of their dialect."[4] Loehe could not understand this at all. For this "master of German prose" spoke "Franconian, even from the pulpit,"[5] as a friend remarked.

Besides this agenda Loehe also put together a "House, School and Church Book" which was meant for both the home country and for America. This work was also close to Loehe's heart. It was, as he said, "the fruit of my life and work in my office; I have nothing better to leave behind."[6] The first part appeared in 1845 and contained, among other things, Luther's Small Catechism with explanations by Loehe. He put together questions and answers about the six Principal Parts and a collection of appropriate Bible passages. In the foreword he gave an exact pedagogical instruction for the introduction of the Catechism. The book was intended for the main service and for parents who "would like to instruct their own children – as is the case with so many who live in the woods of North America."[7]

SOCIETY FOR TRACTS

Loehe considered it very important that the parents teach their children at home. He saw in this "a secret for the education of the people."[8] When the parents teach, they also learn, and their "interest in mental occupation" is aroused. According to Loehe, education of the people "grows" best when "old and young learn together."[9] Therefore Loehe and his friends of the "Tract Society" illustrated posters with biblical pictures as "teaching helps for the parents"[10] and excerpts from an old Bible for children from the 18th century.

The "Society for Tracts" was founded in 1840 by Pastors Wucherer, Kuendinger, Hornung and Loehe. It quickly grew to over 60 members who could be enlisted as coworkers and who helped the enterprise financially. Loehe hoped that the society could support him "especially fitting tracts for pastoral care."[11] In 1842 he took over as editor. He wrote several tracts on congregational life, and he also made use of devotional literature from former centuries.[12]

The small and reasonably priced tracts were being circulated very widely through the support of well-known bookstores in Noerdlingen, Nuremberg, Dresden and Frankfort. They contributed to Loehe's name becoming known far beyond the borders of Bavaria.

EDUCATION OF THE CHILDREN

When did Loehe find the time to do all his writing, besides other daily obligations? About 4 AM when his children were sleeping, he was often standing at his writing desk working on his publications.

He took care of his children as best he could, during night time, and especially if they were sick. During the summer of 1844 he was especially worried about his youngest, one year-old Philipp, who had a high fever which dragged on for weeks. The doctor diagnosed "raging consumption."[13] Loehe had to stand by and look on as the child got sicker all the time. He felt "submerged into an ocean of misery."[14] Philipp died on September 14 after a "long and hard struggle." Loehe wrote to his friend Karl von Raumer:

> My Philipp is at home with his mother and with his Savior. How sick I was next to his sickbed! . . . I ask the Lord not to spare me, but make me ready for eternal life. Only one thing is really hard for me: Helene's departure. Everything else is only an appendix. Only from the perspective of November 24, 1843 has life any meaning for my heart.[15]

Three children remained and he had to be both father and mother for them. Once he called them playfully "my dear *Meerkatzen* (a species of monkeys), but seriously, my beloved children."[16] He decided to teach them himself. In so doing he came to "know them well."[17] They had a great advantage in his eyes: "They are mine." But he was not always happy with them; they caused him much "trouble, cares and worries." Was he always the right educator for them? In a self-critical way he noticed that at times "for fear of doing the wrong thing I become passionate, unjust and tyrannical." He remembered that, toward the end of her life, Helene once criticized him—something she rarely did—because he was "so fearful in these matters."[18]

His oldest son, Ferdinand, who in some way was closest to him, did not seem to be very gifted. He was weak and slow in learning so that his father at times could "weep bitterly," if he were not so ashamed. It took a long time before he understood that he had to take this child, "whom he loved dearly," as he was, and that he had to "carry" him.[19]

Gottfried, called Friedel, was a "different fellow," Loehe stated. He was handicapped since his birth with a "half-lame hand" and a "half lame foot," but "otherwise he is a strong person, full of fiery joy and fiery anger."[20] The child was "full of enthusiasm, full of friendliness, full of life, full of laughter, full of anger and then again enthusiasm, the darling of all in the house."[21] He comprehended things much faster than his older brother. The father let him sit next to Ferdinand and a cousin, to whom he was dictating, and Friedel "with his smeary writing tries to copy everything they are writing."[22]

Between the two brothers there was one daughter Marianne, Loehe's "little girl" whom he called endearingly, "Anndl" or also "Marandl." Loehe characterized her as "passionate, lazy, vain, a dreamer," but he also saw in her "good gifts of mind and emotions."[23] But he also recognized that her education should be put into feminine hands as soon as possible.

When Marianne turned eight, Loehe's sister Dorothea Schroeder, whom he had implored for help, said she was willing to take "poor Anndl"[24] into her house for a while. In July of 1847 Marianne moved to Fuerth for one year. There she had private teachers who instructed her in calligraphy, math, and piano. She also was to learn all the feminine arts and crafts so that "some day she can knit socks for her brothers and mend the holes in their clothes,"[25] as her father hoped. Loehe wrote many letters to his daughter and sent her an evening prayer which she was to say daily. He also admonished her to obey her relatives who had so kindly received her:

"Fare well, my little girl, and make your old man happy by being obedient and by living to love and please other people, as did your mother."[26]

Whether he realized it or not, Loehe wished ardently that his only daughter would be like her mother in her character. None of his letters were without some reference to his departed wife. He didn't realize that in doing so he was putting a lot of pressure on little Marianne. He loved her and tried to see her at least once a month, even though his mother didn't think that this was very wise. But Loehe did not want to break up the "wholesome relationship of a child with its father."[27]

In December of 1847 he wrote a long letter to his sister Dorothea. He was immeasurably thankful for everything she was doing for Marianne. He also asked her to get some Christmas presents for his children, for "in Dettelsau you can't get anything, and we would have to walk all day on our muddy roads." So Dorothea was asked to buy slates for his boys, the kind "that have corners with clean tin," also "a green cord, a little sponge and a dozen colored pencils, the kind which now-a-days are often given to children for fun." Besides that she should have made for each boy some rulers, also stilts and a "simple, but well-made crossbow." Each of the brothers should also get a wide leather belt with the name "Helene" embroidered on it. And don't forget "a toothbrush and tooth powder. Just to use the hand doesn't work very well." He couldn't think of anything for Marianne besides a writing pad—but did Dorothea know of something? He would reimburse her for all her expenses "down to the last penny" even before Christmas. He would also love to give something to his sister: "If only I, an uncouth donkey, with my big nose could sniff out something that would make you happy, I would gladly do it!"[28]

Attempts to Leave Neuendettelsau

During his first ten years in Neuendettelsau Loehe was often urged by his friends to apply for a city church. His great spiritual gifts should not be wasted in that remote village. Following this advice Loehe had applied for a position in Augsburg, in 1839, and in 1842 in Nuremberg; both times without success. Since the children were growing up, a change seemed to be even more urgent. Nevertheless, said Loehe, Neuendettelsau, a name that doesn't sound very nice, will always be a lost paradise for me,"[29] for here he spent his most happy years of his life with his Helene. However in a city the children would have more educational opportunities. In 1846 Loehe applied for a position in Fuerth, his home town and the place where his mother and his siblings were living and therefore especially attractive. There he would be able to go "every morning and evening" with the children "to their grandmother and wish her a good morning and a good night."[30]

But in Fuerth other applicants were given preference. Loehe summed up in a letter to Dorothea: "During the last ten years I have tried three times to find another position . . . and the Lord always kept a place for me here. His thoughts are becoming clear to me, and I will gladly say Amen to His gracious denial."[31]

Except once more, in 1847, he took courage and applied for a position in his beloved Erlangen when the old city church became vacant. But when this position also was denied him, he gave up any thought of further applications. He thought that "God has envisioned for me the way of loneliness."

Of course these disappointments hurt Loehe, especially when he heard what a member of the supreme consistory said about him: His "kind and his direction"[32] would always be a minus point in any application. Thus he learned that he did not have the best reputation in the consistory. That had already become clear in 1843 when the pastors of the Windsbach district had elected him as their senior; but the consistory "didn't like him," as a bitter Loehe wrote at that time, "and therefore rejected the election and put in an incapable older pastor as interim senior . . . a slap in the face for me . . . "[33]

All these experiences convinced Loehe that according to God's will, his place would be in Neuendettelsau forever. He was willing to accept this guidance gratefully. Even after he was rejected in Fuerth he wrote: "Since things are going so well for me in Neuendettelsau . . . I am happy to stay in the place where I have been most happy and most sad. I only hope that my work here will be a blessing for this town."[34]

He was very touched when he heard that some of the peasants had prayed that he would stay in Neuendettelsau. Could it be the right place for him anyway? He was highly respected and much loved in the whole area. The whole village took an active interest in his work for North America. Every Sunday, after Sunday School Loehe reported the news from across the sea and read letters from the "emergency helpers" to his congregation. Everybody knew them, since they used to live in the village and visit the sick in many homes. It was a big thing when Adam Ernst was called to a congregation in Ohio and called it "New Dettelsau." The Neuendettelsau farmers made very generous donations. In 1845 alone the village supported five emergency helpers. Many farmers were signing up to pledge monthly contributions, but because such collections were forbidden, the list had to remain a secret.

There was a similar list of donors in the congregation at Rosstal, approximately three hours from Neuendettelsau. Many of the Rosstal people considered Loehe their spiritual father and made the pilgrimage to Neuendettelsau every Sunday in order to hear him preach.

SCHOOL FOR MISSIONARIES

The engagement with North America spread in ever wider circles from the center of Neuendettelsau. Loehe had some friends among the pastors in the Ruegland area. They offered their help and were willing to take in and instruct some students, since Loehe could no longer handle the growing number of applicants. In 1845 fourteen future *Nothelfer* (emergency helpers) were being trained in Neuendettelsau and another fifteen in the two "*Aussenstellen*" (Branches).

Loehe was in constant correspondence with his "Americans." Not everything there turned out as he had hoped. He had differences with the seminary in Columbus concerning the language of instruction. Should German or English be spoken during class-time? Loehe was convinced that, for the time being, the teachings of the Evangelical-Lutheran Church could be passed on only in German, since none of the basic literature existed in English. He emphasized that he cared more for the Lutheran element than for the German, but since there was "much overlapping"[35] of both languages in America, the work of the Church in America must be done in German. Even though Loehe suspected that in the long run English would prevail in North America, he admonished the German-Lutheran congregations in 1845, in an urgent "call from the homeland"[36] to keep their German language which, next to their Church, was their "most precious jewel."

When the Columbus seminary decided nevertheless that the teaching language should be English, Loehe and his people separated themselves from the seminary and from the Ohio Synod. After a short period of cooperation with the Michigan Synod, Loehe's *Nothelfer* established contact with Lutheran congregations in Missouri who had emigrated from Saxony. A new seminary was founded in Fort Wayne in 1846, and from then on all the students that received their preliminary training in Neuendettelsau were required to go there.

However, the training of the young people got to be more than Loehe could handle. Fortunately he found an excellent man to work with him, Friedrich Bauer, who had been a teacher and catechist at a school in Nuremberg. Thus the "Missionary preparatory school" was founded in April 1846 in Nuremberg. Friedrich Bauer was entrusted with its leadership. Together with other teachers he taught without salary.

A year later the Missouri Synod was constituted during a conference in Chicago. It was a union between the Saxon congregations and those taken care of by Loehe's *Nothelfer*. In a solemn letter to the president, Carl Ferdinand Wilhelm Walther, in September of 1848, Loehe turned over the Fort Wayne seminary to this synod. He laid down some conditions for the transfer: The seminary should always serve the Lutheran Church, the language of instruction should be German and it should not become a theological university but should remain a school for "planting of preachers and pastors."[37] It should also train missionaries to work among the Indians.

FRANCONIAN COLONIES IN NORTH AMERICA

In the meantime Loehe, back home in his middle-Franconian village, was working on yet another plan. While he was caring for the German emigrants, he did not forget his original concern, the missions among the heathen. Should it not be possible to combine both aims in North America, and use a German congregation as a base for missions among the Indians? The idea for such a "mission colony" became "ever clearer"[38] to him. Again he had in mind the example of the Herrnhut Mission which a hundred years previously had started such colonies in Pennsylvania.

One day a candidate of philology, August Craemer from Lower Franconia, showed up in the parsonage in Neuendettelsau. He had studied in Oxford and spoke English well. According to Loehe's judgment he was "motivated, both as a Christian and as a member of the Church" and was determined to "dedicate his life and his strength to the work in North America." Loehe discussed with him his long-standing plan of "combining colonization and mission."[39] The children of the household and the domestics listened attentively. Craemer was immediately enthusiastic about this project. Loehe's domestic servant Lorenz Loesel also declared his readiness to go along as a colonist and so did his "most excellent fiancée" who was also working in Loehe's household. A driving motive for these young people to emigrate was the fact that in Germany they were not allowed to marry. The restrictive laws forbade marriage if a couple could not show enough income.

Lorenz Loesel's fiancée came from the little town of Rosstal, where Loehe had many friends. When the project of a mission colony became known there, "a number of the strongest fellows and girls" decided to join with Craemer. Among them there were four engaged couples who were in the same situation as Loehe's domestics. It was a small but tightly knit group. Their plan found an enthusiastic echo in the surrounding villages. The farmers took a collection and donated two bells for their future church in America. Loehe was happy. "That means that an idea that promises much salvation will become a reality. May God grant His blessing!"[40]

In April of 1845 the young people set out. Craemer, who in the meantime had been ordained, was with them. Immediately after the ship had cleared German territorial waters, Craemer performed his first pastoral act: He married five engaged couples.

South of Saginaw-Bay, immediately adjacent to Indian territory, the young settlers were able to buy a suitable piece of land where they established the colony "Frankenmuth." A year later Craemer was able to buy more land for a reasonable price. It would be home to another newly formed group of colonists from Franconia who established "Frankentrost," and later "Frankenlust," After hard beginnings the colonies developed very nicely.

Frankenmuth especially attracted many emigrants. Often they were friends of relatives of the first settlers. Six years later the colony had 80 log cabins, a saw mill, a grain mill, a doctor, merchants and its own post office.

EMIGRATION—YES OR NO?

Along with the idea of Mission, Loehe and his friends saw these colonies as a solution to a great problem connected with emigration: As Loehe saw it, the stream of immigrants was "disappearing like a vapor"[41] in America. In the loneliness of the woods and prairies of North America people were in danger of sinking into mental and spiritual apathy. Therefore one ought to send out closed groups of the same confession, together with their own pastor, so that in the New World they could immediately start out as a congregation. In order to develop this idea, Loehe in 1848 thought of a "revolving colonization fund."[42] With such a fund one could buy available "first land." Once this was sold, the funds could be used to purchase more land. For "poor engaged couples"[43] who could not marry back home for lack of funds, Loehe planned a colony "Frankenhilf." There they were to be given a piece of land and a cottage, so they could start their own household. When they were able they could pay back these funds.

Not all the projects could be carried out the way Loehe had imagined them. But though he had originally warned against emigration, when he saw the "frightening increase in poverty,"[44] he became convinced that emigration could be a salvation for thousands of poor in Germany. But of course they needed financial support. This should be a challenge for the State, as Loehe emphasized a few years later:

> After an eight-year experience, we find it incomprehensible that government officials and communities do not give more serious attention to the emigration of the poor. While there is no power in the world that can do away with pauperism and the proletariat, and while millions are simply thrown into poverty relief, a barrel full of holes, it would take only comparatively small amounts to take big burdens away from communities at home and to make many poor people happy and content .[45]

FOREIGN MISSIONS

In the meantime the "Franconian colonies" in Michigan did not forget their original purpose, namely to be bases for mission among the heathen. Already during the first year after the arrival of the colony in Frankenmuth, Pastor Craemer started a school for children of Indians which became very popular. On Christmas of 1846 the first three Indians were baptized. In the following year twelve more were baptized.

In 1847 Craemer received help from missionary Baierlein who had been sent out by the Leipzig Mission. Baierlein took over the school and also started services for Indians. Shortly afterwards he accepted an invitation from an Indian chief who asked him to settle in the territory of his tribe. He built a log cabin there where he lived with his family. It also served as a school and a church. Gradually the Indians followed his example and also built real homes, following his instructions. The missionary named this new village "Bethany." He also composed a primer and a first reader in the tribal language for the children that had biblical stories and was greeted with cheerful interest. For Sunday services the whole tribe gathered. At first things were pretty "back-woodsy:"[46] Children were screaming, the women were talking and the men were smoking the peace pipe. Gradually a congregation of baptized Christians was being formed with a church, complete with a tower and a bell. Its inviting sound called the Indians from a distance of up to five miles.

These were hopeful beginnings, and Loehe followed them from the distance with great interest. In several publications he reported extensively about the development in the Franconian colonies. Would he not like to inspect the distant places of his work in person? After the founding of the Missouri Synod, where, according to the words of Loehe, "all are *in dulci jubilo*,"[47] he received a heartfelt and urgent invitation to visit North America. After thinking it over for a long time, he decided to turn it down. He was "not especially gifted for travel,"[48] he once said. But above all he had no private means to pay for such a trip and he would not touch any of the donated money under any circumstances. Even though he might be good and useful there, he would not "travel on the contributions intended for the poor."[49]

8

STRUGGLE FOR A LUTHERAN CHURCH

Revolution in France in 1848! The "citizen king" Louis Philippe had to abdicate. France became a republic. The people won the upper hand over the ruling princes and the nobility. Quickly the revolution spread to other European countries. In March there were rebellions in Vienna and in Berlin. In Munich the people showed their disapproval of the king especially because he allowed his mistress, the dancer Lola Montez, to have more and more influence in politics. There were wild disturbances, and finally the king was forced to abdicate. His son Maximilian II became his successor.

EFFECTS OF THE REVOLUTION

There were disturbances all over Germany. Even the quiet little village of Neuendettelsau was caught up in these upheavals. In the beginning of February there had been great jubilation, because a royal edict, signed by King Ludwig, had ordered the neighboring village, Reuth, to become part of the Neuendettelsau congregation. In the parsonage the boys jumped around in their room, clapped their hands and shouted: "Reuth has been incorporated! Reuth has been incorporated!"[1]

But the great event of the revolution pushed such local events into the background. The pastor's boys now were playing war and their father had to stop them from calling each other: "You Frenchman!"[2]

In his "corner of the world"[3] Loehe was trying to keep peace and quiet. He reintroduced the prayer for peace[4] during the ringing of the bells for the noonday prayer. Many families in the village adopted that custom. At night, while Loehe sat in his study, he heard the drunks on their way home from the tavern shouting, "Freedom,

Equality!" But there never was a real "uprising" in Neuendettelsau. True, the peasants saw that their hour had come to bring some complaints to the lord of the manor; for "everybody wants to grab the opportunity by the hair,"[5] as Loehe stated. But the people presented their cause in an orderly way during a community meeting, and the patron could be relieved that he was not attacked in a worse way.

Even though Loehe rejected upheavals and the use of force, he nevertheless saw a "promising shape" in the revolution: "That which the nations want to enforce seems to me by and large better than the present conditions. A German parliament seems to me to be a saving anchor, without which everything could break in pieces."

Loehe himself spoke in favor of this "saving anchor." In April of 1848 he was appointed as "voting man" for the election at the planned national assembly in Frankfurt. However, he refused to become a delegate. According to his conviction a pastor should stay away from political movements. Colleagues who were all enthusiastic about the revolutions and were running around with cockades, willing to "run away with the peoples," disgusted him.

But Loehe was eager to seize the opportunity of the hour for his Church. He was interested in the possibilities "which can come for the Church out of these political Upheavals." For years he had foreseen that "the godless" might well "destroy the conditions" and "break the fetters" into which "the Church had been put by the princes."[6]

That meant a "reconstruction" of the Lutheran Church and its constitution. Since the beginning of his ministry Loehe had chafed under the disastrous connection of State and Church under the Catholic King as "supreme bishop." The opportunity was now or never to formulate his thoughts and those of his friends and to present them at the appropriate place.

CONFERENCE IN NEUENDETTELSAU

Toward the end of March, Loehe called a two-day conference to be held in the Neuendettelsau parsonage to debate the following questions:

1. What is the relationship of the Church to the present political movements, and how is a pastor to respond?

2. What possible changes in the conditions of the Church should a pastor be aware of during the present political movements?

Nine of Loehe's closest friends were gathered together, among them pastors Leonhard Kuendiger of Petersaurach, Friedrich Wucherer of Noerdlingen, Eduard Stirner of Fuerth, and Georg Wilhelm Volk of Ruegland. The country judge Friedrich Hommel of Heilsbronn was also present.

There was quick agreement concerning the first question, the relationship of the pastor to politics. A pastor should not "stir up things in politics" and should not "bring politics into the pulpit." Church is "neutral territory." It is the "duty of pastors to keep the one, holy refuge of the weary, the holy Church, for the poor people that are being harassed."

Then the second question was discussed: What kind of changes were to be expected within the realm of the Church? All those gathered were hopeful that the Catholic king would no longer remain the *summus episcopus* (supreme bishop) of the Lutheran *Landeskirche*. The Church should be able to administrate itself. But what would the constitution of the Church look like? There was talk about a synod assembly, headed by a *Praeses* (president) who would take care of current business and be responsible to the Synod. He should be a member of the clergy. Up to now a jurist had always been appointed as the president of the *Oberkonsistorium*.

In addition, the "new building of the Church" should be instituted not only by way of a constitution but also especially by a "better formation of the congregations." Here Loehe developed some basic thoughts, based on the earliest Christian congregations. He considered "Confession and Discipline" the basis for congregational life. That meant that a congregation attend to the keeping of the divine commandments and sanctification of life. Loehe would like to revive old apostolic institutions and offices, the deaconate, for instance.

In the past there was a connection between church and school, but it was obvious that a separation would be unavoidable, for the teachers were often only "compelled to serve the Church." Most likely it would be necessary to establish private church schools.

Loehe and his friends were not the only ones thinking about the future of the Church. Given the general atmosphere of new beginnings after the revolution, there were conferences throughout Germany. There was a Church Day in Wittenberg and a Conference in Leipzig. Even though he was invited, Loehe did not want to take part in them. He was afraid that these conferences would lead to a union of territorial churches and an unclear union could only fail again "given our torn Church conditions." Loehe did not expect much from such large church assemblies: "Deeds," he opined, "are being discussed and accomplished much better by just a few that are of the same mind. Then they can be imitated by everyone."[7]

"Society of Lutheran Christians For an Apostolic Life"

Loehe's deliberations after the Neuendettelsau conference in March of 1848 led him a step farther. He recognized that his ideal picture of the Church could not be realized in a large *Volkskirche* (church of the people), especially not in the Bavarian *Landeskirche*, which, in his opinion was beyond hope. Among the clergy there were "Rationalists, Pietists and Mystics, Reformed, United, and Lutherans in a colorful mixture."[8] In Loehe's opinion this was an "evil conglomeration of hostile elements." The best thing would be a commonly agreed upon separation, a "peaceful parting."[9] But there was a large majority that wanted to keep the *Landeskirche* as a *Volkskirche*, and was most afraid that the various parties might go in different directions.

How could one affect a true breakthrough for the Lutheran Church? Loehe designed a "Suggestion for a Lutheran Society for apostolic life, together with a catechism of the apostolic life."[10] He suggested that serious and convinced Lutheran Christians, which means the "better congregational members" within the *Volkskirche*, should join such a society to be the "kernel, light and salt of the congregations."[11] The Church always had such communities in its midst "whenever life was diminishing within it." They became "conscience and salt" for the "lukewarm and dead members."[12]

Apostolical life is the life that "all the apostles in their letters admonish the congregations to keep." In his "catechism" Loehe mentioned three "pillars" of this life: "Discipline, communion, and sacrifice."[13]

What did Loehe mean by the word “discipline” which sounded so repugnant to many? He referred to the “main passage for discipline within the Holy Scriptures”[14] in the gospel of Matthew:

> If your brother sins against you, go and point out the fault when the two of you are alone. If he listens to you, you have regained your brother. But if he does not listen, take one or two others along with you, so that every word may be confirmed by the evidence of two or three witnesses. If he refuses to listen to them, tell it to the church. And if he refuses to listen to the church, let him be to you as a gentile and a tax collector.

This means that every Christian should become a pastor (*Seelsorger*) for his neighbor and should “involve other Christians in ever widening circles to save the soul of an individual.” Instead of the repugnant word *Zucht* (discipline) which is derived from *ziehen* (pulling) one could also say *Erziehung* (education): “Education of the person for his destiny, for holiness.”[15]

The term “communion” also had special significance for Loehe. Again he went back to the primitive Christian Church where communion first showed itself in the “common possession of goods.” Everybody shared with the others, gave voluntarily “what and how much he wanted to give.” Loehe saw here a clear difference from the “communism of our days:” “For present-day communism wants to empower the poor to take what they like, thus removing the difference in possession of earthly goods, which was ordained by God. Christianity, on the other hand, moves its confessors to freely give of their own.”[16]

The disparity among humans, according to the will of God, should be removed not through force but through “love of the brother.” This is the origin of *Diakonie* (diaconate) which had been instituted by the apostles as a special office.” Communion” and *Diakonie* were really one and the same thing for Loehe.

Loehe pointed out the significance of “sacrifice” in many passages of Holy Scripture. It has something to do with “dedication,” but also with worship, praise and thanksgiving, that is, “true worship.”[17]

On these three basic pillars—discipline, communion and sacrifice—Loehe wanted to found his society. Because the form of a “society” bothered many that would be interested—he is not concerned with rules and lists of members—Loehe later chose the name “Union of Lutheran Christians for an Apostolic Life.” Loehe imagined that people who had chosen the apostolic life according to the “catechism” would gather as “free participants” around “free centers,”[18] across the borders of local congregations. He did not want to designate special services or hours of devotion in order not to be under the suspicion of wanting to separate from the *Landeskirche*.

TRAVEL THROUGH NORTHERN GERMANY

Could the apostolic life become a reality without such obligatory elements? The practical Loehe was very much aware of this problem. Even though he hated to travel he made a trip to Northern Germany in the fall of 1848. He wanted to become acquainted with the situation of the Church outside of Bavaria. He also visited the many friends he knew only from corresponding with them, and he wanted to test whether his “proposition” was doable and to discuss it with them. His companion was Pastor Volk of Ruegland who functioned as “travel marshal” and because of his “happy disposition gave much joy”[19] to serious Loehe. He also took along his 19 year-old nephew, Wilhelm Schroeder, the son of his sister Dorothea. The three made a happy travel company.

The journey went via Nuremberg, Kulmbach, Hannover, Bremen, and Stade to Hamburg. In all these places Loehe met with important men of the Church. He was not equally loved by all. There was, for instance, a Bremen pastor who did not want to see the “Lutheran pope.” But in other places in the North the “fiery, witty, practical Franconians” caused a great stir, as Loehe stated. People were astonished, laughed at them, and considered them “crazy customers.”[20]

The highlight and goal of the trip was the Synod of the Lutheran Church in Prussia which had separated itself from the Prussian Union Church. It met in September 1848 in Breslau. For once Loehe decided to take part in a Church assembly and even gave a speech there. He met many leaders who shared his Lutheran position. Toward the end of the Synod all present were filled with deep emotions and a feeling of unity. Even though he was “showered with love,” he still had many doubts concerning the future of this Church. He returned to Bavaria convinced that “by comparison there is still the greatest blessing here, or at least the greatest hope.”[21]

As to his "proposition," he found much agreement, but also some rejection. Again and again there was the objection that the "community for apostolic living" could not prosper without "physically being together" and the "living practice of those basic ideas." But concrete organizations could become a "little church within the Church,"[22] an "*ecclesiola in ecclesia*." That is what Philipp Jakob Spener, the "father of Pietism" called his small group meetings in the 17th century. Even though Loehe regarded Spener very highly, he nevertheless envisioned more in his proposed "community" than only a revised form of Spener's small groups.

After much consulting with his friends, Loehe's "proposition" and his "catechism" were printed, but their practical application was put on the back burner for the time being. Difficult inner-church debates during the following years required all of Loehe's energies.

THE GENERAL SYNOD OF 1849

The year of revolution, 1848, severely shocked the Bavarian *Landeskirche*. As soon as Maximilian II was at the head of the government, a group of Nuremberg radical rationalists under the leadership of the state librarian Friedrich Wilhelm Ghillany petitioned the king to dismiss the president of the *Oberkonsistorium*, Friedrich von Roth. He was charged with hindering the "right to contemporary religious development."[23] The king gave in to the pressure and dismissed the president on April 1, 1848. Roth's successor was the lawyer Arnold who found himself with a difficult inheritance. In October 1848 the Palatinate, which belonged to Bavaria, requested that its church be declared independent of the *Oberkonsistorium* in Munich. As early as 1817 the people of the Palatinate had voted for the Union of Lutheran and Reformed churches. Ever since then they had tried to get out from under the influence of the Lutheran *Oberkonsistorium*. Now the consistory in Speyer definitely wanted to get out of the alliance of Bavarian consistories and achieved this goal the following year. Only the two consistories of Ansbach and Bayreuth remain.

A "general synod" was called in the beginning of 1849 for the renewal of the *Landeskirche*. The new spirit of democracy was demanding its rights in the Church also. This was evident by the fact that as many lay people as clergy were elected as delegates.

Even though Loehe did not hope for much from this general synod, he and his friends put together a petition, based on the deliberations of the Neuendettelsau conference. It presented clear demands, among others the following:

The king must give up the title of *summus episcopus* (supreme bishop) of the evangelical Church. At their ordination all clergy should definitely be pledged to the Lutheran Confession. At official visitations they should be examined whether they were indeed loyal to the Confession. There should be a clear separation between Lutheran and Reformed-United celebrations of the sacrament. Church discipline should be enforced on "openly unbelieving" church members. Loehe also spoke against the planned introduction of "secular"[24] church elders. Instead he proposed the apostolic office of deacons.

25 pastors and over 300 lay people signed the petition which was to be given to some delegates who were friends of Loehe.

Loehe himself was not a delegate to the synod, but he closely followed the events in nearby Ansbach. He sometimes rode over to Ansbach in order to discuss issues with his friends who were delegates.

At the opening of the synod there was a clear "profession for the Confession" of the Evangelical-Lutheran Church. It was received with great enthusiasm with all the delegates standing. But immediately a reformed delegate asked for the floor. He of course could not accept this confession. Then even from the Lutheran side this first confession was weakened enough, so that Loehe talked angrily about a "maneuver," a "farce," and a "comedy."[25]

The Nuremberg Ghillany-group also had a petition for the Synod. They wanted "an improvement of the protestant writings of faith."[26] For them that meant to delete basic Christian teachings, such as the divinity of Jesus Christ and the redemption of people through his suffering and dying. The only doctrines that remained were faith in the existence of God, striving for moral perfection, and hope of an eternal life.

Loehe gave this grim commentary: "One ought to send Ghillany a "thank-you note,"[27] for through his "shameful petition"[28] it has become clear what unchristian elements are living under the roof of the Bavarian *Landeskirche*." His disappointment and anger over the reaction by the Synod was even greater. While the petition was denied with "indignation and hope that the lost ones will return,"[29] no disciplinary actions against the petitioners were considered.

Loehe's own petitions were taken up very late and very briefly when the Synod was about to adjourn. The synod preferred to keep the status quo in regard to the *Summepiskopat* (to have the king as supreme bishop), since there were certain advantages to being under the protection of the King. The other items of the petitions were denied, or "dealt with in a hurry," because many believed that they had already been dealt with sufficiently.

Loehe was deeply disappointed and upset. His hopes for a new beginning of the Church had been destroyed. A few weeks after the Synod he vented his feelings in a pamphlet: "Illumination of the Decisions of the Synod."[30] Once more he described critically what happened. The result: "In comparison with former synods one can find much that is praiseworthy, but one cannot say that there was faithfulness to the Confession, the way it should be in the Church." According to Loehe the *Landeskirche* was not Lutheran, even though it had that name. It was rather "a disunited bunch lacking harmony." "The supreme bishop is Catholic, the church government is of the Union type, the Church is Lutheran, Reformed, United, Rationalistic."

At the end of the "Illumination" Loehe announced that he and anyone likeminded would part from the *Landeskirche*, even though he realized that he would be accused of splitting the Church. He and his friends needed "a minimum of Lutheran agreement" for church fellowship to be possible.

After his experiences with the Synod it became even clearer for Loehe that his ideal of the Church "as it should be" could be realized only by a small minority. The Church "will have no power unless it becomes small. Whatever is not intensive is not extensive."[31]

Loehe considered either starting a Lutheran Free Church or to joining the Lutheran church in Prussia. One of the Prussian Lutherans that he was corresponding with sent him a signal that Loehe already had been suggested for the office of a district president there.

STRUGGLE FOR AN "UNMIXED COMMUNION FELLOWSHIP"

But things had not progressed that far just yet. First Loehe had to face the numerous reactions to his "Illumination." His evaluation of the general synod caused a great stir throughout all of Germany. In a Nuremberg newspaper he was wildly insulted, because he wanted to pronounce the "ban of the Church" over the Ghillany followers: This "arrogant fellow" should not dare "to charge from his village into our city, or someone would throw a bundle of hay at him at the gate to turn him around, so that he would trot home again."[32]

Loehe endured such hateful attacks with relative equanimity. He was much more moved by the negative response of some of his fellow pastors who in general were quite content with the Synod. Three negative articles appeared in answer to the "Illumination." Loehe answered these "friendly enemies" with a paper, "Our Church Situation,"[33] in which he explained his views again.

For the time being Loehe found support from the theological faculty at Erlangen. His professor friends Johann Konrad Hofmann and Gottfried Thomasius were trying especially hard in conversations with him and with their colleagues to prevent Loehe from leaving the *Landeskirche* and splitting the Church.

The faculty declared its willingness to send a petition to the *Oberkonsistorium*. In it they wanted to adopt some of Loehe's demands. He had great hopes for this faculty initiative and was willing to wait for its effect before taking additional steps. But when he finally held their petition in his hand, composed by Dean Friedrich Hoefling,[34] he was very angry about the "despicable faculty petition,"[35] because it contained some nasty insults against him and supported his concerns only half-heartedly.

A disappointed Loehe stated: "There is not much to be expected from the Erlangen people."[36] However at this time, the summer of 1849, he received letters from some committed Lutherans in North Germany, among them Dr. Petri of Hannover and professor Huschke of Breslau. They urged him not to leave his *Landeskirche*. To those outside of Bavaria, church conditions in Bavaria did not seem as hopeless as Loehe saw them.

He took the objections of his friends very seriously. Even though it was difficult for him—and for his like-minded friends—he decided to postpone leaving the *Landeskirche*. However they would not simply wait for better times, but "do everything possible to create conditions that would make it possible for us to remain in the Church. If our work is in vain, we are going to leave and join where one does not participate in the disaster that befalls the *Landeskirche*—that is the idea."[37]

"To do everything possible": During the following years the Loehe-group sent petitions to the *Oberkonsistorium* in order to foster their ideas of a Lutheran Church.

In a "second phase of the struggle"[38] they concentrated their efforts on a petition for the "separation of the Lutheran Church in Bavaria from the Reformed Church and for an independent organization for each of them."[39]

Why was this separation so vital for Loehe? It was mainly the problem of Holy Communion, the "presence and distribution of the body and blood of Christ." For Lutherans this is "the greatest deed of God, our Lord," but for the reformed it is simply a "meal of remembrance."[40] Loehe was convinced that this was not just a matter of different opinions among the theologians, but it was "a great chasm, separated by an entire heaven."[41] He could not understand that the Union Church thought that this chasm could be bridged and that it could conduct common communion services for both confessions.

And how were things in the Bavarian *Landeskirche*? The number of Reformed in Bavaria East of the Rhine was minuscule, no more than 1,500 members. Many of them were from the Palatinate. They had been enticed by the Bavarian government to settle in the peat-bog along the Danube or in Upper Bavaria. There were also some Reformed Christians in the larger cities, especially in Munich. In most cases they did not have their own pastor, so they attended the Lutheran church, but they would like to receive the sacrament according to the reformed rite. For many Lutheran pastors this was not a big problem, but Loehe could not in good conscience abide by such a situation. He could not and would not be a pastor in a *Landeskirche* which tolerated a common communion for Lutherans, Reformed and United, even in "exceptional cases." Such a Church in his eyes was United, not Lutheran. Therefore he was pushing his "gracious superiors" to remove this "blot on our church situation."[42]

Loehe led this fight for the "unmixed communion fellowship" with increased determination. Clergy and congregations paid ever more attention to this with the result that awareness about the problem was sharpened and everyone became excited.

IN LIMBO

The supreme consistory always took months before answering another petition of the "Loehe Circle," dragging on the debate for three years. Often Loehe was about to quit his office, but he always pulled back "the foot that was about to walk away."[43] During this time he occupied himself with the contrast between *Volkskirche* and *Bruderkirche* (a church for all the people, or just for brethren). Once he wrote: "I no longer believe in a *Volkskirche*. The masses are against the Lord."[44] Whereas a church of brethren, a small voluntary church, would be a place where his ideas of community and apostolic life could be realized. Could not a church of brethren be feasible which would be between the Roman-catholic church and the "United church for everybody?" It could be a "bride of Christ with a crown of thorns," a "quiet center" which would "bring salvation all around."[45]

While Loehe postponed his decision to leave the *Landeskirche*, he studied intensively the Lutheran Free churches in the rest of Germany. They already had separated themselves from their United *Landeskirche*. In October 1850 he traveled through Northwest Germany, preached in the Lutheran congregations in Essen, Cologne and Nassau, and during his trip along the beautiful Rhine River he rejoiced that a Lutheran Church was "blossoming anew" there. He became something like a "bishop"[46] for these small, sometimes very small communities to whom they could turn with their problems. He was well-received everywhere. After all the hostility in Bavaria this felt very good. His view was expanded during this trip. He envisioned new opportunities for Lutheranism even beyond the borders of Germany. "It seems as if we old complainers, not loved by anyone except God, would have a lot of opportunities in Europe. We are now going to venture out to Paris, Bordeaux and London . . . "[47]

His trip finally brought him to Mecklenburg where he picked up his son Ferdinand whom he had brought there for a cure half a year before.

The thirteen year-old Ferdinand had been a worry for his father. For some time he showed signs of attacks of spiritual confusion. He tried to throw himself out of a window, or he was lost in the forest and had to be searched for. The doctor had found "traces of water in the head."[48] The family of von Maltzan in Mecklenburg, who had been in contact with Loehe for a long time and were full of sympathy and understanding, had offered to take the patient to their estate Doberan. Perhaps the fresh air from the Sea would bring healing. Apparently this cure was good for the boy. But after returning home, there were more isolated attacks. The worried father clung to the hope which a Frankfurt specialist gave him. He and Ferdinand had visited the doctor on the way home and been assured that within a few years this problem would disappear without a trace, all by itself.

Meanwhile reorganization took place in the Neuendettelsau parsonage in 1849. After many maids, who came and went, an older noble lady, Sophie von Tucher, took over as house matron. She came from an old Nuremberg patrician family. Loehe was good friends with her brother, Gottlieb von Tucher, who had represented Loehe's concerns in the general assembly as a Synod delegate. Sophie von Tucher had come to Neuendettelsau for the first time in 1839. Loehe had the impression that she had looked upon the parsonage with "pity and horror." The difference between his house and the "Tucher palace"[49] in Nuremberg was overwhelming. So Loehe appreciated even more the fact that ten years later, she was willing to take over this service in his house. This also made it possible for Marianne to return home from Fuerth, something she had wished for ardently.

THE DISPUTE WITH THE CHURCH GOVERNMENT BECOMES MORE INTENSE

The *Oberkonsistorium* received five petitions from Loehe and his friends from 1849 to 1852. However, during this period the group became convinced that it should not leave the *Landeskirche* but remain and "continue protesting."[50]

What was the reason for this change of mind? Besides the urging of friends from outside of Bavaria, a letter from pastor Kellner of Hoenigern impressed Loehe greatly. He was the Lutheran pastor who in 1834 had refused to introduce the Union in his village and as a consequence was thrown into prison. He urgently admonished Loehe not to give up his office but remain in the "Lutheran fortress" Neuendettelsau, unless he would be relieved of his office. The feisty pastor emphasized: "I am always in favor of letting yourself be kicked out or imprisoned, rather than ceding the field, or at least the local altar, to the enemy."[51]

The Neuendettelsau congregation itself was a strong recommendation for Loehe. The establishing of a church council, in the meantime introduced in all of Bavaria, had proven better than Loehe at first imagined. He had been against it in principle, but his church council and the majority of his congregation supported his fight for an "unmixed communion fellowship." They even signed one of his petitions to the church government. He could not abandon such a congregation. He made this clear in a declaration to the *Oberkonsistorium.* As always, he considered communion fellowship with "strange believers"[52] a sin and he would deal with the practical consequences of his conviction within his congregation. His friends gave similar declarations.

The church government understood this to mean that this group of pastors wanted to claim an "exception"[53] for themselves. They were told that there would be no special rules for them. They were to obey the orders of the government or resign their office.

Thus things were dramatically coming to a head. Loehe and his fellow soldiers found themselves increasingly isolated. Friends who up to now had stood beside Loehe could no longer continue on this confrontational course. Among them were the revered "father" Karl von Raumer and the old travel companion Leonhard Kuendinger. Not even his family understood him. Dorothea Schroeder became his "enemy" in this matter, and he has become a "stone of worries"[54] for his mother. She had always been so proud of her son in the prestigious office of a pastor. The fact that he maneuvered himself into such an extreme position was a burden to her soul.

But Loehe and his likeminded friends could not do otherwise. They declared to the *Oberkonsistorium* that they have to stand by their opinion and practice. But they would not resign on their own, since their congregations were standing behind them.

There followed an ominous silence from the church government. Loehe did not know it, but there was a petition, both by the *Oberkonsistorium* and the ministry of culture, that he and eight other pastors be suspended. The only thing missing was the signature of the king, the "supreme pontiff."

Here the institution of the "*summepiskopat*," which Loehe had always opposed, proved to be his savior in a time of need. The king had the impression that during these church debates both sides went way too far, and also a split in the *Landeskirche* would be very inconvenient for him, because of his political plans. Therefore the petition for suspension never left his desk. Maximilian II forced the president of the *Oberkonsistorium*, the lawyer Arnold, to retire. In his stead he called a theologian to head the church government, Adolf von Harless, a longtime friend of Loehe.

ADOLF VON HARLESS

Harless was two years older than Loehe, a descendant of a Nuremberg family of merchants. His grandfather was a well-known philologist. Harless also first studied philology, then jurisprudence, and finally theology. When he was a student in Halle he experienced a revival. Later, when he studied the Lutheran confessional books he was "surprised and touched"[55] to find out that everything he read in them agreed with his faith experiences. Thus he followed a path similar to Loehe's. They became both dedicated Christians and Lutherans.

In 1828 Harless came to Erlangen. He became a professor, and together with Wilhelm Hoefling, Gottfried Thomasius and Johann Konrad Hofmann he became the founder of the church-orientated Lutheran Erlangen theology.

In the "knee-bending controversy" Harless led the protestant opposition to minister Abel. He played an important role and gained great popularity. Abel wanted to neutralize him and moved him to Bayreuth in 1845, to serve as a counselor in the consistory, but Harless left Bavaria and accepted a call as professor of theology at the University of Leipzig. In an open letter he bade farewell to Maximilian, who was the crown prince at that time, and he complained that under minister Abel the Protestant rights and liberties had been violated. A correspondence followed between the Leipzig professor and the crown prince, who in 1848 became king. Both came to know and appreciate each other.

For five years Harless was a much revered professor and preacher in Leipzig. Then he was called to Dresden as chief court preacher and vice president of the consistory of Saxony. Thus he was "at the pinnacle of honor and fortune"[56] when the urgent request of the Bavarian king reached him: He was to assume the leadership of the *Oberkonsistorium* in Munich and mediate in the conflict between Loehe and the church government. The king explained that he had been unable to find anyone in Bavaria that would have his trust, and also the trust of the warring parties. After some consideration Harless declared that he was ready to assume that difficult office. In September of 1852 he became the president of the *Oberkonsistorium* in Munich.

What was Harless' relationship to Loehe? They had been friends from their youth. Harless appreciated the great gifts of Loehe. Both were Lutherans. Harless understood Loehe's concern but did not agree with him in all points. He especially disapproved of Loehe's original intention to quit the Church. In 1849 he had written: "I consider this whole kind of nervous unrest, the wish to start a new Church, a feverish product of our time, not a new birth from God."[57] Some ill feeling between the two resulted. However, they were able to move on after a satisfying discussion.

Since then the connection between the two was never severed. For Loehe the fact that Harless was called to Munich was a fortunate turn of events. There no longer was any talk of suspension. Loehe and his friends could quietly hope that things would get better.

The next step was the fulfilling of the wish of the Reformed Church to be independent, not only in the Palatinate, but also in the Bavaria East of the Rhine. They received their own "*moderamen*" and their own Synod. This solved a great problem, according to Loehe's way of thinking. There was a "peaceful separation" of the two confessions in Bavaria, something he had always demanded.

The first general synod under the leadership of Harless in 1853 could rightfully call itself "the first undivided synod of the Evangelical Lutheran Confession."[58] Evangelical-Lutheran from now on is the official designation of the Bavarian *Landeskirche*. During this synod Harless proved himself a wise and skillful parliamentarian who was also conciliatory and friendly. He won the hearts of all the delegates. They praised and thanked God constantly for the spirit of unity in the synod. Matters that had been postponed for decades because of fighting between different factions could now be decided. Among them were a new hymnbook and a common order of service, drafts for which were accepted unanimously.

Of course this synod too could not end without a petition from the Loehe circle. It was not written by Loehe, but he did sign it. Harless was not exactly happy about it and remarked that the time for "stormy and pushy petitions" should be past by now. The preservation of the

Confession was a "matter of the heart"[59] for the new church government as well. In spite of this reprimand, Loehe and his friends were happy with the results of the synod. It meant great progress for their cause. This ushered in a time of quietness during which Loehe could turn his attention to other problems that bothered him.

9

FROM THE MISSOURI SYNOD TO THE IOWA SYNOD

In the summer of 1853 Loehe's elderly mother visited him in Neuendettelsau. Shortly afterwards she suffered two strokes and died on July 6. She was buried in Neuendettelsau. Her son conducted the funeral, as Maria Barbara Loehe had always wished. At the grave he read her obituary, expressing once more all his love and thankfulness for her.

A few weeks later, on August 4, Loehe wrote a very depressing letter to Ferdinand Sievers, the pastor of the Frankenlust colony in North America:

> My dear friend. There are two reasons why I am writing this letter on paper with a black margin. My dear mother died in her 84th year. But this letter also means for me a sort of farewell, referring to a death in a different context. Remember what happened gradually with all the Saginaw colonies; you will also remember how close my heart and my hand were to these colonies. Today not my heart, but my hand says farewell to these colonies.[1]

FIGHT CONCERNING OFFICE AND CONGREGATION IN NORTH AMERICA

What happened that Loehe had to take such tearful leave from the "Franconian Colonies," his very own creation? The pre-history goes back some 40 years. At that time already there were disputes between the Missouri Synod, to which Loehe had turned over all his establishments, and the Buffalo Synod under its leader, Johannes

Andreas Grabau. The question was concerning the position of the pastor within the congregation and the significance of ordination, in other words questions concerning the ecclesiastic office. The Americans who were proud of their democratic liberties in the political arena also demanded that in the Church the individual congregation should have a large voice in the decision making process. One appealed to Luther and his concept of the "priesthood of all believers."[2] Another concluded that the preaching office was entrusted to all Christians by God, and the congregation then conferred it on a single person, their pastor. The congregations who provided the support of the pastor demanded the right to choose their pastor, to call him and, under certain circumstances, to dismiss him. Ordination and installation were to be nothing but the affirmation of the call.

When the Missouri Synod was constituted in 1847 the clergy agreed to this concept and the demands of the congregations. Loehe at that time already had raised great concerns against the "strong interference of democratic principles"[3] in a letter to the president of the Synod, Carl Ferdinand Walther. In Loehe's opinion this did not agree with the example of the first Christian congregation. However, he understood the situation of his colleagues in America and wrote to his former "pupils" that they could join the Synod without any qualms of conscience. "If I were over there, I would also join."[4]

Loehe was concerned for the unity of the young American congregations. He did not want to jeopardize that unity by his different understanding of the office of a pastor. But in North America, pastor Grabau objected fervently to the Missouri Synod theory of the pastoral office. In 1839 he had emigrated from Prussia to America, together with a large number of members of Lutheran congregations. He wanted to get away from the Prussian Union and had started his own Synod with the center in Buffalo. He considered ordination a divine order and emphasized the importance of the spiritual office to such an extent that he demanded from the congregation absolute loyalty and obedience toward their pastor. Congregational members who did not want to subject themselves to this hierarchical claim were excluded from the Synod. Often they were gladly received by the Missouri Synod. This intensified the clash between the two synods.

Aphorisms Concerning the Offices in the New Testament

Loehe was constantly kept informed about what was happening. After all, these were his former "pupils" who had received preparatory instruction in Neuendettelsau and then went to Fort Wayne to finish their studies. Then they had taken over the work in the congregations of the Missouri Synod. The debates in North America motivated Loehe to thoroughly research once more the relationship between office and congregation in the New Testament. His ideal was the early Christian Church, as it is described in the New Testament. He published the result of this research in 1849 under the title "*Aphorismen* (thoughts) about the New Testament Offices and Their Relationship to the Congregation."[5]

After the time of the apostles who were witnesses to the resurrection of Jesus, there remained only the office of the presbyter. The presbyters were the "elders" of the congregation, supervisors and teachers. Their office was identical with that of the bishop (episcopate), the office of overseer. Loehe was convinced that this office of the presbyter—the word "priest" is derived from it—was instituted by Christ Himself in order to administer the "means of grace," word and sacrament. Therefore the office ranks above the congregation and cannot be bestowed or taken back by the congregation. Earlier Loehe had formulated it this way:

> It is not a claim of arrogant pastors, but an irrefutable experience of ancient and modern times: Without leadership of the office of the shepherd, no little flock of God's children, much less large congregations, can escape serious damage to their souls . . . Therefore the shepherd must be and remain the center of the congregation, not just because of human right, but because of divine order . . . [6]

The presbyters are to pass on the office to suitable successors. Of course the witness of the congregation should be heard, but the congregation has no right to make a decision. Loehe considered ordination, installation with prayer and laying on of hands, a divine ordinance. For him it meant more than just the public affirmation of the call to the office.

In addition to the office of presbyter, the ancient Church also knew that of the deacon. The apostles had instituted it so that charitable gifts of the congregation could be administered and distributed. It was Loehe's fervent wish to reintroduce this New Testament office. In the ancient Church the deacons were chosen from members of the congregation in contrast to the presbyters. Therefore Loehe saw here a "democratic element of the early Church constitution," while the office of presbyter could be called "a sacred aristocracy of the Church." The inferior rank of the deacons was clear for Loehe: "The office of the shepherd is above all, even above the deacons."[7] Thus Loehe derived a Church constitution from the New Testament. It was built on the office of presbyters and deacons. In addition, there was the Church assembly, the Synod as it took place in Jerusalem and is described in the Acts of the Apostles (ch. 15). The congregation may and should take part in it and speak its opinion, but the last word belongs to the presbyter. Loehe considered decisions by a majority in the Church inappropriate.

No wonder then that there were loud protests against the "*Aphorismen*," especially by the Erlangen faculty. Was Loehe representing a hierarchical understanding of the office? Was he approaching the teaching of the Roman-Catholic Church? He, the arch-Lutheran, had to suffer the accusation that he had distanced himself from Luther's understanding of the office and of his theses of the "priesthood of all believers." Loehe energetically rejected the claim that he was "catholicizing:" "I have never been as anti-Roman and as apostolical."[8] But he readily admitted that he could not agree with Luther who, in his letter to the Bohemians in 1523, wanted to permit any baptized Christian to "preach, baptize, administer communion" because of the common priesthood of all Christians."[9] But Loehe could prove from other examples that Luther did not hold this opinion in later years, because it would open the floodgates to any misuse. On the contrary, Luther emphasized the call and the office of the pastor. Lay people should be permitted the exercise of the office only in emergencies.

Thus Luther's opinion concerning the office is not unequivocal, nor do the confessional writings give a clear answer. Even in Luther's days there were different opinions among Lutheran theologians concerning office and ordination. For Loehe, this meant that there had been no conclusion about this subject in the Lutheran Church. For the time being it should remain an open question: "The ancient teachers do not agree, the Symbols have no common and sufficient orders, the Scriptures in the passages that apply are not commonly understood. The doctrine concerning ordination is one of those that always found different opinions within the Lutheran Church . . . "[10]

Why not simply leave the matter alone, since it could not be cleared for centuries? "The Lord will not deny light and peace to the sincere and upright. That which we have received as an open question, He will graciously solve through His Spirit which leads into all truth."[11]

An Attempt to Mediate in America

Loehe maintained this conciliatory attitude toward the warring factions in America as well. The debates between the Missouri and the Buffalo Synod had sparked the discussion concerning the relationship between office and congregation. Since Loehe had become convinced that these matters were still in flux, not yet "ready," this question should not be a reason for the separation of the two synods. Loehe tried to mediate, but it was not very easy for him. For though he had rejected the superlative claims for the office by Pastor Grabau, he nevertheless in his "*Aphorismen*" had assigned a dominating role to the office over the congregation.

This did not suit the Missourians and their self-assured congregations. On the other hand they were closely connected with Loehe. They saw in him "the old, most faithful friend of the Lutheran Church in North America, the most eloquent intercessor of the same . . . The Missouri Synod really has to honor him as its spiritual father."[12] Many pastors of the Missouri Synod were former students of Loehe. However, when it came to the question of the office most of them stood with their American congregations.

An urgent invitation to come to America was sent to Loehe. He must help to clarify the debated questions with brotherly conversation and also personally form a picture of the conditions of the congregations. Loehe had to decline. It was 1851, the time of his most severe conflict with his church government.

VISIT OF THE AMERICANS

Thereupon the Missourians went the opposite way. They sent their two distinguished pastors, Walther and Wynecken, to Germany in the fall of 1852 in order to clarify matters with Loehe. The "Americans" visited Loehe and Wucherer in Neuendettelsau and also met with Wucherer. The relations were so congenial that Loehe afterwards could say hopefully: "Dear brothers: We gladly will go for you and with you! May Jesus and His Spirit unite us and you forever."[13]

Walther also admitted that "unfortunate prejudices" with which he came to Loehe's house, "have completely disappeared."[14] However, they could not agree on the disputed questions concerning office and ordination. Loehe admitted that, based on Luther's thesis about the priesthood of all believers, one "could easily arrive at the Missouri teaching concerning the office."[15] But he remained of the opinion that the New Testament witnesses were a foundation for a greater importance of the office. He was willing to leave the solution of these questions for the future: "I do not want to be more ready than is possible. I believe in a development in the Lutheran Church."[16]

Unfortunately the "American brothers" were of a different opinion. They considered their teaching concerning the office "complete," because they could appeal to Luther and a few sentences in the confessional writings. In spite of this, the talks continued in a friendly atmosphere. Both sides were hoping that in spite of differences "we can shake hands as brothers and continue to do the work of the Lord together."[17]

It was agreed that in addition to the seminary for preachers in Fort Wayne a seminary for teachers for the Missouri Synod should be established. Loehe promised to raise the necessary money. However, for the time being he wanted to remain in charge of the Fort Wayne seminary. His experience had been that once he turned over to the Missouri Synod the seminary for preachers and the Franconian colonies, he lost all rights and any possibility of being an influence in his institutions. He would be permitted only to continue to support the Fort Wayne seminary financially and to send seminarians from Germany.

Loehe wanted to have things handled in a different way with the seminary for teachers. It opened in the fall of 1852 in Saginaw under the leadership of Georg Grossmann, one of Loehe's most faithful students. It was not turned over to the Missouri Synod, but for the time being remained directly under Loehe's supervision. This was an untenable situation for the Missourians, and it caused the final breakup between Loehe and their Synod. Pastor Wynecken wrote to Loehe that the seminary was a sign of mistrust and disunity. Without using many words he asked him to "take the seminary away from Saginaw."[18] With that, the separation of Loehe and his faithful few from the Missouri Synod became unavoidable. Loehe was deeply hurt and disappointed. These were his students, his colonists who were turning away from him, joining the Missouri Synod. That Synod declared categorically that in any state in America where there were congregations of their Synod, no other Lutheran congregations should be permitted to exist. Whoever adhered to Loehe's doctrine of the ministry must move to another state.

In his letter to Ferdinand Sievers, Loehe used his blessing as a farewell to the Synod, but he also vented his feelings:

> I am standing with you, as I always have stood. As to the teaching concerning the ministry you are and remain my close relatives. I am happy for your Synod, for your life. I bless you and pray that no curse will come over you because of your unjust, unholy and nasty behavior toward us; that you may be kept safe and be a blessing. The Lord be with you, and his holy peace . . . You are acting in the free mission areas as if they belonged to you. You cannot stand anyone next to you who does not share your teaching about the ministry, even though he agrees with you in many and especially in the principal matters. And you dare to make the preposterous statement that church fellowship among brothers is not enough if they have reasons not to bow under your regiment . . . You have your own way, your system, you are complete, and it's taken for granted that we and the likes of us are at least erring Lutherans and brothers! But you are great and very happy, convinced that you have the truth and victory! Almost all of you, together with your congregations, have come out from us. Now you rejoice in your loneliness: "I am wiser than all my teachers!"[19]

FOUNDING OF THE IOWA SYNOD

Loehe wrote his former students Georg Grossmann and Johannes Deindoerfer and advised them to move the seminary for teachers to Iowa since the Missourians no longer wanted to have them in Michigan. He did not want a public altercation that would confuse the simple colonists who would not be able to understand the theological issues. "Whoever loves them has to take care not to make fanatics out of them over a matter which they do not understand."

That meant a peaceful departure. Perhaps the vile behavior of the Missourians might even have had a positive side: "In the end our departure is more appropriate for our calling as missionaries than to remain," Loehe concluded, for he had already envisioned a new mission model for the planned new beginning: "Two pupils who divided office and school between themselves and two or three Christian brothers have gone into an area that was well settled and bought some fine acreage, financed by us." They would hold services and keep school and form a "Lutheran congregation of brothers who will not be Herrnhuters, but will live together according to the intentions of the Society for Apostolic Living." Such "cells" should be formed among German emigrants and as "mission farms" among the Indians. "The plan is to found one such church settlement after another."[20]

Thus Loehe saw an opportunity to realize in America his "proposition for a society for apostolic living." In Germany it had not been possible thus far, but his young emissaries had to deal with great difficulties. In the fall of 1853 Grossmann, Deindoerfer and a few others started out for Iowa. Grossmann located a new place for the seminary in Dubuque on the shore of the Mississippi. Later it would be called "Wartburg Seminary." The others moved on farther West and founded the colony "St. Sebald by the spring."

These were difficult, poor beginnings. The houses and fields that were left behind in Michigan could not be sold as quickly as expected. The new settlers lacked capital. Loehe borrowed as much money as possible in Germany. He was surprised and thankful when he found out how much trust he enjoyed: "All the lenders require is a piece of paper with my name on it."[21]

A year later Loehe could send two more "pupils" from Neuendettelsau; and then, in the summer of 1854, the Iowa Synod was founded in the little parsonage of St. Sebald by the spring. According to Loehe's wish it was decided that the Iowa Synod should confess all the Symbols of the Evangelical-Lutheran Church. But during the inner-Lutheran discussions concerning the direction the Church should take, it was decided that the new Synod should cling to the direction "which strives toward a greater completion of the Evangelical-Lutheran Church, based on the Word of God."[22]

That meant that they would hold to Loehe's idea of the possibility of a further development within the Lutheran Church, in contrast to the unbending and intolerant attitude of the Missouri Synod. Of course that meant many disputes with the Missouri Synod in the years that followed.

In spite of the difficult beginnings, the Iowa Synod was able to consolidate. Within ten years it included fifty congregations. However, Loehe's plans for an apostolic church of brothers and for brotherly mission farms could not be realized. The pastors of the Iowa Synod were working with immigrants who for a long time had no spiritual guidance and were "beginners in their Christian faith."[23] And in spite of Loehe's frequent admonitions, the Synod did not find the strength for mission work among the heathen until 1858. A mission station was erected at the Powder River, but the Indian tribes there were at war with each other. Because they had previous bad experiences with white people, they did not trust the missionaries. In 1860 missionary Moritz Braeuninger was murdered by Indians.[24] A few years later it became necessary to give up the mission among Indians.

Mission Institute in Neuendettelsau

But back to the year 1853, when Loehe developed his new plans for mission. During that year the "Missionary Preparatory Institute" moved from Nuremberg to Neuendettelsau. Friedrich Bauer gave up his teaching in Nuremberg and assumed direction of the new "Mission Institute."

"Preparatory" had to be stricken from the name, since the seminary in Fort Wayne was no longer available for completion. Friedrich Bauer had to enlarge his curriculum. For the young people had to receive a complete training in Neuendettelsau before they were sent to the Iowa Synod in North America as preachers and missionaries.

For the time being the students were housed in the "*Gasthaus zur Sonne.*" But space was very limited. Bauer pushed for a separate building for the Institute, while Loehe did not want to enlarge the project before he could see how things were going to continue with the Iowa Synod. He favored temporary solutions which could be altered, if necessary. Finally Bauer took the initiative and bought the "*obere Wirtschaft*" in Neuendettelsau with his own money.

Since he was now the "upper innkeeper," as the peasants called him, he even continued the tavern business for a while. It was a really old village inn. On the right side was the entrance to the dining room and on the left there was the barn for the cows. Above, there was a dance hall, which was changed into a classroom. It also served as Inspector Bauer's office. The students slept in very drafty rooms in the attic.

"SOCIETY FOR INNER MISSION IN THE SPIRIT OF THE LUTHERAN CHURCH"

Bauer was paid a modest salary by the "Society for Inner Mission in the Spirit of the Lutheran Church." This Society had taken over the finances of the mission institute. A few years later it also reimbursed the inspector for the house he purchased. What kind of a society was this, and what was the meaning of that long, clumsy name?

Originally it was the old circle of friends of Loehe, some of whom were his supporters in his fight against the *Oberkonsistorium*. They met on September 12, 1849 in Gunzenhausen. It was the group that for many years had taken care of emigrants for North America and had published pamphlets in Germany, without any firm organization. Now the "Society" was to receive a definite form and statutes. It was to be enlarged by many new members. Four sections were established: Service of traveling preachers, spreading of literature, care for emigrants, and *Diakonie* (deaconate). Each section was given an "*Obmann*" (leader), namely Pastor Stirner, Wucherer, Loehe and Dean Eduard Bachmann of Windsbach.

The founding members formed the inner circle. The plan was for a larger circle of local societies to follow. For their first anniversary the "society" presented itself to the public in Nuremberg with five festive addresses. Two of those were delivered by Loehe.[25]

The four sections of the "Society" assumed the many tasks which had been tackled by Loehe and Wucherer's private initiative with the help of the circle of friends. Membership increased from year to year until it reached its highest number in 1866 with 564 persons.[26] Pastors and teachers, many educated and well-to-do lay people, and also peasants and artisans joined. Lists of members show that the members of the congregation adopted the goals of the society and made them their own. The "Society" published a "correspondence paper," also the "*Freimundkalender*" and, since 1854, the weekly "*Freimund*" (free mouth).[27] The editor was Pastor Wucherer of Noerdlingen.

JOHANN HINRICH WICHERN

Loehe had a special reason for starting the "Society" precisely in the year 1849. He also has given careful thought to the name "Inner Mission in the spirit of the Lutheran Church." "Inner Mission" had been the slogan which Johann Wichern used in his famous speech during the Church Day in Wittenberg in 1848. There were some 500 people present, and they were electrified by that speech.

By that time Wichern was already a well-known personality. As a young candidate of theology and a Sunday school teacher he had become acquainted with the horrible poverty and neglect of children of the proletariat and their families in his home town of Hamburg. In 1833 he founded the "*Rauhe Haus*," a rescue mission for male juveniles who came from totally degraded circumstances and already had police records. A few years later a "*Bruederhaus*" (house of brothers), where deacons were trained as educators and coworkers in the church, was established. There was a great stir throughout Germany when Wichern and his "brothers" went to Silesia in 1848 to help there. Typhoid, caused by starvation, was raging among the impoverished weavers and mine workers. The government was overwhelmed trying to care for hundreds of orphans after countless parents had died. Wichern, with great energy and wisdom, saw to it that they were placed in homes of the State and of the Church.

In the year of Revolution, 1848, people were frightened by social unrest. They were more open to listen to reports of the terrible problems among the lowest classes. That made Wichern's words on the Church Day very persuasive. He held before the eyes of the Church people the great task of "Inner Mission." Wichern demanded that, in addition to Christian faith, there should be "saving love."[28] His charge that the Church should make "Inner Mission" its own task and get busy with it was accepted with joy and applause.

Wichern developed a program for "Inner Mission." Its basic purpose he wrote down in a "*Denkschrift*" (memorial) in 1849[29] was that there should be a "Central Board for Inner Mission" that would establish as many societies in the individual German lands as possible.

In the summer of 1849 Wichern traveled through Bavaria in order to promote his program. In this basically Lutheran *Landeskirche* of Bavaria he expected tough resistance to his interdenominational project. But wherever he spoke, in Wuerzburg, Erlangen, Nuremberg, Augsburg and Munich he found churches filled with interested people. Even the *Oberkonsistorium* urged the clergy to cooperate with the "Inner Mission."

But Loehe felt forced to swim against this common stream of enthusiasm. He was of the opinion that the cause which Wichern promoted was a "confused concept of Inner Mission."[30] "It just delights the world, namely the Christian world." Loehe was concerned and wrote to Karl von Raumer, who also showed great sympathy for Wichern: "I am sure you trust that I have some understanding of the misery which surrounds us. Perhaps you also believe that I do not want to stand aside where one can help relieve this misery. However, Wichern's plan, as it is put down in his book, is risky and dangerous. The works should be done, but the plan is wrong."[31]

What were Loehe's objections to Wichern's "Plan?" Did he not himself try to help with many burning social issues? And did he not save many people from misery and poverty with his work in North America?

Loehe's first concern was a clarification of the concept "Inner Mission." Christ Himself had given the command for Mission to His Church. Thus Mission is an intrinsic part of the Church. With Foreign Mission she goes to the heathen, those not yet baptized; with Inner Mission she goes to baptized Christians, both those who are staying with the Church and those who "have fallen away or are in danger of falling away."

But what did Inner Mission among baptized Christians mean? Was it only to "lift social needs and untenable conditions?" Loehe admitted that in all of Europe, including Germany, "physical misery" to an unimaginable extent existed. In his opinion it was "the consequence and unavoidable punishment for the lack of morals and for falling away from the Word of God." Therefore, if Inner Mission was only concerned with improving outward circumstances, it would accomplish very little, it would remain "a drop in the bucket of misery." Rather, it should attack the root of the evil, unbelief and moral decay, which can only happen through the Word of God. Therefore Inner Mission must first take care to spread the Gospel "through speech and writing, through pastoral care and discipline." After that, it should tend to the physical well being of people. It has to address the "whole person who exists as body and soul."[32]

But preaching and pastoral care are the tasks of the spiritual office, which brought Loehe back to the "New Testament offices." He took it for granted that Inner Mission is first of all the task of the presbytery and from it emerges the deaconate to take care of physical needs. Translated into modern times this means that Inner Mission is the work of the Church, entrusted to the ministry. It should not be a separate organization, sort of a society next to the Church, as Wichern imagined it.

Loehe was also worried that such an all-inclusive organization, such as Wichern's plan, could promote a Union of the *Landeskirchen*, since it would not be a matter of confession, but only of aid in social conditions. This "*Werkerei*" (work, busy-ness) could easily be done by "completely unchristian people." The important offices of the Church, ministry and deaconate, that belong together like husband and wife, would be separated; "the Church is blown apart." Loehe was determined to fight against this: "I am going to resist this Plan with a clear conscience, through word and writing and deed, as much as I can. But I will also do my utmost to do away with misery."[33]

Loehe's "resistance" and alternative to Wichern's Plan was his "Society for Inner Mission in the Spirit of the Lutheran Church." He called it "Society" (*Gesellschaft*) on purpose so that even the name would be different from Wichern's "alliances" (*Vereine*). An alliance has a "democratic base;" members make decisions by majority vote and they can join or leave whenever they want to. The "Society" on the other hand was made up of like-minded friends who had worked for the "goals of Inner Mission" for a long time and would continue to do so. The inner circle, made up mainly of pastors, makes the decisions. The societies that join have no vote. According to Loehe's opinion this "aristocratic form" was the best guarantee of consistency and the best way to make "possible the formation of a wholesome tradition."[34]

This Society would do "Inner Mission" differently from the way Wichern did, namely "in the spirit of the Lutheran Church." The care of the poor and the sick, the social work, the *Diakonie*, formed a part, a "division" of Inner Mission. It was subject to the preaching of the Word. As a result, in ranking the tasks of the Society, Loehe gave it the fourth and last place. For the time being the *Diakonie* should be limited to the local congregation and be under the pastoral office. Its status had to first develop and grow. Loehe imagined that something like an arch-deaconate could result later from this fourth division.

However, it didn't take long before this "modest" fourth division, the *Diakonie*, assumed a controlling position in Loehe's activity.

10

THE DEACONESS INSTITUTE

> Whenever we pastors go out to our villages to call on the sick, we always find some women who take better care of the sick and those in misery than others. Somehow they have a gift that motivates them; they are following a natural inclination. Many of these women could be deaconesses in the biblical sense if only they could be given the proper training.

Thus Loehe wrote toward the end of 1853 in his "*Bedenken*" (thoughts) concerning a female deaconate within the protestant Church of Bavaria.[1] With "deaconesses in the biblical sense" he meant women like those in the earliest Christian congregations who took care of the poor and the sick, like Phoebe and others to whom Paul sends greetings in chapter 16 of the letter to the Romans.

Writing about such "souls of deaconesses" he thought, among others, of the widow Anna Maria Meyerin in the village Bechhofen which belongs to the Neuendettelsau parish:

> As often as the pastor came to a sickbed in Bechhofen, he could find her there. She knew everything and could often report better than the family of the sick person whatever the pastor needed to know to fulfill his office. Nor did she take care of physical needs only. She had a spiritual gift to talk about God's Word. One could only wish that she had more training so that this gift could have become a true Christian virtue.[2]

But in his "*Bedenken*" Loehe also thought of yet another group of women, those who enjoyed a special social position in the villages, like the daughters of pastors and teachers. The sons of those houses of course received a proper professional education; they were sent to schools or universities. But the daughters were usually kept at home, a welcome help in the house. There was always the hope that they would marry well, but if this didn't happen, they became "old spinsters" and were in a difficult situation. They had no chance to earn a living, they had no insurance in old age, and they were looked down upon socially.

At the same time Loehe was aware of terrible conditions in the run-down country hospitals. They were often only "caricatures of what they are supposed to be."[3] He also saw little children who were in need of schooling and supervision, and many retarded children who grew up without any help.

Could not the Church help not only those above-mentioned women, but also the sick and the children by training the women as nurses and social workers, thus giving them a necessary and meaningful occupation? Loehe concluded: "To train women who have a special gift to serve suffering humanity is a '*pium desiderium*' (a pious wish) and a challenge for the Church."[4] Thus Loehe laid an urgent problem on the conscience of the Church, just as he had done in the case of help for needy emigrants. Along with this he headed toward reintroducing the apostolic deaconate, which had been a matter close to his heart for some time. He was sure that it would be especially appropriate for women to carry on this service. The fourth division of the "Society" already revealed the beginnings of such diaconal activities since it was founded. A few influential women who belonged to the "Society" had also pointed out to Loehe how urgently a Church- sponsored education for women was needed.

In his "*Bedenken*" Loehe presented a detailed plan of what such a "training place" for women should look like: It would not be like the usual institutes for "daughters of the upper classes, where all kinds of things are being taught," but only "the already existing talent of women for loving service would find further education." It didn't matter whether the girls, after receiving their education, would return to their families or get married or receive further training and become "fulltime deaconesses" and work as caretakers in hospitals and asylums or teach small children or do other vital services. In every case they would be a blessing for the country, "helpful counselors for those around them, examples and sources of true female education."[5]

"LUTHERAN SOCIETY FOR A FEMALE *DIAKONIE*"

Loehe's "*Bedenken*" were printed in the newsletter of the "Society" in December 1853. That same year a group of women and men met in Windsbach to found a "Lutheran Society for a Female Deaconate." Already in March 1854 the society received governmental permission. To get such permission was no longer as difficult as it was in Loehe's younger days for King Maximilian II, himself, was engaged in Christian social issues and had a benevolent attitude toward charitable activities.

There were three women at the head of the Society who were to form "the inner center of the whole." Loehe emphasized that "all the business should be conducted by women. Men should be called upon as helpers only if needed." "Male and female helpers" meant especially pastors and their wives, but also included Lady Sophie von Tucher. Together with the leaders they formed the "Mother Society." However, in the Society the male "helpers," with Loehe as their head, still exercised the overseeing, so that one could not exactly claim a female independence.

The name "Mother Society" implied that there was hope for the founding of many "Daughter" or local societies who all would serve a common purpose: "A reawakening and formation of a concern, especially among women, for the service of suffering humanity among the Lutherans of Bavaria." It was Loehe's wish that "the spark that is being lit here will cause a fire throughout the land," that in Bavaria "there would be societies for female *Diakonie* everywhere, and that a "fire of love and mercy"[6] would spread throughout the land.

FOUNDING OF THE DEACONESS INSTITUTE

In Neuendettelsau proper, Loehe wanted only an educational institute for daughters of the rural middle class, as he had mentioned in his "*Bedenken*." They were to be trained in the theory and practice of nursing and other diaconal services. They were also to receive a general Christian education and then return to their home towns. There they should care for the sick and poor, in cooperation with the local society. The Mother Society should provide only the "initial spark"[7] for many independently working groups.

This Institute had its beginning in the *Gasthaus zur Sonne*, which was just vacated by the students of the Mission Institute who had moved to their own home. Years later Loehe was still thankful for the energetic support of the innkeeper: "There are not many inns in this world (perhaps none) which have rendered such service to the Lord Jesus. This honor will probably belong exclusively to the *Gasthaus zur Sonne* and its faithful host Johann Michael Ottmann."[8]

The three supervisors, Caroline Rheinbeck, Amalie Rehm and Helene von Meyer moved into the upper rooms of the "*Sonne*." With them were seven student-deaconesses and eight girls who did not want to become deaconesses but wished to have a "deaconess education" and then return to their "hometown conditions."[9]

The Deaconess Institute was opened with a festive service in the Neuendettelsau church on May 9, 1854.

THEODOR FLIEDNER AND KAISERSWERTH

What was the relationship between this newly founded organization and the already existing deaconess institutes in Germany? The most famous one was founded already in the 18th century by Theodor Fliedner and his wife in Kaiserswerth. Fliedner started by taking care of discharged prisoners. He also started a school for little children. Then he and his wife began an "Institute for Evangelical Caretakers" to improve the untenable conditions in German hospitals. The "care" in these hospitals was often in the hands of uneducated male and female keepers, often of disreputable character. The buildings were dirty and neglected. No wonder that only the poorest of the poor or abandoned, lonely people were housed there; any other sick person would prefer the poorest care at home to these hospitals. These conditions changed abruptly when Fliedner's Kaiserswerth "deaconesses," as he called them, took over a hospital, such as the Station of the Charite in Berlin where women with syphilis or scabies were housed or the insane asylum in Marsberg.

Fliedner's "educational Institute" in Kaiserswerth became the model for the typical mother house deaconate. The training place was also to give support and protection to the deaconesses. It was to be a "mother house." It should also represent their interests over against their employers wherever they were serving.

But with this "centralizing" the office of deaconesses was taken away from the congregations and turned over to the Deaconess Institute. Therefore Loehe had his reservations about a deaconate that was based in a mother house. He wanted the deaconate to be firmly rooted in the congregation as an office of the church. His ideal, as always, was the congregational deaconess of the apostolic Church.

"That business of Fliedner's deaconesses has become a power" Loehe opined, but he regretted that it was not "more churchly." Just like in the case of "Inner Mission" he was afraid that the care of the poor and sick would be taken out of the hands of the Church and become a Christian organization without any confessional ties. He expressed this clearly with the image of concentric circles:

> The widest circle is called human. The second smaller one is called Christian. The third and smallest one is called churchly. In the center of all of them is Jesus who sends his rays into all the circles, as they are able to receive. They are rays of grace and of blessing. To do away with begging is human, not anti-Christian. To help all the sick and to direct them to the Savior is Christian. But do not forget that the Christian element finds its completion in the Church. If you are connected with all Christians through the bond of baptism, nevertheless the closest and most perfect bond unites you with those that share with you the body and blood of the Lord in Holy Communion . . . Do not forget that a common love for all people flows out of the love of the brothers (2 Peter 1:7) and that you have the divine command to do good to all, but chiefly to those of the household of faith.[10]

Loehe confessed later that he wanted to "put a block in the way of the uniting tendencies"[11] with his new foundation in Neuendettelsau, even though he genuinely admired Wichern and Fliedner. Of course he was well-informed about the Kaiserswerth institutions. In fact one of his supervisors, Caroline Rheinbeck, had been a Kaiserswerth deaconess for a few months. She had to leave there because she could not stand the climate in Kaiserswerth. She informed Loehe about the work in Kaiserswerth, but he wanted something different from the motherhouse deaconate. He emphasized that there was great respect in Neuendettelsau for "Fliedner's great and rightly famous work," but that here "we do not want to imitate other deaconess institutes."[12]

Therefore he refused to visit Kaiserswerth or to read reports about it. He wanted to base his work on the needs and possibilities of his Lutheran Church. He did not want to have grandiose projects for the future but to make a modest beginning by training some young women. Neuendettelsau was to be the base "not forever, but only for the time being."[13] Even later Loehe would always emphasize that his original plan was to be something temporary, of a provisionary nature.

IN THE "*SONNE*"

In the inn "*zur Sonne*" there was soon a "busy and happy life." Soon after the opening of the Deaconess Institute, Dr. Schilffahrt of Windsbach began classes in nursing. Later, Cantor Guettler taught singing. All other subjects—Bible history, catechism, calligraphy, and math—were taught by Loehe himself.

The supervisors "went over" the lessons with the students and "ruled the house."[14] A mentally retarded boy from the neighboring village Reuth was also taken in, for they planned to start as soon as possible to work with such children.

All the "pioneers" who were there in the "*Sonne*" from the start would remember those days as an especially blessed time. The mood was upbeat because of the new beginning and there was great enthusiasm even though conditions were very cramped. There was great interest in the new Institute in Neuendettelsau and many new registrations. Loehe felt that "this deaconess business"[15] met approval everywhere and the leaders soon had to look for a separate house for the new institution. First Loehe tried to rent the mansion in Neuendettelsau which had been empty since the death of Baron Karl von Eyb in 1851. But the heirs would not agree to this.

Therefore the "Mother Society" had to venture to erect a new building. This was very risky, since only 1,200 *gulden* were available from donations and the estimate for the new building was 13,000 *gulden* which had to be raised largely through loans. A building site was purchased on the "highest point in the area," a field where hops were raised. "The Deaconess Institute should not forget its beginning in an inn!"[16]

Building of the Deaconess House

On June 23, 1854, there was a festive laying of the cornerstone for the deaconess house. The building went up incredibly fast with the help of people from the country. To find cheaper building material Pastor Loehe hired a workman to start a special brick factory. Here the farmers could learn how to make bricks, which would help them later when they wanted to build their own houses, said their village pastor happily. He had an eye for the future.

For the construction of the two-story main building plus a side wing 125,000 bricks were needed, and a well had to be dug. These were anxious days until finally water was found at a depth of 57 feet. Pastor Loehe carried all the burden and the duties of a contractor. He often moaned about the time he had to spend with the building project, in addition to the duties of his office, the hours of teaching in the mission institute and with the student deaconesses. But what worried him most were the enormous debts connected with the building. They caused him sleepless nights. Often "the waters of worrying come up to his throat."[17]

In spite of this on October 12 there was a happy feast of dedication with many guests.

After the service of dedication all joined in a "love meal" in the chapel of the new house. The "widows and the poor of the congregation" were also invited. Over a hundred guests were fed a "delicious and satisfying Rumford soup."[18]

Within a year the deaconess house held 110 persons, among them 60 students.

Institute for Mental Patients

Of course the retarded boy who had lived with the deaconess students in the "*Sonne*" moved with them to the new house. His training and education were the first "practical task" for the future deaconesses. He was not the only one for long. Many parents wanted to bring their mentally handicapped children. Within a year there were already 28 children, and it became necessary to look for new quarters. Two small houses close to the parsonage were bought for the "imbecile place," as it was called in those days. By 1864 this institute already needed its own new building which was larger and taller than the deaconess house for the housing and education of mentally retarded people proved to be one of the most important tasks of the deaconesses. Loehe later on considered it an act of divine providence that this was the first kind of work in which his deaconesses could "labor, practice and suffer hardships."[19] He had learned by experience how many forms of mental handicaps there were, especially in the country. The members of the "Society" reported frequently that there was no one who would care for the "necessary education, especially in religion" of mentally ill children and that in the villages they were kept "just like animals."[20]

Thus Loehe's deaconess institute was connected with the work with mental patients from its very beginning. In order to gain more knowledge in this field, Loehe traveled to Winterbach in Wuerttemberg where there was a home for mental patients. He had long discussions with the doctors there. He became convinced that mentally handicapped people were better off in institutions and had better opportunities for development than in their families.[21] The establishment in Neuendettelsau became the first protestant institute for mental patients in Bavaria.

The Schools

But the training of the future deaconesses included more than work with the mentally handicapped. They were to learn how to take care of the sick, how to teach smaller and older children, and how to run a household. In addition they should acquire a good general and a religious education, "because," said Loehe at one time, "a deaconess should be able to do the most lowly job and the highest. She should not be ashamed of the lowly job and should not hesitate to take on the highest work a woman can do."[22]

Such an all around education for women also attracted girls who did not want to become deaconesses. They lived harmoniously with the proper deaconess students under one roof in the deaconess house. In addition younger girls eventually came who had not yet been confirmed, who formed the so-called "little school." Older students were trained to become teachers by teaching the younger.

Eventually there were three grades in these Neuendettelsau schools: The younger girls formed the "red school"; they wore a red ribbon around the neck of their black Sunday dress. Then there was the "green school" with a green ribbon for girls that have been confirmed, and finally the "blue school" with a blue ribbon for future deaconesses.

Since at this time the State was doing very little for the education of girls—there were no State high schools or seminars for female teachers—the schools in Neuendettelsau attracted wide-spread attention and many applicants.

During the first years sick people were also accepted into the deaconess house, so that the students could learn nursing at their sick-beds. Almost more important was the ambulant care of the sick in the surrounding area, for the country people did not like hospitals where there were rules for hygiene, and one had to be "embarrassed." However, the old and infirm were receiving such poor and reluctant care in the farm houses that for them a "village hospital" was started in Neuendettelsau in 1857.

The institutions soon needed their own "farm" in order to raise their own produce. A bakery was started. A gardener was hired who gradually transformed a field next to the deaconess house into a beautiful park with trees and blooming plants. Loehe, who greatly appreciated natural beauty, found daily pleasure in the bushes and flowers. Of course there had to be a vegetable garden also. In order to raise the money for the manure beds, Loehe had his seven "Sermons for the fasting days" printed. Through "a strange metamorphosis they were changed into manure beds."[23]

The Mother House

It was a joy to see how the institutes in Neuendettelsau were developing and growing. However, one also had to see that there was little development of branches of the "Mother Society." No other new institutions began in Bavaria, as Loehe had planned. In the year of the founding of the Deaconess Institute, 1854, a few such local societies had started: In Nuremberg, Hersbruck, Memmingen, Altdorf and Noerdlingen. Among other things they sponsored a soup kitchen, a nursery, a home for female workers, and a children's hospital. But then for years things came to a halt. In the following decade only two new societies were added. All in all the "Society for a Female deaconate" remained a "very weak plant,"[24] to Loehe's regret.

Three years after the founding of the Deaconess Institute Loehe had another reason to realize that his concept of *Diakonie* was "not practical." It proved not to be a good idea to send out the deaconesses after their graduation to their places of service and leave them on their own. Their school had to remain in constant contact with the deaconesses. It had to be a refuge for them, a place where they could return. It had to be their family. The annual report of 1856/57 stated:

> Our friends know very well that at the beginning of the deaconess work we were totally against the idea that our students should become some kind of closed sisterhood, or an order. But now we must confess that after some time we have come to a different insight. The student that gives up the close connection with the motherhouse and with her peers will always get into thc same trouble. She forgets the motherhouse, the ideas she received there, the high opinion of her calling which has very little support in the present congregations; and so she gradually sinks to the state of a hired servant and becomes a child of this world…Therefore we have begun to let go of our reluctance for a sisterhood…All deaconesses should recognize their motherhouse as their home from which they go out and to which they can return when they are sick or weak. From it they should receive what is needed, as children would from their parents.[25]

So Loehe decided to take over elements of the motherhouse deaconate. The "educational institute" became an "institute for leadership and government, for supply, food and care" of the deaconesses, in other words a motherhouse.

This "closer connection and the permanent relationship"[26] between motherhouse and deaconesses brought new structures. The deaconesses in their assigned areas and cities joined together in "chapters," a "spiritual society" which met once a week to read the Bible ("chapter"), for prayer, and for "mutual admonition and pastoral care."[27] The "chapters" would be regularly visited by one of the leaders from the motherhouse, who also visited the hospitals and institutions.

The places of work would no longer pay the "salary" to the deaconesses but send it to a fund for deaconesses at the motherhouse. The deaconesses received their clothes and some spending money from that fund. That made them all equal financially and independent of their employers. A uniform dress was introduced which was similar to that of the local farmer's wives: Black dress with a blue apron on workdays and a white one on Sundays. First they wore a white veil but this turned out to be impractical, so it was soon changed to the white deaconess cowl.

The deaconesses who had completed their training were to be addressed as "Sister." Their leadership was now in the hands of the "*Frau Oberin*" (Mother Superior). That meant that instead of three supervisors there was only one. Since Karoline Rheineck died in 1855 and Helene Meyer had left the deaconess society temporarily, Amalie Rehm, until then called "Miss Rehm," was consecrated as first *Oberin* on February 2, 1858.

Rector of the institute was Pastor Wilhelm Loehe. In 1857 a candidate of theology Ernst Lotze, was employed as co-rector. That meant that among the supervisors males prevailed, even though, according to Loehe's original concept, men should be only helpers of the "female workers." But it was clear to everyone that the overwhelming personality of the "*Herr Pfarrer*," as he was commonly known, was putting its stamp on the Neuendettelsau enterprise, and that his powerful will always won out in the end.

All these new orders and the close tie to the motherhouse necessarily resulted in the fact that the deaconesses were no longer able to join or quit without a lot of formality, as was the case during the first few years. The motherhouse in turn had to take greater care and probe more thoroughly into which of the young women were suitable for a permanent relationship with the Deaconess Institute.

THE CHAPEL

The little village church in Neuendettelsau gradually became too small for the fast growing congregation of thc Institute. The farmers felt cramped by the large number of deaconesses and students. A carpenter finally made the exaggerated claim that "from the breath of so many women there is more humidity in the church, and the beams are rotting."[28] Loehe laughed at this prophecy of doom, but he recommended that the village congregation enlarge the church. The farmers would have to help with this by furnishing "labor and transport," but they would not be burdened with financial contributions. In spite of this, the church administrators rejected the proposition.

That left no other solution but to build a separate chapel for the congregation of the Institute. In 1858 the cornerstone was laid next to the motherhouse. Many friends and supporters of the Institute as well as deaconesses themselves, contributed financially. Loehe donated the royalties from his new book “Months of Roses of Holy Women.” But the building progressed very slowly. Finally, on Christmas Day of 1859, the first service was held in the new chapel. But to conduct a main service there, including Holy Communion, the permission of the *Oberkonsistorium* was still needed.

11

NEUENDETTELSAU AND THE *LANDESKIRCHE*

What was the attitude of the Church leadership in Munich toward Loehe's institutions, this new center of Church life that was growing in Neuendettelsau? At first "this business with the deaconesses has found approval from all sides,"[1] Loehe stated contentedly. In 1855 he sent the report of the Deaconess Institute to his friend Harless and listed all the places where Neuendettelsau students were already at work.

Ever since Harless became the head of the church government in Munich, Loehe's relationship to the *Landeskirche* had become much more relaxed. All the decrees of the *Oberkonsistorium* during the years after the general synod of 1853 met with Loehe's approval. There was need for more order in the life of the Church in Bavaria and more uniformity, since there were still great differences within individual regions, for instance in the way services were conducted. A new hymnbook was introduced in all the congregations of the *Landeskirche* in 1854. To achieve a more unified form of the service, an "*Agendenkern*" (agenda kernel) was put together. It was based on ancient reformatory orders of service. With it the congregations were to become reacquainted with liturgical forms such as the responsive chanting of the psalms.

THE "*AGENDENSTURM*"

(STORM OVER THE AGENDA)

For some years it was left up to the congregations whether they wanted to use the new order of service, but in June of 1856 the church government declared that it must be used. In July of the same year the

Oberkonsistorium sent no less than five decrees to all the pastors. Among other things there was the recommendation to continue private confession where it was being practiced, but between the lines it was apparent that the *Oberkonsistorium* would also like to see that it would be introduced where it was not yet practiced. Certain remnants of church discipline should also be reintroduced: People who openly "despise the Church" should not be allowed to act as god-parents, "fallen bridal couples" should be married "without any ostentatious display,"[2] and in certain cases a church funeral should be denied.

For Loehe's congregation such things as liturgy, private confession and church discipline were nothing new. Their pastor had introduced all this over the years. No one knew better than Loehe how difficult it was to bring about such changes in a congregation. In 1855 he had written to Harless that, in spite of his "extraordinary love for liturgy," he would counsel to use "caution and slowness"[3] when introducing the new agenda. And now this multitude of decrees, which were directed to pastors, had reached the public through some indiscretion.

There was a storm of indignation, first in Nuremberg where the "protestant zeal" was waging so red hot "that all the taverns are humming and growling with loud voices and noises so that the innkeepers were hardly able to bring up enough beer to quench the roaring flames."[4]

The "*Frankische Kurier*" called for a protest against church coercion under the headline: "Harless wants to make us Catholic!"[5] The paper defended the achievements of Rationalism in regard to faith and Church, namely: "Everybody should consider as truth only that which he can consider true after receiving instruction and based on his own insight." The clergy should stick to their preaching, "proclaiming the greatness of creation, the teachings of wisdom and virtue, and love and justice for all people."[6]

This appeal from Nuremberg found a tremendous echo in other Bavarian cities. A complaint with over 7,000 signatures was sent to the King. It requested that the offensive new orders be canceled and the present Church government be dismissed. In Nuremberg violence reached extremes: After a service there was a riot and the railing leading up to the Church of the Holy Spirit was ripped down.

The "*Agendensturm*" came as a total surprise to the *Oberkonsistorium*. They had misjudged the mood in the congregations, especially in the cities. The members of the consistory thought that the newly awakened Lutheranism would find many supporters among church people and that they would react favorably to stricter Church ties. The Church government had not realized that the spirit of rationalism was still so much alive among the liberal citizens of the larger cities; that they would insist on their "protestant freedom." Had they anticipated the storm they would have proceeded more cautiously.

Harless was in big trouble. His enemies at the royal court attempted to use the occasion for all kinds of intrigues with the King, but King Maximilian II stood by his president of the *Oberkonsistorium*. The evangelical Queen Marie also supported him. However, the church government was forced to make some concessions; especially the introduction of new liturgical forms was left up to the congregations for the time being.

Loehe was shaken by these events. He did not expect such violent opposition to the new Church edicts and was shocked that "the true face of the *Landeskirche* . . . has been so glaringly revealed."[7] According to Loehe all supporting the hostile attitude toward the Church should be put under church discipline, but this did not happen. They were allowed to remain and considered themselves members of the Evangelical-Lutheran Church.

To have communion fellowship with such people was unbearable for Loehe and his friends. Again they prepared a petition to the *Oberkonsistorium*: They wanted to remain in the *Landeskirche*, but they asked for permission to join with like-minded Christians who were faithful to the confessions and to have communion fellowship with them. Loehe's vision of a communion of true believers within the *Landeskirche* was again surfacing here.

He sent the petition, together with a personal letter, to Harless, but Harless foresaw a violent reaction within the *Oberkonsistorium* if the demands of the Loehe-circle were brought up for discussion. For from the view of church politics this would mean that any member of a congregation would be free to choose his own pastor and confessor, and free to choose the congregation where he would receive Holy Communion. The church government certainly could not allow this for everybody. It would destroy the structure of the local congregation. At the most one could imagine a few exceptional cases.

Harless in his answering letter to Loehe described the difficulties that this petition would make for the *Oberkonsistorium* and for him personally. He already had to fight against the accusation that he had been converted by the ideas of his friend Loehe.

After a detailed friendly exchange of letters[8] Loehe withdrew his petition. Surprisingly there were no more petitions of the Loehe circle to the general synod in 1857.

Anointing of the Sick

But beginning as early as 1858 Loehe had become another "case" for the *Oberkonsistorium*. An elderly noble lady from the Baltics who was a patient in the deaconess house in Neuendettelsau had asked Loehe in the summer of 1856 for an "anointing of the sick." She had received such an anointing while ill in her Baltic homeland. Loehe asked for time to think about it since this was "unusual and apparently daring"[9] in the Bavarian *Landeskirche*. He discussed the matter with his church council and his coworkers Friedrich Bauer and Ernst Lotze. Then he decided to honor the urgent request of this patient. He found a justification in the New Testament in the 5th chapter of the epistle of St. James (James 5:14–15): "Are any among you sick? They should call for the elders of the church and have them pray over them, anointing them with oil in the name of the Lord. The prayer of faith will save the sick and the Lord will raise them up . . . "

Luther also did not object to the anointing of the sick, but he did warn that it should not be elevated to a sacrament, as the "extreme unction" in the Catholic Church.

So Loehe performed the anointing of the sick in September of 1856 in the presence of the church council, the above mentioned pastors and *Frau Oberin*. He had composed a special liturgy for this titled "The Apostolic Visit of the Sick." The matter would not have caused any stir if Friedrich Bauer had not published this liturgy in the paper of the "Society" toward the end of 1857 under the title "A Liturgical Experiment."[10] It was done with Loehe's permission, and no one imagined what a controversy this would produce.

The *Oberkonsistorium* was very indignant over this unsanctioned action by Loehe and demanded an explanation. In public he was accused of having taken one more step toward Catholicism with this "anointing." True, the "*Evangelische Kirchenzeitung*" in Berlin explained the matter correctly: One could rather understand the anointing of the sick as a protest against the practice of the Catholic Church, since it was meant to bring about healing, while the "extreme unction" is only given to the dying. Professor Ernst Wilhelm Hengstenberg, the author of this article, spoke up for Pastor Loehe. Loehe was a man "whom one has to forgive much and grant him freedom of action so that the rich gifts he is endowed with can be freely developed. God has put his seal on him. No one can deny that Neuendettelsau is the brightest spot within the Lutheran Church in Bavaria."[11]

Loehe provided the *Oberkonsistorium* with the requested explanation, but he could not hide his surprise that he, "a representative and promoter of Lutheranism for the last 28 years," should be accused of unlutheran behavior. Besides, it was not his intention to "emphasize especially"[12] the anointing of the sick and, so far, no one had asked for a repeat performance. Nevertheless the church government "categorically and forever" forbade the practice of anointing the sick. Loehe received an emphatic reprimand for his "unsanctioned behavior which undeniably has caused far reaching offense."[13]

Confession of Children and Church Discipline

Even worse than the reprimand was the renewed suspicion and mistrust by the church government. What in the world was this Pastor Loehe doing in those institutions he started in that village in the boonies? Did he do nothing but introduce forbidden novelties? Did he present strange ideas in his classes? His immediate superior, the Dean of Windsbach was ordered to clarify these matters. Loehe was to hand in copies of his lesson plans. Then there were reports that Loehe had admitted students who had not been confirmed to private communion and that he had introduced special forms of church discipline. He was to answer these accusations as well.

Loehe was deeply hurt that he was put under the supervision of the deanery, but he immediately sent his good friend, the Dean, his plans for instruction. As far as the offensive "confession of children" went, he replied as follows: In cases where he had been asked, he did "indeed from time to time, but without any compulsion and without emphasizing it, admit young people to confession and absolution, even though they had not yet been confirmed." For "children sin as much as grownups," so they want to confess and repent and the absolution is for them "a mighty mean of grace," even more than for adults. Pastor Loehe is sure that

> he has acted according to the will of the Lord, also that he did not violate any church order . . . because a single tear from the eye of a child who has been absolved is enough to remove any doubt of a father, a teacher, or any member of the church government and . . . to thank the Lord that His divine word of peace is for everybody, including children.[14]

As far as church discipline was concerned, for instance admission to the Lord's Supper, the Neuendettelsau congregation acted according to this principle: "Any public sinner who has offended the congregation should do away with the offense through a public confession."[15]

In practice that meant that a "public sinner" on the day of communion would come to the altar before the service, confess before the pastor and the church council, and receive absolution. After a prayer he would be "dismissed in a brotherly and friendly way." Loehe had been asked by such members to enter the day of their repentance in their hymnbook. This "proves in what spirit all this was done."

When people came to announce themselves for communion there were always members of the church council present with the pastor. Sometimes they revealed to the Pastor some "public sins"[16] of a certain member which he did not know about. In each of these cases Loehe offered to present the matter to the governing authority of the Church, but so far everybody rejected this suggestion. That also proved to the Pastor that no member had felt treated unjustly.

Loehe was determined not to give up the practice of "children's confession," nor to "take back" anything in the question of pastoral leadership of the congregation. He would rather ask to be permitted to give up his ministry and be restricted to the leadership of his institutions. He ended his declaration to the deanery with these words:

> I am a Lutheran and am known for being zealous for establishing Lutheran conditions and orders. My love for the

> Lutheran Church . . . has opened my eyes for what is lacking and for misuses that have existed for centuries . . . If I am not permitted to serve my Church in the best way I am able, I am not going to impose what little strength I have on my Church, but will leave peacefully to my rest.[17]

After several more letters in which Loehe explained his practice in greater detail, the church government was somewhat satisfied and quietly consented to let the Neuendettelsau pastor do his work. But a mistrust of Loehe remained in Munich. This could be seen, for instance, when the new chapel of the deaconess house was finished toward the end of 1859, and Loehe asked the church government for permission to conduct not only services for the house, but also complete church services including Holy Communion. The congregation of the institute had to wait for this permission until May, 1860, because Loehe was constantly under suspicion that he planned to separate himself from the *Landeskirche*. It took a while before the *Oberkonsistorium* was convinced that the new chapel was not going to be "the first church of a separated congregation."[18]

Suspended from Office

That same year, 1860, Loehe found himself in conflict with the existing laws concerning marriage, just like 23 years earlier, when he was a young vicar, because he refused to remarry a divorced man in his congregation. He was a young artisan, a notorious drunkard, who had mistreated his first wife and thrown her out of the house, after all her money had been used up. After a year-long court case the man finally won a decision that placed all the blame for the broken marriage on his wife who had "maliciously left him." The entire village was outraged over this decision. Both spouses received permission to marry again. The man in the meantime had fathered two children with another woman; but now he did not want to marry the penniless mother of his two children but another, more well-to-do woman. He needed the money, he told the pastor quite openly.

Loehe knew such cases only too well from his experience as a village pastor. Some men had fathered illegitimate children with "three, four, five women," but did not provide for them nor care about them. Often a man lived seemingly with a good conscience in a

Christian congregation, but "does not dream of remembering his abandoned illegitimate children."[19]

The pastor immediately told the groom that, according to the well-known principles of his congregation, he would not perform this marriage, even though the court gave the man permission to marry again and so he had the law on his side. Nor was Loehe willing to issue an official "demission" so that another pastor could perform the marriage. He felt "bound by the Word of God." it was his duty "not only to act as he does, but also, as far as he is concerned, not to let someone else act in his stead. It would be immoral for him if while not to committing a sin himself, he made room for someone else to do it."[20]

Everybody involved knew that the church government in such a case was obligated by law to suspend the obstreperous pastor. In order to resolve the matter with as little trouble as possible, the suspension was issued officially on July 1860 and Loehe's friend, Pastor Kuendinger from the neighboring village of Petersaurach, was nominated as supply pastor. He issued the "demission" and believed that this would end his status of interim pastor. In this way the groom could be married in the distant place of residence of his bride by the local pastor there, Loehe could take up his office again and the whole business of suspension could be settled before it caused much attention.

But the groom now wanted to flaunt his victory over Pastor Loehe. It suddenly occurred to him that he did not want to be married in another place but here in the church of his Neuendettelsau congregation. The church council and a majority of the congregation objected to this in a letter to the deanery. They were all upset that their "revered Pastor" should no longer be permitted to exercise his office "on account of such a rascal."[21] However, as long as the matter had not been resolved the suspension could not be lifted.

Loehe did not take this matter lightly, but he decided to use this time as "a vacation given to him by God." But who was going to conduct Sunday services? Except for a few dissidents the congregation decided that they would not acknowledge a substitute for their "only rightful pastor."[22] They expressed this in writing to the *Oberkonsistorium*. When poor pastor Kuendinger appeared reluctantly as a substitute in Neuendettelsau, the atmosphere in the village was ghostlike: the bells were rung for the service, but no one showed up. The streets were empty. The Neuendettelsau people held their own devotions at home. Only a few curious people came; and of course the wretched bridegroom and his partner who considered herself "queen of the church" on this day.

But the rest of the congregation refused to accept the services of the interim pastor. A seriously sick man refused, at first, to receive Holy Communion. A father would rather himself perform emergency baptism of his infant. Others considered whether they should leave the *Landeskirche*. The congregation offered a quiet, passive but very effective resistance. Finally it accepted the Sunday sermons and other emergency services of Vicar Ferdinand Weger, who had been assisting Loehe for some time.

The vicar also at first refused to intervene, but agreed when Loehe urged him. The neighboring pastor no longer showed up in the village; he had "plenty to do"[23] with his Sunday sermon.

The suspension lasted eight weeks, and Loehe was not completely without blame. For the Church government had decided after only two weeks that the disputed wedding should take place not in Neuendettelsau but at the place of residence of the bride and that the suspension should be lifted. But now it was Loehe who hesitated to take up the duties of his office again. He would have preferred "not to be pastor anymore." He felt tired, exhausted, and offended. But he could not abandon his congregation. He considered his ties with his people a "divine matter."[24] His people had stood by him so faithfully. But in order to be able to continue working, his authority had to be repaired. The opposition party should not be allowed to feel victorious, as if the Church government were on its side. So Loehe demanded that the consistory issue an official reprimand to the groom, who in the meantime had been married and "recognized that the pastor acted correctly." Of course the consistory could not admit that it had acted unjustly. Therefore the matter dragged on for weeks.

The redeeming formula was finally found. Loehe asked the church government to declare "whether according to its judgment a man with his convictions was able to continue in his office." The governing authority answered that it fully appreciated the gifts and achievements of Pastor Loehe, except in the present case. It also appreciated his sacrificial activities, his dedication and conscientiousness which he had shown in the exercise of his office." It esteemed and honored him, even though it repeatedly had "to remind him to follow the existing norms which were established for all by the order of the Church."[25]

That pretty much describes the relationship of the *Landeskirche* to Loehe. On September 17, exactly two months after his suspension, he took up his office again. His good qualities were known, but he frequently caused trouble. Even among his colleagues in Bavaria there were different opinions about the Dettelsau pastor. There were some ardent "*Loeheaner*" (followers of Loehe), but others rejected his ways: Neuendettelsau with its strict practice of Holy Communion and its rich liturgy had become a stumbling block for them.

Even though he was well aware of his reputation in the *Landeskirche,* Loehe continued unperturbed. The general synod of 1861 had to deal with another petition, signed by Loehe and 20 other pastors. They complained that there were still congregations within the Bavarian *Landeskirche* that practiced communion fellowship with Reformed and Union churches. The petition demanded that the church government make a clear separation in regard to the sacrament of the altar to stop all that "communion mix up."

This petition of the Loehe circle was considered "disgusting" in the synod. A motion was made that the "the reverend synod should skip the request of Pastor Loehe and the other signers and return to the order of the day."[26] This was accepted by the majority and the petition was simply dropped.

Loehe and his fellow soldiers were very upset over this abrupt dismissal. They gave up "further public attempts," but kept their principles and practice within their own congregations. They would "not tolerate any mixing when it comes to the sacrament."[27] The congregations agreed and the church government was wise enough to let the matter rest.

Sicknesses

During Loehe's suspension the Neuendettelsau congregation and the deaconesses became painfully aware of how important Holy Communion had become for them. They feel "the lack of the sacrament and of confession."[28] Thus their joy was all the greater when Loehe started hearing confession again. Since the beginning of the Deaconess Institute, the number of those who went to Loehe for confession had multiplied many times. The deaconesses, in contrast to the farmers, also expected counseling when they came for confession, so Loehe had to set aside times for confession not only on Saturdays but also during the week.

Because of this his workload increased. In addition to his pastoral duties, he taught daily in the deaconess house, took care of a large correspondence, and was busy as a writer. He visited deaconesses in outlying stations. Since 1859 he was allowed to have a vicar, Ferdinand Weber. With Candidate Ernst Lotze, who became co-rector in 1857, he received a close coworker for the institutions.

This help was urgently needed, for Loehe had severe health problems. In 1855 a type of typhus had severely weakened him. In late summer of 1857 felt faint during a sermon and after that he was sick for a long time. His kidneys gave him trouble and he went for a cure in Karlsbad both in 1858 and 1859, from where he returned home refreshed. His Neuendettelsau people all agreed that he "lost a lot of weight," but he looked "much brighter, happier, better." A farmer's wife delightedly exclaimed that he "turned out so beautiful—*su schaei*,"[29] as it sounds in the Franconian dialect. But the troubles returned and would not leave him again for the rest of his life. One night he lay on the floor with "terrible kidney trouble,"[30] but nobody was aware of it because he was home alone.

What bothered him even more was a sickness of his tongue and the larynx. For a while it prevented him from speaking and made it impossible for him to preach. Some sort of paralysis of the larynx often forced him to stop in the middle of a sermon. Sometimes a helper had to read his sermon.

Marianne

He also worried constantly about the health of his only daughter, Marianne. Since she returned from Fuerth in 1848, she lived in the parsonage and was instructed by Miss von Tucher in leading the household. Five years later Miss von Tucher found a separate apartment in Neuendettelsau, and Marianne took over her duties. She was 14 years old.

Everybody took it for granted that it was her duty to keep house for her widowed father. Loehe found it very pleasant that his daughter, not some stranger, was in charge in the parsonage. He called her his "little maid." There was also a "big maid," but when the big maid was sick, "all that work" had to be handled by Marianne alone. Loehe accepted the situation by thinking that this work was "good for her body" and that it served "her soul" well if she had to be "low and humble."[31] Once he proudly finished a letter with the words: "My cook, Anndl, is ready to serve dinner now."[32]

But in the spring of 1855, her father suddenly decided to take Marianne to Greiz in Thuringia where he had some good friends. Ostensibly she was to learn languages there, but in Neuendettelsau the rumor was that there was an incident with a certain young man, and that Loehe thought it best to remove his daughter from Dettelsau. Loehe took his daughter to the family of a *Schulrat* (school inspector). After he left her there he begged her in a letter for understanding: "My child, let me have the only joy of my life here on earth, that you are of one mind with me, you and your brothers. I need no other fortune on this earth than this one thing."[33]

There was not much progress learning languages. Marianne, who previously had suffered from rheumatism, became ill in Greiz and was confined to bed for weeks with a "sneaking nerve fever."[34]

A year later she needed a three month cure in Bad Reichenhall because of some eye problems. While she was gone, an acquaintance from Greiz, Cantor Dietel, wrote and asked for her hand in marriage. Loehe discussed this with his sister-in-law Emilie Fresenius who happened to be visiting in Neuendettelsau. Both agreed that Marianne, only 17 years old, was too young for marriage. Besides she was sick with "this business with her nerves."[35] The worried father thought of Marianne's mother who died so young. She also had married very young, and apparently Marianne inherited her "very weak nerves." Therefore Loehe believed that he has to give a negative answer to her suitor. He wrote therefore to his daughter and left it up to her to make a different decision. But Marianne voiced no objection.

She was home for a year, but then treatment for a bronchial condition became necessary. Bad Lippspringe near Detmold was chosen, but her condition grew worse there. Loehe was desperate that she "had to spend her youth" in such a way: "Instead of furthering your education and gracing your father's house as a leader, you have been sick, unable to do anything . . . "[36]

During a stopover in Frankfurt Marianne once more was examined by two doctors. She had to pass on this devastating report to her father, "that the lung is badly damaged . . . in the lower half of the right lung one can no longer hear any breathing . . . the bronchia and the larynx are sick . . . "

As a "last resort"[37] the doctors recommended a long stay in a Southern climate. After much debate they chose Cannes. In October 1858 Loehe accompanied his daughter there. *Frau Oberin* Amalie Rehm also accompanied them, a great relief for Loehe, since in contrast to him she spoke French very well.

It was Loehe's first trip abroad. The beautiful scenery around Cannes delighted him, "the view of the ocean and the landscape full of villas"; "The roses are in bloom, also lemons and oranges. There is a wonderful smell in the air, and the scenery is like a mixture of fall and spring. But they tell us that it is winter, even though one can work with the windows open . . . "[38]

Since there was no Lutheran church in Cannes, Loehe visited churches of different confessions. He liked the Anglican church best, and Marianne could find a spiritual home there. But following Loehe's conviction, she was not allowed to attend communion with the Anglicans.

Marianne was well taken care of in the house of Dr. Severin who also was her physician, so Loehe's mind was at ease as he started home with *Frau Oberin*. Their route led them via Turin and Milano, where they both enthusiastically climbed the tower of the cathedral. They did not miss any of the sights. Then they travelled back to Germany via the Gotthard Pass.

Later Loehe wrote to Marianne about an exciting travel adventure:

> The way from Airolo to the hospice on the Gotthard was cold. On the North side, toward Germany, there were always two people in a sled. It was snowing, there was a freezing cold wind, and we were glad when we arrived in Andermatt in time for a delicious meal, where we could warm up with a glass of wine. When we were back in the sled, racing downhill, I saw a strange bridge. I asked the travel guide who himself was driving: 'what kind of bridge is this?' He answered: 'The Devil's Bridge' . . . At that the sled raced unto the bridge, spun around and tipped over—*Frau Oberin* fell on me; the travel guide also fell. The horse didn't want to stop because the other sleds were ahead of us. *Frau Oberin* screamed, since she thought that I was hurt, but I was calm. The devil, who is supposed to spook around Andermatt in general, had thrown

> me under her, but the angel of the Lord spread his hands under me. I got up, completely unhurt once my burden was gone. Then came the 'hat rascal' which dwells on that bridge and wanted to blow my hat into the raging river below, but I caught it again. I had already left my umbrella and my cap in Cannes and the belt for my topcoat in Turin. (*Frau Oberin* left a package with laundry.) What if I had lost my hat as well! But man and hat got off without harm.[39]

Marianne spent almost two years in Cannes. Again and again the doctor counseled that she extend her stay. For a long time pneumonia with a high fever delayed the beginning of the cure with ocean baths. Besides that she seemed to be happy in the society there. She had been received in a very friendly way by the Anglican congregation. She studied English and French and was surrounded by "interesting people."[40]

In spite of his tremendous workload her father wrote to her faithfully at least once a week. Her long absence depressed him. He worried about her physical condition but also about the state of her soul. Has she been exposed to "moral temptations"[41] in Cannes? Are there any men in her life? She cannot avoid seeing some "male beings" in Cannes. Loehe admonished her to be "very cautious, pure, chaste and modest." Since he knew that she did not like to read such admonitions, he also asked her not to be upset by his "fatherly word."[42]

In Neuendettelsau he had to listen to a lot of advice about Marianne's long illness. Some people expressed the opinion that a "simple life back home" would be more helpful for her. Loehe explained the common opinion: "People would like to see you as a healthy and happy administrator and a deaconess in your father's house. They consider that such a position would suit you best and would be a perfect fit for you." But Loehe himself did not want to urge her to take this "position." He simply wanted a "blessed calling for her, no matter in what occupation."[43]

There were other well-meaning friends who urgently advised her to return, especially since in 1859 France was at war with Austria, and it looked as if Germany would become involved on the side of Austria. Then Marianne would be in "an enemy country." But there was no sign of war in Cannes. Marianne extended her stay into 1860, even though there was no improvement in her condition. Loehe finally became convinced that the different climate could not help her.

Besides that, he was moaning about the financial burden of this endless cure. True, Marianne inherited some money from her mother, the same as her brothers. Loehe administered it since the death of his father-in-law, but he hated to dig into the "motherly emergency penny."[44] As long as he was able he wanted to finance the cure of his daughter himself. Marianne thought otherwise. She thought that it was "most natural" to pay for the expensive stay in Cannes out of her own means: "If the stay here makes me well, my health is worth more to me than millions. If the Lord does not want to give me health, He will take care of me even if I have nothing. And if I die, I won't need the money any longer . . . "[45]

Loehe's father-in-law, Ferdinand Andreae, had lost his life in an accident in 1857. He saved his wife and her children from some shying horses, but they stomped on him and dragged him along and he died the next day from his wounds. Loehe, whose relationship to his father-in-law was always somewhat tense, was very much impressed by the noble deed which caused the death of the old man. Loehe traveled to Frankfurt for his funeral and saw "how much respect the man enjoyed and how much sympathy there was." When the will was read Loehe was relieved to know that "from now on he would be able better to take care of his children."[46]

LOEHE'S SONS

Of course that applied to his sons as well. Ferdinand was confirmed in 1852 and Gottfried in 1855, and after confirmation they had to choose a profession. Neither one of them seemed cut out for a liberal arts course of studies. Ferdinand had overcome his childhood sickness and turned out big and strong. His father thought for a while that he should become a merchant of books and found an apprenticeship for him in the Sebald print shop where they were printing the new Bavarian hymnbook. But Ferdinand was unhappy in this profession. His entire love was farming.

Loehe realized that his son had to follow the path which he "chose with such constant love in spite of many obstacles."[47] Karl von Raumer, Ferdinand's godfather, also urged the young fellow to follow his inclination. So Ferdinand worked for the time being on the farm that belonged to the parsonage in Neuendettelsau and also on the "*Oekonomie*" (estate) of the Deaconess Institute. Later he attended the agricultural schools in Wiesbaden and in Munich.

Loehe's second son, Gottfried, started an apprenticeship as a book seller in the C. H. Beck publishing house in Noerdlingen in 1857. Because Loehe had a good relationship with this firm since they printed many of his writings, the son was not charged any fees for his apprenticeship, to the great relief of his father. Gottfried had to study for three years and then serve an intern year in the business. In contrast to his brother he was happy in the book trade. He was "ambitious, strong, and developing nicely"[48]—the most outgoing and the happiest of all the Loehe children—in spite of his physical handicap that bothered him even in his profession.

Loehe's relationship to his children was often difficult. Marianne complained that there were too many admonitions in his letters. Ferdinand rebelled against his father and often argued with him "without restraint" in the presence of others. There were some scenes where Loehe could only hope "that God may have mercy." Loehe knew how difficult it was "for a young person to find insight and peace when he is not free of worldly matters and yet mightily under a spiritual influence."[49] Only gradually Loehe understood that he was at times oppressive to his children, that they had to cut themselves loose, and that one could therefore understand Ferdinand's "drive for independence." Once he wrote to Marianne: "My children, as you well know, love their father more when they are away from him. The old man is a burden for them."[50]

12

THE "DEACONESS FATHER"

Loehe and women—that is a chapter all by itself. His image of a woman was formed by his unforgettable Helene. With her image forever before him, he published a little booklet, "About Womanly Simplicity"[1] in 1853, ten years after her death. It appeared just in time for him to present his daughter Marianne with a nicely bound dedication copy as a confirmation present.

"ABOUT WOMANLY SIMPLICITY"

Loehe gathered "all the glory of women in the word *simplicity* . . . it includes everything, should give unity and clarification to everything."[2] "Simplicity" as Loehe meant it, had nothing to do with simplemindedness or limited knowledge, but it is "the virtue that leads all things to a goal."[3] It meant the state of innocence and completeness in Paradise before the Fall, an attitude which is directed unwaveringly toward a center, the Creator, and has eyes only for Him. Only through the Fall a person drifts into "discord and diversity" because he "seeks his own."[4]

And what makes "womanly" simplicity special? According to Loehe man and woman have the same "goal of the heavenly calling," but as long as they live on this earth there is a "difference between the male and the female calling." According to the order of creation the man is the head and the woman the helpmate of the man. "Womanly simplicity agrees with this difference, wants to be a wife, accepts the husband's peculiarity, and does not desire or imitate it."

"A woman's degeneration (*Ausartung*) is independence and manly character. Her greatest honor is simple femininity, to joyfully and without a heavy heart subject herself, to be content, not wanting to be more than she should be."[5]

A woman's calling in this world therefore is to be "a helper for the manly life." That applies both to married and unmarried women. Both should "serve and want to serve as women." Her simplicity means that she agrees with what was given in creation. In Protestantism until now "all womanly fortune and completion" was found in marriage, but this led to a depreciation and disdain of unmarried women. But Loehe called for a new understanding: "The unmarried women, virgins or widows, can give all their labor in the service of Jesus and his congregation, even more than married ones."

In this connection Loehe reminded his readers of the "deaconesses of the ancient Church," although one should not overestimate the single state. The married and the unmarried states have the same dignity, the same "simplicity:" The wife serves her husband, her family and therefore Christ. The single woman is free for service "in hospitals, in schools, at sickbeds and with the elderly."[6] Her only goal also is to serve Christ.

In the last chapter of the little booklet Mary, the mother of Jesus, is described as an example of womanly simplicity. Of course Loehe rejected the "calling on" Mary and her "idolatrous" veneration in the Roman-Catholic Church. But he also considered the "protestant scornful indifference" toward her an extreme, since she had "out of the mouth of the angel received blessing and preeminence over all women of all times and countries."[7] All women should follow her example and "learn to mirror her." Her answer to the angel's announcement, "Behold I am the Lord's handmaiden; let it be to me according to your word" is, according to Loehe, "a wonderful witness to the highest and most profound, most humble and high minded womanly simplicity that one could imagine."[8]

The little book "About Womanly Simplicity" was also called a *Marienbuechlein* (a little book about Mary) and it became Loehe's "Program for the essence of the female deaconate."[9] The state of the unmarried woman was elevated appropriately, lifted to the same level as that of the honorable state of the married woman. At the same time Loehe saw a clear ranking of the sexes, based on the creation: The husband is the head, and the woman is the helpmate of the man. Requests for equal rights for women, which were raised already at this time in the early women's movements, were not acceptable in Loehe's view. The "beautiful, holy, patriarchal relationship"[10] between a pastor and his congregation was also unequivocal for Loehe.

The domineering position of the rector of the congregation of the Institute in Neuendettelsau as the bearer of the spiritual office was also unquestioned. The woman's role as a helper, her willing subjection to the man, was an unquestioned condition of the Deaconess Institute.

How did women get along with this? How did it look in the practice? How did Loehe act as teacher and pastor of so many women?

THERESE STAEHLIN

One of them, Therese Staehlin, described very vividly in many letters to her family the life in the deaconess house.

Therese belonged to the group of women whom Loehe had in mind at the founding of the Deaconess Institute. She came from a rural parsonage in Weiltingen near Dinkelsbuehl, one of 14 children. Four of her brothers were studying theology. The oldest would later become president of the *Oberkonsistorium* in Munich.

Therese, a small roundish person, smart and energetic, was fortunate to receive a good education. Her parents placed her with a married sister in Augsburg where she attended the Stetten Institute for girls. At age 15 she graduated, but nobody knew "what to do with her." Shortly before, in February of 1855, the father of that large family, Pastor Martin Staehlin, died. Two daughters still lived with the widow, 12 year-old Marie and Julie, who was blind. They moved with their mother into a small apartment in Noerdlingen. But what to do with Therese? At that time they heard an enthusiastic report of a friend about the new institute in Neuendettelsau. A letter was sent, and Pastor Loehe was willing to receive Therese, even though he was receiving more applications than he could accept.

In the fall of 1855, a year after the founding of the deaconess house, Therese came to Neuendettelsau. In spite of the great enthusiasm because of the new beginning, there was a lot of confusion. Pastor Loehe was sick, the supervisors were very busy, and nobody really cared for the young Therese or told her where she could be used. She struggled with "painful homesickness."

The situation changed the moment *Herr Pfarrer*, only half recuperated, appeared again and took up his teaching. For Therese this "opened a new world."[11] She could not talk enough about Loehe in her letters, especially about his classes where "simplicity is connected with so much depth."[12] In the afternoon there were always "pastoral hours," and the whole community took part: "Old and young, deaconesses and those still on probation, teachers and students, emotionally sick, patients and guests of all kinds." Usually the subject was biblical stories. Loehe knew in an inimitable way "how to touch all present in their diversity, to interest and advance them."[13] When he asked questions, the dignified *Frau Oberin* was just as anxious to answer as the youngest student. Already in the first week Therese was charged with the honorable task of keeping a diary of these hours. She also copied Loehe's sermons every Sunday.

Her homesickness was blown away. Suddenly she was "completely at home" and "extremely happy." She could not "thank God enough for having led her to this house where the inner person receives so much nourishment." She befriended other students, among them the four daughters of the von Tucher family.

Loehe at this time was 48 years-old, but he seemed much older. He called himself the "old pastor of Neuendettelsau." At noon he came to the deaconess house to eat, but he was careful to pay for his meals. After dinner he was available for any sister or student with a problem. He had a quick eye for the talents of his female coworkers, and he knew where to put them to work. The 16 year-old Therese took part in the lessons, but at the same time she was to teach French in the "Little School" and also help with sewing lessons.

The *Herr Pfarrer* became more and more important for Therese. She was glad that he still addressed her with "*du*," because she "was not so big."[14] Once he came with some visitors to her class and introduced the "little person" as teacher and then said smiling: "She is terribly upset that she is so little. We feed her every day, but she just doesn't grow."[15]

After just a few weeks she was invited to the parsonage where every Sunday afternoon a circle of friends and coworkers gathered around Loehe. Such an invitation was very desirable and a "longtime wish" of young Therese. Toward evening a group of students came. They could hardly find any space for all of them but Loehe invited them kindly: “Just sit down; it’s going to work somehow. It’s not my fault that the carpenter made the room so small!”[16]

But the *Herr Pfarrer*’s greatest importance for Therese was as her pastor. She was confused about herself, struggled to find the “right repentance” and the way to sanctification. After much painful inner wrestling, she asked to speak with Loehe. He had already noticed her sadness. He listened, and by questioning her he led her to the “right knowledge” and gave her “the most wonderful counsel and the sweetest comfort.”[17] As for countless other women Loehe became for Therese an indispensable father confessor.

Training of a Deaconess

After just a few months in Neuendettelsau Therese decided to become a deaconess. According to Loehe’s plan she had to learn additional womanly skills, besides her teaching, among them domestic work and nursing. From now on she attended Loehe’s classes on “spiritual care of the sick.” She worked long hours with handicapped children and then was charged with starting an “industrial school” for children in neighboring villages.

On April 4, 1857, Therese Staehlin was consecrated a deaconess, but that did not end her period of learning. Besides teaching her own classes, she continued sitting in Loehe’s classes. During these early years the students showed great interest in learning, and this inspired Loehe to ever new experiments in teaching. For example the deaconess students were learning Greek, in order to be able to read the New Testament in its original language. Loehe wanted to prove that “the female sex is by no means as stupid and incapable as most people think.”[18] His principles concerning a “purely womanly education”[19] were pushed into the background in response to the desire for knowledge and the enthusiasm of his students for each new subject. They were learning middle high German, poetry and theory of verses, history, and mathematics. Loehe had a special love for calendars, from the farmers’ almanac to the calendar of the saints. Whatever he lectured or dictated his students put down in their notebooks.

After his return from Cannes, Loehe gave the sisters an enthusiastic report of his trip and suggested that all should emphasize the learning of foreign languages. For in Cannes he constantly “stood around with a sheep-face and like the ox on a hill"[20] because he did not know French.

Calligraphy was part of the program, beginning with the correct cutting of the quill, the hair lines, and the circles. Loehe was a stickler for details. His sense for what was proper and beautiful extended to the last shelf in the wardrobe of the pupils. There had to be painstaking order. Lists were to be kept about the laundry which had to be folded just so, with right corners. Every deaconess had to learn to keep books of finances and inventory so that she could supervise and administrate a station or a home by herself.

One day Loehe came up with the idea of an "academy." The sisters were to gather material for a certain subject and read books and reports so that they could give a report and discuss it. One day eight reports were given about persons in the history of the deaconate, such as Elisabeth Fry. Loehe was especially proud of these "academic hours," for many visitors said that the academy was "the crown of the institute. What is being taught comes alive and is digested here."[21]

Arts and crafts should not be neglected. Upon Loehe's suggestion a "society for altar hangings" was founded for the "decoration of sacred places."[22] The participants created *Paramente*, altar and pulpit hangings with fine embroidery which were selling well in the congregations of the *Landeskirche*. This was considered the high school of womanly crafts. Only the most skilled sewers and knitters "advanced" to it. In 1858 the society for altar hangings also started a "bakery for communion wafers," after the institute had received the machinery for it as a gift.

Development of the Deaconess Institute

Neuendettelsau gradually became famous because of the good, all around education of its sisters. The requests for deaconesses came from everywhere, and it was impossible for Loehe to meet the demands. Two were going to North America to serve in the congregations of the Iowa Synod. They were received with open arms, but in a very short time they were married, and new cries for help by congregational deaconesses were heard. But all the sisters whom Loehe sent to America were "landing in the harbor of marriage,"[23] so that in Neuendettelsau he applied the brakes on further sendings. One deaconess went to Odessa as an "educator of the daughters of a prince.”[24] A few years later there were requests for sisters from Slovakia. But most of the requests were from Bavaria and they received preferential attention, for Loehe did not forget his original concept that his deaconesses be trained especially for his own Bavarian *Landeskirche*.

In the meantime, the government also became aware of Neuendettelsau. Pastor Loehe received a request to accept girls between 12 and 18 years, former prison inmates. An institution was opened for them in 1862.

The initiator of this idea was the princess Elise von Hohenlohe-Schillingsfuerst. She was a long time correspondent with Loehe. For a while she entertained the thought of becoming a deaconess herself, but her family objected to this plan. But she remained an important supporter of Loehe’s work. She expressed the wish to start a “Magdalenium” in Neuendettelsau. “Magdalenium” designated a home for “fallen girls.” Loehe really did not like this name. In his opinion the tradition that made Mary Magdalene “the patroness of repenting and sinful women” was not justified. But, he opined, “Often one must unwillingly follow a use of the language that should really be rejected.”[25]

The Deaconess Institute had already for some years received a few such women, often members of the upper classes for whom an illegitimate child always was a special problem. But also “Magdalenes” from the lower classes had found a home in the Deaconess Institute. But Loehe insisted on receiving only those women who desired to come to Neuendettelsau out of their own free will.

With a generous gift from the princess a special home for the “Magdalenes” could be built and was dedicated in 1865. The inhabitants took care of the washing, patching and ironing for all the institutions.

Besides all of this there was a small “rescue house” for orphaned and neglected girls. For them and for former young convicts the industrial school was established where they were taught to keep house and to learn arts and crafts.

As a result work increased constantly in Neuendettelsau. Therese Staehlin, who found her “life’s true fulfillment” in the calling of a deaconess and identified herself totally with the Deaconess Institute, received the new developments with hopeful expectations. However, other sisters were skeptical toward Loehe’s constant new “great ideas.” For example, he wanted to reorganize the whole hospital system, because there did not seem to be any real progress. The country people found the daily rate of 24 *Kreuzer*—about the equivalent of 30 eggs—much too high. Therefore Loehe offered to receive all the sick of the neighboring Heilsbronn district without charge. In exchange the deaconesses should be permitted to collect gifts for the poor and sick twice a year in all the villages of the district. Loehe hoped not only to cover the cost for the nursing of the sick, but also to establish close contact between the country people and the sisters. They would converse with the farming population, tell about the life in the Deaconess Institute and thus combat many prejudices against the “*Akonissen*” as the deaconesses were called. They could also distribute tracts, writings, and pictures. Perhaps many sick persons who needed good care would lose their fear of the hospital and agree to be driven to the hospital in the green deaconess coach.

Not all the sisters supported this idea. Therese Staehlin, together with another deaconess, was brave enough to try and they started out “with the beggar’s bag.” They were succeeding with this enterprise “much too well. We were respected and cared for like no other beggars.”[26] Other women who tried to gather collections were often treated poorly and had to bear insults from the farmers. But finally, this collecting proved cumbersome and in a few years was given up.

To receive the expected influx of sick people, a hospital for men was built in 1867, and a hospital for women in 1869, both at the East end of the village. However, they filled very slowly. Mainly the old and feeble made use of the nursing care.

Loehe’s Influence on the Deaconesses

“*Herr Pfarrer* was so much the soul of everything,” Therese Staehlin wrote, “that it was difficult for us to distinguish how much we were purely devoted to our deaconess profession, or how much of our service was determined by the fact that we were mightily attracted to our great teacher.”[27]

One can hardly say more clearly what central significance Loehe had for his deaconesses. He was the “father” who gave direction, so that they felt like orphans whenever he was sick or on a trip. When he left for Karlsbad in 1858 for an eight week cure, all the deaconesses and the students formed a lane at the edge of the forest where his coach passed by. He also passed a row of the mission students, although it was "considerably shorter."[28]

However, Therese was not uncritical of her revered teacher. Sometimes she was hurt by his "strictness," especially when he criticized her in front of others. At such a time she told him or wrote quite openly how she felt. Once he showed understanding and asked her to be nice to him again, after she was "mad" at him. But he also rejected an exaggerated sensitivity: "You should be a building which is not immediately threatened by collapse when it is touched with the finger of truth and of fatherly love."[29]

Therese sighed: "Our *Herr Pfarrer* is a powerful man. He can pull you down and he can pull you up."[30]

She experienced a totally different Loehe when he was sick: "The distant one, feared by all, pushing through his iron will in any matter, not tolerating any resistance when his opinion seems right (and of course he is right!), in his sickness and also in letters is suddenly mild and soft, approachable and full of love, almost more than that."[31]

Therese Staehlin held to her love and loyalty for the *Herr Pfarrer* all her life. In times of sickness, if Marianne was not at home, she cared for him like a daughter. For this he thankfully promised her his "fatherly blessing."[32]

But she would also play an important role in Loehe's work. At age 21 she was made the leader of the "blue school" and kept this office for 20 years. She would pass on Loehe's legacy to many classes of deaconesses. She was thankful that "God in His grace found her worthy" to "bring her poor insignificant life into relationship to that great one."[33]

In 1883, after the death of Amalie Rehm, Therese Staehlin was elected by the sisters as the second *Oberin* (mother superior) in the history of the Deaconess Institute.

MARRIAGE AND SINGLE ESTATE

But back to the 1860s. Therese Staehlin has chosen the full-time occupation of a deaconess and with it the single estate, with full conviction. She wrote: "A deaconess has it a thousand times easier in life than someone who is married!"[34] But Loehe emphasized again and again that he considered the single and the married estate as being completely equal: “One can live married or unmarried. Marriage and virginity have exactly the same dignity; they deserve praise and glory according to their circumstances. Nothing is forbidden, except to seek one’s salvation in such things.”[35]

Loehe emphasized that the protestant deaconess was a novelty who therefore would have a more difficult time in society and in the Church. He compared her to a sister in the Roman-catholic Church, who makes a vow of poverty, chastity, and obedience and as “God’s bride” receives the veil, “ring and crown” from her bishop. Through “tradition, education and power” of her Church she has a highly respected station, higher than the estate of being a wife. The Protestant Church, on the other hand, lifts up the “glory of marriage” and often stubbornly “treats the single estate with disdain. Thus single people are filled with shame . . . Indeed, the Protestant Church still owes something to her daughters.”[36]

But how about the vows of protestant sisters? Poverty, chastity and obedience are likewise pillars of the deaconate, but are “completely voluntary.” Loehe rejected vows, even though this would make things “much easier” for any community. Christ and His disciples did not know any vows: “For us to walk the way of the Lord is not easier but more difficult, but also more evangelical and more spiritual . . . You are a free order, carried by the great love for your Lord, for His work and His goal, and you dedicate yourselves in poverty, chastity and obedience . . . ”[37]

Loehe was convinced that this voluntary dedication by the deaconesses would create a new tradition in the Protestant Church. Therefore he often emphasized his principles to his fellow pastors: “I do not build a cloister. I leave it up to each one whether to marry or remain single. As head of the Deaconess Institute here I refused to demand even half a year, or a quarter of a year, or even four weeks of service as a virgin. Nobody is stopped for even an hour from changing her estate, if that is what she wants, even though this principle already cost the Deaconess Institute dearly.”[38]

But what the motherhouse did require from all deaconesses was a “vow of honesty in all matters pertaining to sex.” That meant any relationship with a man leading to the intention to marry should be communicated to the motherhouse as early as possible without being asked. It was emphasized that this was not a “vow of a nun,” but the purpose was “to save the deaconesses and their profession from sexual carelessness, bad repute, or malicious gossip.”[39]

KAROLINE POESCHEL, NEE STEINLEIN

The memories of another pastor’s daughter, Karoline Steinlein, also tell how Loehe stood on the question of marriage vs. virginity. She entered the Deaconess Institute in 1859, four years after Therese Staehlin. Her sister Elise was already living in the motherhouse as a deaconess.

At age 34 Karoline Steinlein was not exactly young any more. When she was 17 she had been engaged to a student of forestry. Marriage was made difficult for them because the groom had to make a large security deposit, or he had to work for 12 years before being permitted to marry. Since there was no money, the two of them agreed to wait for 12 years. Shortly before the date—they had already rented an apartment in Munich—the groom died of cholera.

It took Karoline a long time to get over her loss. After a few years she decided to follow her sister to Neuendettelsau. Shortly before leaving Neumarkt, where she was living with her mother, she received a letter from a Pastor Poeschel of Loepsingen in the Ries. His wife had died recently, leaving him with nine children. He had heard of Karoline and he asked her to become his wife and the mother of his orphaned children. Karoline’s conscience was greatly troubled because she had decided on a totally different path for her life. Her family was strictly against this union and thought it would be like “throwing herself into an abyss.” Finally she turned Poeschel down in a letter. Shortly afterwards she learned that Pastor Poeschel had become engaged to a “lady from a distinguished family.”

Karoline was relieved, packed her belongings and traveled to Neuendettelsau, where Pastor Loehe greeted her with these words: “We have expected you for a long time.” Loehe became the revered teacher and pastor for Karoline also, and she attended his classes with great interest. When he once said to her: “Karoline, it is not easy for you to sit in a class again,” she immediately answered: “It all depends on who the teacher is.”

Karoline sensed that she enjoyed Loehe’s confidence. She was happy in the motherhouse and felt at home there. Everything apparently pointed to her joyfully entering the deaconate.

Then a second letter from Pastor Poeschel arrived unexpectedly. His fiancée panicked just before the wedding and fled in face of the gigantic task of taking over a parsonage with nine children. Now the distressed man and father asked Karoline Steinlein a second time for her hand in marriage and for help in his desperate situation.

Karoline was frightened. Didn't her brother, Vicar Gustav Steinlein, comment on her first refusal: "If we didn't do God's will, He certainly will do what He did with Peter: The vessel (with all those unclean animals, Acts 10) which Peter did not want to accept was let down a second and a third time."[40]

She talked with her sister Elise who urged her strongly to refuse this proposal. All her friends in the motherhouse were also upset: This pastor with all those children could find a wife wherever he wanted but not in their house where women were preparing for the important profession of a deaconess.

Did Pastor Loehe agree? Karoline decided to make him the arbiter. She asked for an appointment and presented her cause, leaving the decision totally to him but "hoping secretly" that he would "say a definite 'No' " like all the others in the motherhouse.

But after thinking about it briefly, Loehe answered: "If you find the courage to raise these nine children in the fear of God, you will have done more than any sister. I will gladly lift my hat before a deaconess, but before a pastor's wife with nine children, I will lift it twice."

Upset and timid Karoline could only say: "Yes, I would love to have the children, but the man!"

Loehe smiled and said: "Usually one takes the children for the sake of the man, as a bonus, so to speak. But you make them the main reason!"[41]

Karoline accepted Loehe's decision as the will of God. She wrote a "courageous Yes" to Pastor Poeschel and received a "thankful answer." On April 17, 1860, a quiet marriage was celebrated in Neumarkt, and Karoline Poeschel moved to Loepsingen as the pastor's wife.

She quickly established a close relationship with the children—the youngest was not yet three—and also with her husband. She had a good but very short marriage. After a difficult illness that dragged on for months and during which he was cared for by Karoline alone, he died in the summer of 1861.

Now Karoline was alone in the world, a widow with nine children. Thinking back about that time she wrote: "The most difficult thing was that I could no longer understand the ways of my Lord."[42]

The fate of the orphaned family raised a sympathetic response everywhere. The orphanage for children of pastors in Windsbach took in the four older sons. The widow was allowed to stay in the parsonage for a while. Then Loehe offered her the opportunity to move with the younger children to Neuendettelsau where the Deaconess Institute let her have a small house close to the church.

She now was a member of Loehe's village congregation, and her children grew up before his eyes. Mrs. Poeschel soon became an important person in Neuendettelsau, for Loehe knew how to use her in his service in a friendly but determined way. During these years many guests came to Neuendettelsau to experience the famous services. Especially on holidays the parsonage and inn were often fully occupied. The additional guests were then sent to Mrs. Poeschel who somehow had to house them. At other times, if Loehe asked her, she took in extra borders for weeks. By serving in this way she became acquainted with interesting people. A young mission teacher from Riga lived in her house for two years.

One day Loehe had the idea to start a "soup institute" for the children who came to school from outlying villages and for the "roamers," the poor apprentices who traveled about. He suggested that Mrs. Poeschel should take this over and on every school day cook 100 liters of nourishing soup with some meat in it. One portion should not cost more than a *kreuzer*. Even though Mrs. Poeschel explained to Loehe that it was impossible to produce the soup for that price, he was not dissuaded from his *one-kreuzer-portion*. Mrs. Poeschel was very inventive. She asked the farm children to bring potatoes and vegetables from home, if the parents could afford it. The children gave her this produce before school started, and at 11 o'clock the steaming soup was ready in a hundred little bowls placed on long tables. Pastor Loehe came almost daily to eat, stood with his bowl among the children, and consumed the simple soup "with the best appetite."[43]

Loehe showed himself a great friend of children in other ways. Whenever he walked through the village, little children ran to him and stretched out their hands toward him. Loehe was happy that they were so trusting and said: "They are all my children, because I baptized them, and they would be beautiful if they were not so dirty."[44]

Thus Karoline Poeschel became Pastor Loehe's faithful coworker for many years. After her children were grown, at age 50, she took the position of housemother in a boarding school for boys in Oettingen. For the last years of her life she returned to Neuendettelsau, where she died in 1906 at age 81.

13

YEARS OF SICKNESS

On Pentecost Sunday 1863 Loehe preached the festive sermon in the overflowing village church. It was very hot and humid; the preacher was struggling for air. During the distribution of Holy Communion he suffered a slight stroke. He trembled violently and spilled the wine when he tried to refill the chalice, but he was able to finish the service and dragged himself back to the parsonage. His hearing was reduced, and at times he had no feeling on the left side of his body. The doctor ordered absolute bed rest. Loehe felt close to death. He asked to be given the sacrament.

But gradually he and those around him realized that he would live, but with reduced strength and many handicaps. This realization was hard for him: "To die seems more beautiful to me than leading a broken life. And yet the latter is my task."[1]

CONVALESCENCE

The doctor advised travel to a place where he could recuperate. Marianne accompanied her father to the *Hohen Peissenberg* near Weilheim where they both could live in a hospice. They picked this place because Ferdinand was working nearby on a farm which Loehe could see from the mountain where he was staying. His son often came for a short visit. Slowly Loehe felt that he was getting a little better. Once again he could hear the church bells as they "ring harmonically." His left foot obeyed again when he tried to walk, though everything felt different from the way it was before. His thoughts dwelled totally on the question of whether he would be able to resume the work he loved. Would he be able to "work as usual?" He longed greatly for his home town that seemed so abhorrent to him when he first visited it in 1836. In the long years of working there it had become very dear to his heart.

"In my eyes there is no place sweeter or more lovely than Dettelsau. I would not want to exchange it for anything, whether I live there, am sick, or die."[2]

After returning, he still felt weak and dragged along in his "invalid life." On his left hand, which remained a little lame, he now wore a black silken glove. His editor in Stuttgart, Theodore Liesching, encouraged him to start working again. Loehe sadly wrote to him: "I do not have the courage or the time, and in general I believe that my writing career is over. You yourself know that I have lost my touch, even though you do not mention that . . . You touch on pastoral matters. That is the only area where I can still serve. But everything works very slowly."[3]

In July of 1863, a second trip for recuperation became necessary, this time to Bad Schachen at Lake Constance. Then Loehe tried to take up his work again.

Co-Rector Lotze

Loehe knew that he had to slow down, he no longer could accomplish as much as before. What was going to happen to the many people in the institutions who all depended on him? He had to consider seriously how to divest himself of a large amount of his work. He had to entrust many tasks to the hands of others.

He would like to have Co-Rector Lotze, who was 36, as his successor. Since 1856 Lotze has been his faithful and indispensable fellow worker. Together with Loehe he built up the schools of the Deaconess Institute. He was especially instrumental in developing singing lessons for the deaconesses and the students. His choir of well-trained female voices sang chorals, motets, ancient litanies, and parts of the classical literature for choirs in the services, such as Bach's St. Matthew Passion or Mozart's Requiem.

Later Lotze remembered how Loehe, after the first performances of the newly founded choir, exclaimed enthusiastically: "That is real artful singing!" But after a while he would criticize one thing or another of the choir's singing, even though he was "a complete layman when it comes to music." His liturgical speaking sounded like music, but he could not sing "a single line of a choral." Lotze was offended. He correctly assumed that some envious people had whispered things about him to Loehe and that this was the reason behind Loehe's sudden inclination to criticism. Fortunately the visit of a famous expert was imminent, Gottlieb von Tucher, a good friend of Loehe and author of a well-known work about "Evangelical church singing." He had announced his coming for Lent, but unexpectedly he was sitting in one of the "quiet half hours" which were held during those weeks at noon in the chapel. The quiet time of meditation and prayer was framed by singing.

Herr von Tucher was very favorably impressed by the singing of the choir of sisters and thanked them after the devotion with these words: "I had not expected something like this. Your singing moved me deeply. They do not sing any more beautifully in the Sistine Chapel." He had often listened to the famous Sistine choir in Rome.

With this, Lotze as choir director and his work were clearly reaffirmed. At the next assembly of the Institute a contrite Loehe openly expressed his appreciation: "I was wrong and take back all my criticism of the choir. Herr von Tucher was greatly satisfied."[4]

Following his stroke Loehe wanted to train this deserving young theologian and music expert to be his substitute and successor. Therefore he gave him a newly created position of chaplain for the House and the Institute. The *Oberkonsistorium* approved the new position for the Deaconess Institute in 1864. That meant that the new chaplain conducted Sunday services in the chapel for the congregation of the Institute, while Pastor Loehe preached in the village church. The deaconesses found this intolerable! On Sundays they wanted to hear their spiritual father preach, no one else, no matter how much the poor "stepfather"[5] tried his best! The sisters expressed their disapproval very clearly in such a way that the unhappy chaplain was badly hurt. On Sundays the majority of the house congregation was streaming over to the village church. And Lotze could read in the faces of the sisters who remained that they also would much rather sit under Loehe's pulpit.

Somewhat half-heartedly Loehe attempted to mediate for basically it was very hard for him to "slow down and let things go."[6] There was also a certain mistrust, wondering whether the younger man would "spread out so much"[7] that the old rector would eventually be pushed out. The fact that the sisters insisted so vehemently on receiving pastoral care only from him, in spite of his dwindling strength, was a comforting assurance for him.

It became clear that the time had not yet come for Loehe to pass on the spiritual leadership of the institutions. But that made Lotze's relationship to Loehe and to the sisters ever more difficult. Finally, after severe personal struggles, the Co-Rector asked to be dismissed in the summer of 1865.

Loehe was shocked. In a self-critical mood he stated: "I am just not able to train a successor for myself. I am just not lovable or attractive enough."[8]

In the spring of 1866 Lotze left Neuendettelsau and returned to Thuringia, where three years later he was made *Superintendent* (the equivalent of a bishop). Loehe sent him word through a friend that he had the "wish and the certain hope" that after Loehe's death Lotze would return to Neuendettelsau. In 1872 Lotze indeed received a call from Neuendettelsau to be Loehe's successor but after much soul-searching he turned down the call.

POLSINGEN

Lotze left for Thuringia "in deep peace"[9] with the position of co-rector remaining vacant for the time being. Loehe assumed his usual great workload again. Johannes Deinzer, who until then was a teacher in the mission institute, became his vicar and Loehe utilized him increasingly for the Deaconess Institute. The sisters noticed that the young man was "the apple of the eye"[10] of *Herr Pfarrer*. There was harmonious cooperation between the two. When the vicar received a call to be an instructor at the University of Erlangen, he refused and gave this reason: He loved and revered Pastor Loehe more than anyone else, and he could not imagine a better call than Neuendettelsau. Loehe was deeply touched by such devotion and said: "Now I know that I have three sons and that there is more love and unity every day."[11]

In 1865 the Deaconess Institute opened its first branch in Polsingen near Oettingen. Loehe's son Ferdinand purchased the baronial estate Polsingen for a very reasonable price. Estimates claimed that it was worth at least twice what he paid. It was a beautiful possession with a "magnificent manor house"[12] which

Ferdinand wanted to lease to the Deaconess Institute, since he lived in another house on the estate.

In June of 1865 Ferdinand married his cousin Johanna Andreae. Her father was the brother of Loehe's deceased wife. The new owner of the estate and his young wife entered Polsingen triumphantly, as proud father Loehe reported: "The village administration received him with a mounted escort and with banners. Some wagons with flags also led him into the village. Near his house the road was covered densely with flowers. The entire congregation stood there, singing 'Now thank we all our God.' "[13]

Just a few days after this entrance Loehe traveled by coach from Neuendettelsau via the "*Hahnenkamm,*" a forested hill. The trip took him eight hours. He was welcomed joyfully and immediately attended a conference of the village administration where the use of the mansion was discussed. The rector of Neuendettelsau would like it to house "institutions of mercy." Loehe suggested a home for children for the village of Polsingen, a "rescue house" for the whole district and a "place for incurables."[14] The Neuendettelsau deaconesses would have a field for future endeavor there.

With this beautiful estate Ferdinand received "his purpose for his life"[15] and the Deaconess Institute received an impressive branch. Loehe was very much in favor of this purchase, but the financing brought Ferdinand and his father, who supported him faithfully, many problems for years to come. Again and again new deadlines loomed when payments were due, and there were anxious questions whether Ferdinand would be able to hang on to the estate. Ferdinand's uncle and father-in-law, Adolf Andreae, initially was very skeptical about this purchase until he finally visited the place. Then he was prepared to raise money among relatives. In spite of this there were always times when money was tight. Loehe himself had no savings, but he asked Gottfried and Marianne to loan their brother money from their inheritance, which Ferdinand would pay back from the income of the estate.

Gottfried Loehe's Bookshop

But Gottfried also wanted to become independent. On January 1, 1866, he opened a store for "Books and Arts"[16] in Nuremberg. It was not easy for the young business man to begin there, for other

Nuremberg book merchants were against it; and after he succeeded in starting the business, he ran into financial problems. At the end of 1866 Gottfried had to pay the printer and asked his brother Ferdinand to pay him back the 2,000 *gulden* Gottfried had loaned him. Ferdinand did not have the money at the moment, so he rode through the night to Neuendettelsau to ask his father for help. Loehe eventually was able to raise the necessary funds from relatives.

Thus Loehe always found himself in the "strange" position that he, the "broke and poor man," had the task of raising money.[17] Yet he knew no other way but to finance the ventures. He also had the great joy of seeing the sons getting along better with each other and with their father.

"Since Friedel's ability, wisdom and energy have been proved, he gets more respcct from Ferdinand. And that is wonderful . . . One can also see their Christian attitude reflected in their businesses: Ferdinand's understanding of institutions of mercy and Friedel's love for Christian literature. It makes me very happy."[18]

Gottfried Loehe desired to specialize in his bookshop in the "spreading of protestant-theological and ascetic literature." He could count on the faithful support and the good counsel of his father. When he asked him whether he should publish a collection of sermons of Loehe's friend Wucherer, Loehe answered immediately: "I think that you don't even have to read it. Just go ahead and print it. I would be very mistaken if this would not be good business for your store . . . I will be honored and happy to write a preface for Pastor Wucherer's best book and your first one. Please give him my best regards."[19]

This collection of sermons with Loehe's preface was the first book that appeared from the new publishing house. Gottfried was also interested in publishing writings of his father. He thankfully wrote to his father that his business was doing well, thanks to his proficiency and also because the name "Loehe" was "capital."[20] During that same year that he started his business, Gottfried also married. His choice was Agnes Liesching. She was from the Liesching family of publisher Liesching in Stuttgart with whom Loehe had business relations for many years, who also was a good friend. Agnes attended school in Neuendettelsau and was confirmed by Loehe. Gottfried asked his father to speak on his behalf to the future bride, and he did so successfully. The wedding was celebrated in Neuendettelsau at the end of July 1866. Shortly before, Ferdinand's first son, Johann

Konrad Adolf Wilhelm Loehe, was baptized by Vicar Deinzer in Loehe's house. Loehe was godfather and held the baby over the baptismal font. Everybody claimed that the little one "looked just like" his grandfather. Loehe also noticed a "high forehead as the most prominent part," but he also found: "The nose is crooked, just like mine. The upper lip is long . . . it is a serious looking Loehe face."[21]

The War of 1866

A dark cloud hovered over Gottfried's wedding. Guests from abroad could not come, because there was war in Germany. On July 3, 1866 the Prussians defeated the Austrians near Koeniggraetz. Bavaria had been on the side of the Austrians and parts were occupied by Prussian troops. At the wedding banquet, everybody cussed the Prussians. Loehe, who "does not want to belong to any party," was considered "Prussian friendly."[22] This was not entirely unjustified, given his friendly connection with Prussian Lutherans and his abhorrence of this "war among brothers." At the beginning of the war he offered the services of the deaconesses to the Bavarian minister of war, which were gratefully accepted. Even though no field hospital was established in Neuendettelsau, as originally planned, the Neuendettelsau deaconesses were nursing the many wounded in a field hospital in Kissingen in amiable cooperation with Prussian deaconesses and Catholic sisters of mercy.

The newly married Loehe couple had planned a modest honeymoon in Goessweinstein in Franconian Switzerland, but on the way they were stopped by Prussian guards and had to return to Nuremberg. The Prussians were billeted there, while farther South Neuendettelsau was occupied by a battalion of Bavarians. The officers and soldiers were quartered everywhere, including the parsonage. They were interested in the institutions and were shown the schools. They were very moved by the mentally retarded. One soldier was deeply shocked and said to Loehe: "*Herr Pfarrer*, I would rather be killed in battle than to become such a poor human being."[23]

Many of the soldiers attended Loehe's evening services, even though they were Catholic. But in spite of the fact that they behaved decently, the village was happy when they finally left. Gottfried's business in Nuremberg at least benefited from the longer lasting

Prussian occupation: The soldiers bought a lot in his bookshop, especially the "Wartime prayers," written by Loehe.

MARIANNE'S SICKNESS

Loehe reported all these events in long descriptive letters to Marianne, who again was taking a long cure. She had not been able to attend the weddings of her two brothers, nor the baptism of her little nephew. After returning from Cannes she kept house for her father for a few years, but since May 1865 she needed another cure. She alternated between Karlsbad and Alexanderbad where stomach ulcers and other ailments kept her for two years. Repeatedly there were life threatening sicknesses.

These long and expensive cures added to Loehe's financial problems, but he worried more about her physical and spiritual well-being. Did she always keep the proper distance when relating to men? The worried father had heard that she had smoked cigars with some men. He was afraid for her good reputation: "A woman's honor is like flowery dust."[24] On the other hand, he understood that the fact that her brothers having married and started families also created in Marianne a longing for a husband and a child. But Loehe had great qualms when he thought of her being married because of her unstable health and because "as a girl she is already advanced in years."[25]

"You are going to be 27," he wrote to her in 1866, "and your youth is past. Even if you were healthier there would be less chance for a marriage. You are not going to be a fool and start chasing after a man now."[26]

Repeatedly he admonished her to put her trust in God: "God can lead you, make you happy, so that the misery of an unsatisfied heart will not eat you up."[27]

She should not worry about her future. As long as he lives she will always have a home with him, and she should not have to work so much in the household any more: "Once you are back you can take it easy. We let the people in the deaconess house cook and wash for us, and I will keep a maid or some occasional help. So you can relax and don't have to ruin yourself again."[28]

But she should not under any circumstances think that she had to dedicate her young years to her "old and sickly father": "If God shows you another profession which you can love, be it within or without marriage, I am perfectly content." Most important for him was that she be happy. During her "long and frequent absences he has become perfectly adjusted to being alone."[29] An elderly maid came every day to take care of the most necessary chores in the household. He was going to redecorate the rooms in the parsonage. After Marianne returned she was to pick the most beautiful one. Then there would also be a "Polsinger" and a "Nuremberg" room for the families of her brothers.

But what would happen to her once he died?

"I can think of no other solution than for you to find your best refuge in the deaconess house. If you get well again, you may find a profession . . . But if you are sick, you certainly will find better care in the deaconess house than elsewhere."[30]

During these years, when he felt that his life would end soon, Loehe thought often of his relationship with his children. It was a great misfortune for them that they lost their mother so early. "Perhaps you would have found with her a center for your love. I am sorry that I could not be that for you."[31] He made mistakes, especially toward Marianne, and was well aware of them. She often had to listen to how different she was from her mother. During her last stay in Karlsbad, in 1870, her father wrote: "In spite of all my mistakes, I am still your faithful father. I am sorry for all the mistakes which I made while bringing you up, in spite of my intentions. I wanted what was best for you, but I should have acted differently. May God have mercy on you and on me!"[32]

Loehe considered it a great blessing that during recent years his relationship with his children had become much more cordial. All three knew that he was interested in how they were doing and appreciated his help and his support. In Polsingen he was happy that Ferdinand "treated him so lovingly,"[33] in Nuremberg Gottfried acted "with the most tender attention" toward his father. He was also "very happy"[34] because of the way Marianne responded during his visit in Karlsbad. He felt especially close to her, so close that he foresaw in a dream whenever she had "another attack" of sickness.

Charismatic Gift

Did Loehe possess special "magnetic"[35] charismatic powers? The host of the inn "*Gasthaus zur Sonne*" claimed repeatedly that he saw demons "around the *Herr Pfarrer*" during a sermon, or "the chancel full of angels during the sacrament," or "a brightness around the *Herr Pfarrer* when he stands at the altar.[36]

Dettelsau people believed that the prayers of their pastor worked wonders. Two parents told how they had fetched Loehe in the middle of the night because their child was suffering from diphtheria. He saw that the two year-old was near death and started to say the prayers for the dying. But the mother implored him to ask God to let her keep this her only child, since several others already had died. Whereupon Loehe prayed "with hands uplifted" for the life of the child. The little one was already in a coma but then opened his eyes and started crying. Loehe gave him a piece of sugar which he ate "with great pleasure." A few days later the child was well. Later Loehe could not walk past that farmhouse without the mother lifting the child through the window toward him, showing "her thankfulness and her joy."[37]

An "indestructible calm" and "deep peace"[38] emanated from Loehe's person. Because of this he had a special benevolent influence on mentally or emotionally sick people. Many people with such illnesses came a long way to Neuendettelsau, or were brought by their family. Loehe housed them in the village, and talked and prayed with them. Some became better quickly, others had to remain longer, but all spoke gratefully about the calming influence when they met with Loehe.

Some "possessed" people were also brought to him, starting many stories that made the rounds in the village. A farmer's boy from the Altmuehl valley had several bad attacks and had tried many kinds of cures. Finally his family, with his permission, wanted to bring him to Neuendettelsau. At that a voice "with horrible tones" had spoken out of him: "I don't want to go to Dettelsau. I'll go anywhere else but not to the preacher in Dettelsau. He is most cunning; I want him to leave me alone."[39]

His family had great difficulty bringing this sick person to Loehe, but he is reported to have helped him by praying with him and making him say the Creed and the Lord's Prayer.

Was there a "time of miracles"[40] in Dettelsau? Loehe tried to stop such stories from spreading. He did not want to be known as a miracle healer. He knew best how powerless he often stood at sick beds and beds of dying people. But the healing power of prayer is something that often occupied his mind, as was already seen in the case of the "anointing of the sick." Sometimes he was convinced after praying that he had been heard. At other times he found "within himself only a deep silence."[41]

JOHANN CHRISTOPH BLUMHARDT

In 1861 Loehe visited the Wuerttemberg Pastor Johann Christoph Blumhardt (1805–1880) in Bad Boll. He had already healed many sick people through prayer and the laying on of hands. He was a popular figure of Swabian pietism, and beginning in 1852 he became the house father of the sulphur bath in Boll. Many sick seeking help were praising the beneficial, spiritually intense and yet also free atmosphere of that house. Loehe had heard a lot about Blumhardt and wanted to get to know him. There were existing prejudices between the two theologians. Loehe found Blumhardt's attitude toward the confessions too liberal and non-binding. Blumhardt on the other hand criticized Loehe's "narrow understanding of communion"[42] because it binds consciences. But he did admire Loehe's achievements and thought he could be "the greatest man of our time" if he did not have this "perverted side."[43]

Their personal acquaintance brought the two closer together. Loehe wrote in his diary about Blumhardt: "I liked the man better than I had feared."[44] Two years later Blumhardt returned the visit to Neuendettelsau which Loehe experienced as "very refreshing." "The childlike man assured (me) many times that he was very happy."[45] Blumhardt, on the other hand, wrapped up his impressions of Neuendettelsau in one sentence in a letter to his son: "I liked the institutions very much, but there were too many crucifixes and altars for me."[46]

CELEBRATING ANNIVERSARIES

During these years when his strength was waning there were two anniversaries which caused Loehe to look back on his life's work. In 1864 there was a festive celebration of the tenth anniversary of the work with deaconesses. In a paper "The Tenth Year of the Deaconess Institute in Neuendettelsau" Loehe remembered the speech he gave at the dedication of the deaconess house in 1854. At that time he thought that "the house would be worth the money it cost to build it if it would fulfill its purpose for even ten years." He had thought at that time that "perhaps the Deaconess Institute might last only ten years, and that its little light would then be extinguished." Now he was convinced that the institute was still in its infancy. Should one wish and pray for a longer life for it?

"Of course there are some people," Loehe said, "who are upset over the continual expansion of the Deaconess Institute and only wish that it would finally quiet down, do its little work peacefully, and that should be it . . . That is just as if one would say to a strong young man who is struggling to find a career: Just stop all this business, don't bother so much, sit down in your grandfather chair and be quiet . . . The One who gives hours and days to everything and writes it into His book, He is the Lord, the Lord alone. His ways will cut through the loose talk of humans like a wagon goes through the dust toward its goal. The Deaconess Institute will end some day, since nothing temporal lasts forever, whether it is good or bad. But when, and after how much time, who knows?"

Therefore, at this 10 year anniversary, Loehe gave to each deaconess this encouraging exhortation: "Forward, toward the goal. Work, as if there were no end. Accept from the beginning every success and every blessing, every sickness, suffering and dying, as it may please God."

But what was the goal of the Deaconess Institute? Was it mission work, "which is so close to the task of deaconesses, if one understands it correctly?"

"The office of a deaconess from the beginning is joined to that of preaching, just like Eve was given to Adam. A church that does God's work among the heathen without *Diakonie* seems to me like a person with only one leg."

But for the time being Loehe did not want "to set the goal too high." The Deaconess Institute did not yet have a call for mission, but a "sure and secure call to serve here in our Franconian homeland, in fact in all of Bavaria." Here it should put the "roots of its heart deeply into the ground"[47] and only later spread its branches to farther places.

With these words Loehe formulated vividly how closely *Diakonie* and mission, his two great fields of endeavor, were connected as signs of life in the Church. He had been able to withdraw gradually from the Mission Institute because Inspector Bauer had energetically taken charge. But when the North American mission work celebrated its

25th anniversary in October of 1866, its founder Wilhelm Loehe again was the center of interest.

On the day of this other anniversary a festive procession moved from the Mission House, which was all decked out in flowers, to the church where Loehe conducted a celebrative service. Before the sermon he was very anxious: Will his voice last? But afterwards he wrote joyfully: "God gave me joy, strength and cheerfulness so that I could speak as in my younger days and with richer content."[48] People crowded up for Holy Communion in such numbers that Loehe waived his otherwise inviolable rule for previous announcement.

After the service the guests assembled in the beautifully decorated chapel of the Motherhouse. Loehe was also asked to give an address that summarized the history of the mission work. He remembered the first years of the mission work in America and how it had "unifying strength" at that time. It was a painful disappointment for Loehe that his connection to the Missouri Synod had been severed, even though Loehe's "emergency helpers" had been the co-founders. In spite of this, he was happy "that there is a Missouri Synod," for their congregations have "the pure word and sacrament." When visitors from the colonies reported that people there were better off than in the old homeland and that they had good church leadership, this was sufficient reason to thank God. And of course, there was the Iowa Synod whose workers were trained in the Mission Institute in Neuendettelsau. Loehe closed his festive address with these words:

> Most glorious is this . . . The messengers of the gospel of eternal peace are still going into the forests of America, the scattered are still gathered, congregations are established, children are baptized and instructed, the dying are comforted. The blessing of Word and Sacrament has remained. . . . Nothing happened according to our plans, but everything happened so that salvation and blessing are proceeding to this very hour. The Lord has not withdrawn his hand from the work of our hands.[49]

Decorations

The War of 1866 ended in August of that year with the peace treaty of Prague. But the wounds of those hurt and of the amputees did not heal as quickly. The Neuendettelsau deaconesses continued nursing in the field hospitals in Wuerzburg and Veitshoechheim for many months. Everywhere people talked about them with great respect. During a visit by the Queen-Mother Marie, one of the sisters, as a representative of all deaconesses, was honored with a "decoration."

Even greater honor was bestowed on the rector of the Deaconess Institute "in recognition of his activity in the area of *Diakonie* and for his merits in caring for the wounded of the war of 1866."[50] The chief of the local government in Ansbach presented Loehe with the knight's cross of the order of St. Michael before the assembled congregation of the Institute in the chapel. That was a big thing for Loehe and for Neuendettelsau. The whole village was afoot, six trombones blared "so that the chapel almost fell down," as Loehe wrote to his daughter. Poems and hymns were dedicated to the new Knight of St. Michacl. Thc *Oberkonsistorium*, the *Konsistorium*, and the *Decant* all sent their best wishes. According to the desires of the *Oberkonsistorium*, all Bavarian pastors should be informed of this honor. Loehe did not quite know what was happening to him: "Congratulations from all sides, and I don't really know what for. — But of course the institutions are promoted by this in the whole country. That is the important thing."[51]

The granting of the order had great significance for Loehe's work, which suddenly appeared in a new light because of this honor. Loehe described the decoration in a letter to Marianne: "It consists of a golden cross with eight broad points, enameled sky-blue." But he would not wear this "child's toy" under any circumstances: "It rests well in its case."[52]

Loehe's Munich friends urgently advised him to take advantage of the favorable mood of the government and the church agencies in the city of the royal Residence to found a deaconess station in Munich. So Loehe made a trip with *Frau Oberin* (the mother superior). In Munich he was received by the family of Baron von Tucher "not just benevolently, but with great joy." For a whole day, from early in the morning to late at night, he acted as a "real busybody from Dettelsau," since his concern was to prepare the ground for the new station. He visited President von Harless who was "heartily happy and glad" to see his old friend. Then a visit with the president of the ministry of the interior, the Prince von Hohenlohe, was required. He was the brother of Princess Elise von Hohenlohe-Schillingsfuerst who had been a friend of Loehe's for years. She wanted to accompany him in person to see her brother. Besides that, Herr von Tucher, with the help of the Court Marshall, had secured an audience with the queen-mother. But Loehe's friends stated that the wardrobe of the village pastor was in no way good enough for the court. The most necessary items had to be loaned to him, as Loehe reported in comical despair:

> Herr von Tucher loaned me his hat, Dean Meyer his *Amtrak* (official clergy garb) the white gloves—thus I was properly equipped, even for the Queen. Tucker's hat was too small for me and there was an ugly wind. When Princess Elise came to bring me to her brother, the *Ministerpraesident*, the wind took the hat and drove it far away and the two of us had to gallop after it.

The prince received him kindly. Afterwards Loehe visited all the clergy in Munich "in order to reconcile them with the Neuendettelsau deaconesses, who were considered the best, but were also feared."

In the evening there was the audience with the Queen-Mother. She was the widow of King Maximilian II who had died in 1864, and she was the mother of the ruling King Ludwig II. Queen Marie had often expressed the desire to get to know Loehe personally. He reported about the audience:

> For the first time I visited a queen—without any heart palpitation. I enjoyed walking through all those body guards and liveried people. I was hoping I would be through in five minutes, but I had to stay for an hour and a half. The kindhearted woman enjoyed my presence . . . The next morning she sent me her album, and I had to write something in a spot designated by her. I wrote Psalm 21:1–8 for her. I liked that. When I returned in the evening to Tuchers, there was a group of noble women who wanted to start a society. Perhaps there will be an upswing of things now, especially in Munich.—I was so tired from talking that I drank a glass of beer.[53]

The society "for Deeds of Mercy" did indeed get started with Loehe's help. That same year Neuendettelsau deaconesses started working in the new station in Munich.

THE FRANCO-PRUSSIAN WAR OF 1870/71

Tragically another cry for help came very soon from the Ministry of War to Neuendettelsau. The request was again for nursing sisters in the field hospitals. The Southern German states had joined the North German Alliance; Prussia and Bavaria went to war as allies against France. Loehe was able to free almost a third of the sisters—at that time about 150, including those on probation—for service in the field hospitals. Some of the sisters were sent to France in a medical train. They were to pick up the wounded there and return them to field hospitals in Germany. Other sisters were deployed immediately after the heavy fighting near Woerth in the Alsace, and they found the wounded there in "nameless misery." They were lying on straw in private homes. "O God, now I know what a war theater is like!"[54] one of the sisters wrote home, deeply unnerved. Emergency field hospitals were erected as quickly as possible.

After the German victory over France, some Neuendettelsau sisters were working in a field hospital that had been established in the castle of Versailles. There the proclamation of the empire took place on January 18, 1871. The Prussian king Wilhelm I was proclaimed German emperor by Bismarck. Five Neuendettelsau sisters succeeded in hiding behind the flags and watching the entire ceremony.

When the sisters, after the peace treaty of Versailles had returned safe and sound, a peace festival was spontaneously arranged in Neuendettelsau. A service of praise and thanks opened the festival. In the evening all the houses were decorated with lanterns and lights, a torch parade marched through the village, and there was music and singing. Neuendettelsau was shining with festive glory like never before. Loehe let himself and a few friends be driven in an open carriage through the village, back and forth. He was sharing the joy. Some musicians had come from Windsbach; and before returning home at night, they serenaded the *Herr Pfarrer* with a somewhat frivolous song. Against all expectations he received it in good humor.

THE LAST YEAR

During this time Loehe had a hard time walking or standing for an extended period of time. In 1870 his doctor forbade him to preach for almost a year because of his physical weakness. This was harder for him than all other suffering. When the bells rang on Sunday and the vicar went over to the church in his stead to hold the services, the eyes of the old pastor filled with tears. About this time he wrote in his diary: "Even though I know that I am no good for anything, that I am weak everywhere, it is clear that I have a hard time giving up and sitting around as an old man, and that I am a hard man. May God help me in his mercy . . . How it is going to end with me I do not know. If only I were truly ready to die. My time is running out . . . "[55]

In January of 1871 he once more mounted the pulpit for a short sermon. But his deaconesses, who listened with sympathy and worries, no longer were happy because they recognized his "serious and sad"[56] condition.

Marianne had been back at home since the fall of 1870. Even though she herself was sickly from time to time, she cared for her father who increasingly was in need of nursing care. In October 1871 he was pushed through his beloved village in a comfortable wheelchair every day. Next to him pattered his little grandson who had come for a visit from Polsingen. It was a touching picture. Passers-by paused and greeted him full of sympathy.

An attack of weakness shortly before Christmas 1871 signaled to Loehe that his end was near. He prepared for death and asked his vicar to give him the sacrament, but he was still alive as 1872 began. On New Year's Day he sat in the corner of his couch and received many visitors who came every year to wish him well and were happy that apparently he was doing better. A sister wished that he would be able to walk again in the New Year, but Loehe had an even greater wish: "It would be even better if I could preach again!"[57]

Death and Burial

Would the many friends, deaconesses and members of the congregation suspect that their New Year's visit would also be their farewell visit with their beloved pastor? In the afternoon the sad news travelled through Neuendettelsau: *Herr Pfarrer* had suffered a serious stroke. After dinner he had been put to bed, suddenly he grasped his head with both hands, and then his arms dropped lifeless.

He was unconscious, breathing heavily until the afternoon of the following day when the end came. He never revived from the coma.

At his deathbed there was singing of hymns, psalms, and litanies. His children were with him during these last hours. Gottfried wrote to his wife in Nuremberg on January 2, 1872: "Dear Agnes! Just now, at quarter after five in the evening, our dear father died after a prolonged struggle. God will reward him through all eternity for all the indescribable good deeds he did for me—for all of us . . . "[58]

On January 5, Loehe's body was laid in the tomb in the village cemetery where so many of his loved ones were already buried. His express wish had been for a funeral like for a deaconess, which meant only a liturgical celebration at the grave without a preceding service in the church. In that way all eulogies and speeches to honor him should be avoided.

The fulfilling of this request was hard for the congregation of the Institute, also for all the prominent mourners who had come from afar. But the departed had impressed this on his children "with an uplifted finger" just a few months earlier: "No one should make a speech at my grave. I do not want to have a funeral sermon. Give me a deaconess funeral."

After many deliberations whether one should perhaps have a service in the church anyway, the Windsbach Dean Mueller decided to respect Loehe's wishes: "He wanted to avoid human praise, and there is sense and wisdom in this order. Besides, what can poor human words add at this grave?"[59]

Only a "Parentation," a short memorial service with the reading of the obituary as was customary for deaconesses on the evening of the day of the funeral, was held that evening for an intimate group in the chapel. The larger sorrowing congregation had to cling to the words of the Bible that were read at the cemetery: "Many of those who sleep in the dust of the earth shall awake, some to everlasting life, and some to shame and everlasting contempt. But the teachers shall shine like the brightness of the sky, and those who lead many to righteousness, like the stars forever and ever." (Daniel 12:2–3)

14

IN RETROSPECT: "A CRY FOR THE PERFECTION OF THE CHURCH"

"There is a cry for perfection within me," Loehe once wrote, "but I speak of the perfection and corporeality of the Church here and in the world to come."[1]

This longing for completion and perfection of the Church ran like a red thread through all of Loehe's life and work. The Church of God here and there, the pilgrimage to the heavenly Jerusalem, the "communion of saints" was his great love and passion. He was able to inspire and win people for this vision, all who had been turned off by their disappointment in the religion of rationalism held by so many pastors of the 19th century. From this perspective one can understand much of what seemed strange and incomprehensible in Loehe to his contemporaries and to the following generations.

The Church becomes visible and concrete in the world through people who remain faithful to God's Word and the sacraments. Even though Loehe was well aware of wrongs and shortcomings in the Church; he was able to say: "It is the garden of all good, in spite of all the trouble and pain one has with the weeds."[2]

In the "Three Books about the Church" Loehe as early as 1845 awarded "the prize for the greatest amount of truth"[3] to the Lutheran Church, out of all the "*Partikular* churches." Its confession corresponds most closely with the Sacred Scriptures. "For no one could ever prove that our confessions are in error even in one single point."[4] Luther's teaching and the confessions of the Lutheran Church had become the inviolable basis of the faith for this young theologian. According to his opinion the Lutheran Church "is complete in its doctrine. It is incomplete in the consequences of its doctrine."[5] He meant that it has to become aware of its own importance. Once it has recognized its teaching as the right one, it must give it "full application in all aspects."[6] It was Loehe's concern to fill the Lutheran confession with life, translate it into practice in the congregations, the mission and the *Diakonie*. Therefore it was so important for him to work toward a Lutheran mission and a Lutheran *Diakonie*, and not to turn these "life signs of the Church"[7] over to inter-confessional organizations.

ACCUSATION OF "ROMANISM"

Loehe became known as an upright and strict Lutheran. How could he then be accused of Roman-Catholic leanings? How could "Romanizing rumors" cling to his feet "like the dust of the street?"[8]

Like the German Reformers, Loehe saw the Lutheran Church as the legitimate continuation of the "ancient pure Church of the Occident."[9] It had been cleansed of the "novelties and misuses" of the papacy. Therefore, he also claimed for the Lutheran Church the "cloud of witnesses of the ancient world,"[10] the pious men and women of the first centuries after Christ. He had a great love for the calendar of saints, also for calendar literature in general, which played an important role in rural areas. Loehe called the calendar the "most beautiful union of nature and grace," because it shows "signs, times, days, and years" and the "stars in the sky of nature and of grace."[11] The names of the saints and martyrs in the calendar, the "stars in the sky of grace," can teach the people much of the history of the Church if they are properly explained.

This is what Loehe had in mind when he published the "Months of Roses of Saintly Women" for the Deaconess Institute in 1860. It contained 60 biographies of female saints, most of them from the early days of the Church. Almost immediately he had to defend himself against harsh criticism that he was "Romanizing." He expressed his conviction that as a Lutheran and "firmly standing on the confessions, one could nevertheless appreciate reverently the ancient Christians,"[12] those who lived before Luther's reformation "at a time when one had to make his own choice of the ways of sanctification and righteousness."

In this connection he spoke of the relationship of the different confessions:

> I therefore cannot be indifferent when it comes to confessional differences, because there are points of agreement between the confessions and because so many join me in bending their knees before the same Son of God. On the other hand I consider it a wrong kind of confessionalism to insist on the different teachings we have received by the grace of God and then trample on the undeniable truth that there exists a common union between Christians which transcends confessional differences. Therefore one must nourish the relationship which exists between those who worship Jesus in spite of the different confessions.

Since Loehe foresaw that his conciliatory ecumenical attitude would surprise people, he added belligerently: "It is a matter of total indifference to me if some say that earlier I did not strike this chord. It is hardly worth the trouble to point out that I did strike this chord a long time ago, for instance in the Three Books about the Church. I just did not have any cause to repeat it too often."[13]

Loehe brought up this subject once more in the "Church Letters" of 1861 which are a justification of his theological direction. He emphasized especially that he knew himself to be "free of all Romanism" and that he was "always faithful to himself:" "Within the border lines of my understanding I became clearer and firmer. In some small details I changed because of better insight. But you cannot call this a change; it is a continuing development."[14]

He realized that he "once was maligned as a very rough cut Lutheran," and now he is considered an apostate. He believed the reason for this was his "Less antagonistic mood" toward the Roman Church, in the tolerance between the confessions that was possible in his century, and in contrast to the vehement debates of the 16th and 17th centuries:

> I am opposed to Rome as much as anyone. But the way I feel, this opposition does not prevent me from seeing much that is laudable in less important things on the other side and much that is perverted and wrong on our side. Precisely because I find myself completely separated from the Roman Church, as also from other Church parties, I dare to notice the good things, and I do not shy away from saying it.[15]

MOVING AWAY FROM LUTHERANISM?

A second accusation against Loehe charged that he distanced himself from Luther's teaching and from the Lutheran Confessions. This accusation came especially from some in the Missouri Synod, on the one hand because of Loehe's teaching concerning the ministry, on the other hand because of a famous/infamous sermon by Loehe in 1857 based on Philippians 3:7–11, which he entitled: "Meeting for the Resurrection of the Dead."[16] At that time Loehe had been sick a long time and was occupied greatly with death, resurrection, and the second coming of Christ. He could not deliver the sermon himself. It was read from the pulpit, and because of the urging of friends, it was published.

Loehe believed that in this passage Paul assumed there would be a first and then a second resurrection. In between, the thousand year kingdom of Christ as described in the book of Revelation would exist. This understanding raised a touchy subject "chiliasm"—belief in a thousand year kingdom—that had often played a role in sects and enthusiastic movements in the history of the Church. The Augsburg Confession expressly rejected it.[17] Therefore Loehe was angrily attacked after publishing his sermon, especially by some Missourians who accused him of "having completely fallen away from Lutheran teaching."[18] In a letter to a Missouri Synod pastor who had asked him to explain his position, Loehe showed a certain degree of understanding for the Missourians but admitted that he had gone through a period of development in his attitude toward Luther and the confessional writings:

> When I was younger and had recognized the doctrines of the Lutheran Church as correct, I also acted like my brothers in Missouri. Because of my great and justified confidence I accepted everything that they (namely Luther and the Lutheran theologians) said. Even if I was not satisfied with everything, I did not dare to trust my own eyes when I was reading the Word of God. But eventually I could no longer resist the light of the divine Word. The more I was convinced of the purity of Lutheran teaching in its main points, the more I recognized that God, the Lord, wanted to give to his poor Church in our own days a greater light and more beautiful clarity on some points than our fathers had.[19]

In the "Church letters" Loehe affirmed that he would subscribe to the Lutheran symbols as much as he had 10 years before. After the Reformation the Confessional Writings had clarified the position of the Lutheran Church toward the Roman Church and toward the sects. That was their historically necessary task. They had great significance for Loehe himself in his youth. Disappointed by the rationalistic interpretation of the Bible, he had found truth in these confessional writings: "The Tradition became clear to me sooner than the Scriptures. The light of the Church brought me to the fountain of truth."[20]

But once he started an intensive Bible study of his own, he found on the one hand that "the decisions in the symbolic books of the Lutheran Church did indeed correspond to the Scriptures." On the other hand it became also clear "that for the understanding and devout reader the Scripture is clearer and plainer in all main points than its interpreters."

Thus Loehe confessed that in his theological development "he received the final and strongest conviction through the Holy Scripture."[21] It is "brighter and clearer than any human words."[22] It became for him the rule and norm against which he checked Luther's teaching and that of the confessional writings: "I do not want to believe something just because Luther and the Lutheran Church believed it. But I am heartily glad to be able to believe and confess with the Lutheran Church, because I discovered with my own eyes and through my own research that her confession is faithful to the Word."[23]

Nevertheless Loehe cast a critical eye on some of Luther's pronouncements. For in Luther, also, there was gradual development; he "wrestled over time toward the complete truth."[24] The Symbols also are bound to their time in certain aspects. So the Church must always in every age search anew the Scriptures:

> As long as there is a Church, one must study the Word of God. Light upon light will be given to those who are willing to learn from the Word, as the times require it. There will never be a time when one can conclude searching and learning and say: "Well, now we are done; we have learned everything that the Spirit of the Lord has put down in his Word.[25]

Loehe emphasized again and again in his later years this tension between "steadiness and movement within the Church:"

> There are some unchangeable things in which the Church will always remain the same. We sum them up with the rightly understood words 'Confession and administration of the sacraments.' But there are many things in which the Church is free, capable of movement, changeable and in need of development. In these things one must not be too conservative; otherwise not only the freedom of Christians is bound but also love and unity are disturbed whenever there is any movement.[26]

THE SACRAMENT OF THE ALTAR

Among the "unchangeable things in which the Church must always remain the same" Loehe counted Holy Communion in the first place. The "glory of this sacrament," the "teaching of the bodily presence of the Lord," is the "center of the Church in this world," its "principal doctrine."[27] There can be no compromise. Luther had rejected church fellowship with the Reformed Church at the religious colloquy with the reformer Zwingli in Marburg in 1529 because of the different teaching concerning communion

Loehe wanted to "trumpet with a clear horn into all the world"[28] that Luther was right when he severed ties with the Reformed Church. The different understanding of the Lord's Supper was for Loehe the "real point of separation" from the Reformed Church because, according to its teaching "the true body and the true blood of Jesus Christ are not truly present and distributed."[29] For the Reformed Church this difference in doctrine was not essential. According to Loehe it had a "cold view of the sacrament,"[30] while Luther clung with passion to the real presence of Christ in Holy Communion.

However, Loehe repeatedly emphasized his otherwise friendly attitude toward the Reformed Church, especially when he thought of his teacher, the Reformed professor Christian Krafft: "Should I hate Reformed Christians, when I am indebted to one of them for (having found) my Christ and their Christ?"[31]

Loehe also had "noble friends in Reformed areas,"[32] whom he had come to know in Switzerland when he had twice been there for recovery. But in spite of his friendships he was in favor of a clear separation because of the Lord's Supper: "It is possible to be together without confessing the same; one can love, without letting the other have his say in all parts. Two can walk together hand in hand even if there is a fence between them . . . "[33]

The Reformed Church, on the other hand, with its "cool" standpoint has no trouble having communion fellowship with all the confessions that emanated from the Reformation, including the Lutheran. In Loehe's eyes this made it the "mother of all Union," while the Lutheran Church considers the doctrine of Communion as something that separates the churches. What Loehe really attacked was not the Reformed Church, but the Union, because it thought it was possible to neglect important differences in doctrine.

In this "main point of confessional life" the Dettelsau people were "very strict," according to Loehe.

"Whoever comes to us from other churches and wants to go to the Lord's Table has to first convert. That goes for the Reformed and United as well as for the Romans."[34]

No one could accuse Loehe of a lack of confessional awareness in this regard. Unflinchingly he lifted up "the banner of unmixed communion fellowship."[35] In his later years Holy Communion became for him the center of his Lutheran faith. In 1865 he said:

> Formerly for me to be a Lutheran meant to confess the Symbols from A to Z. Now all of Lutheranism is wrapped up for me in the Sacrament of the Altar . . . It is not so much the Lutheran doctrine about the Holy Supper, but the sacramental living and the experience of the blessing of the sacrament which is made possible only through frequent participation. This is now the main thing for me. My progress is summed up in the words "sacramental Lutheranism.[36]

The deaconate and the mission should also be practiced "from the altar and in its honor." Therefore there has to be a Lutheran deaconate as well as the work of Wichern and Fliedner. Loehe revered and admired these men "most sincerely" and wished them "success a thousandfold."[37] He was also very much in favor of contacts with other, non-Lutheran motherhouses. In 1865 the Deaconess Institute Neuendettelsau received an invitation to the general conference of deaconess houses in Kaiserswerth. Loehe thanked them "respectfully" and sent *Frau Oberin* (mother superior) Amalie Rehm and Sister

Therese Staehlin as delegates. They took part in the conference "full of delight and joy."[38]

A few years later Loehe signed the Kaiserswerth appeal asking young women to become deaconesses. This was in conjunction with other deaconess houses, including some of the Union and Reformed churches. Some strict Lutherans were offended that the Neuendettelsau rector had signed this. The Rhenish-Lutheran weekly raised a "brotherly complaint because of the disturbing of consciences." Loehe had to defend himself against the accusation that he "esteemed the fellowship of the same labor higher than the fellowship of the Church."[39] He emphatically declared that "the fellowship of the Church and the Altar meant more than anything to him," and of course he wanted new sisters especially for the Lutheran deaconess houses. But he added:

> Because it is apparent that the Lutheran Church furnishes so few sisters for the service of the Lord, we wish—and we are not afraid to say this—that we would rather see another 500 eager and capable workers in Kaiserswerth than to see the whole Protestant world with all its needs denied help because of a sparcity of Lutheran sisters.[40]

Volkskirche and *Bruderkirche*

(Church for All People vs. Church for Brothers)

Loehe's longing for perfection of the Church often showed itself in his desire to form a communion of believing, dedicated Christians within the larger Church. Ever since his "Proposition for a Lutheran Society for Apostolic Living" Loehe had attempted to realize this ideal. There were times when he suffered so much from the conditions in the Church at large that he was determined to leave the *Landeskirche*, to form a Free Church, or to join one of the existing Lutheran free churches. What kept him from taking this step was mainly his faithful Neuendettelsau village congregation. Also his work was given increasing recognition and the church government gradually gave him a free hand in his field. Thus Loehe remained within the Bavarian *Landeskirche* until the day he died. He strongly shaped this Church and challenged it again and again to debates concerning questions of the Church. He made discussions about the essence of the Church and the sacrament of the altar the main battlefield where he warred against Rationalism and churchly indifference.

Toward the end of his life, his relationship to this *Landeskirche* became more positive and more peaceful. He wrote in 1865:

> I always emphasize my obedience and my faithfulness toward my *Landeskirche*: God's providence has given us this regime, and we have no other, no better . . . Here we build the kingdom of God. No one hinders us (or only seldom), and we are awaiting spring-time blossoming that will sprout at the proper time.[41]

In his struggle to build the kingdom of God in Neuendettelsau, Loehe found something close to the realization of his ideal of the Church in the Deaconess Institute and the congregation connected with it:

> If you want to know what we really desired, you have to look at the Deaconess Institute. But you should not think only of the sisters. We wanted an apostolic-episcopal Church of Brothers. Lutheranism is not a party matter for us. What makes us Lutheran with all our soul is the Sacrament and the doctrine of justification. We are not Lutherans in the sense of the Missourians, nor in the sense of the *Altlutheraner* (a Lutheran orthodox group). We are very old and very modern. What we really wanted in the final instance was for of Lutheranism to progress to an apostolic-episcopal Church of Brothers.[42]

15

LOEHE'S WORK AFTER HIS DEATH

How did things continue in Neuendettelsau after Loehe's death? From the start it was clear that his two offices—being pastor of the village church and rector of the Deaconess Institute—could no longer be handled by one person. They had to be separated. Ferdinand Weber, who had been Loehe's vicar from 1859 to 1863, became pastor of the village church in July 1872.

THE DEACONESS INSTITUTE

Finding a successor for the Deaconess Institute was more difficult. Mission inspector Friedrich Bauer had taken charge temporarily until the election of a new rector. Ernst Lotze was the first elected, but after thinking it over for two weeks he declined the call. In a second election city Pastor Friedrich Meyer of Michelstadt in Hessia was called with a large majority of votes. He was a declared Lutheran who revered Loehe greatly and who led the Deaconess Institute faithfully in the spirit of his predecessor. The liturgical services that Loehe had introduced were especially close to his heart. In contrast to Loehe, Meyer was gifted musically and built up the worship life in Neuendettelsau even more. The sisters who felt like orphans after Loehe's death quickly learned to trust their new rector; for he "is not only a clergyman through and through, he is also a very precise, clear, energetic business man,"[1] according to Therese Staehlin.

For almost 20 years, from 1872 to his death in 1891, Rector Meyer led the ever growing work in Neuendettelsau. When he assumed his office in 1872 he found 147 sisters who worked in Neuendettelsau, Polsingen, and in 31 external stations. In 1890 there were 331 sisters in 40 stations.

Meyer's successor was the eminent theologian Hermann Bezzel who later became president of the *Oberkonsistorium*. In spite of his admiration for Loehe, his great predecessor, he put the stamp of his own personality on the work in Neuendettelsau. He knew how to integrate the Deaconess Institute into the *Landeskirche*, more than had been the case previously. During his administration the work was "enlarged and with more depth."[2] Bezzel paid special attention to the schools. The number of deaconesses increased to more than 700.

It is impossible to include all the details of the subsequent history of the Deaconess Institute in this Loehe biography.[3] But a quick glance at today's *Diakonie Neuendettelsau* may be appropriate. It rose out of Loehe's Deaconess Institute and celebrated its 150th anniversary in 2004.

DIAKONIE NEUENDETTELSAU

Today the *Diakonie Neuendettelsau* is one of the largest social institutions in Germany, with about 5,600 co-workers. Its central goal is to "form life in the name of Jesus Christ."[4] About 2,000 children, young people, and adults are taken care of in the institutions of the mentally challenged, as one can read in the annual report of 2001/2002. There are homes for 1,600 seniors that include nursing care. More than 20,000 patients per year are treated in the hospitals in Nuremberg and Neuendettelsau. Some 4,000 young people attend the various schools, from general schools to trade schools and academies.

The "*Diakonie Neuendettelsau*" also works in other European countries. In Romania it is involved with a training place for nurses and caretakers of seniors since 2000, in cooperation with the Romanian diaconal work. Similar projects are planned for Poland and Spain.

Those are impressive figures. Professional, modern management has come to Neuendettelsau. The *Diakonie* has to compete with many secular social institutions. It has to show its own "diaconal profile" and yet work economically.

When it comes to maintaining a diaconal attitude, most important are the co-workers, both male and female. How are things today with the deaconess community? What kind of development has there been in the "deaconess business?"

Ever since Loehe's times the "Deaconess Motto" of the first rector has continued to give direction to the deaconesses. It was published after his death in 1873 in the Correspondence Letter:

> What do I want? I want to serve. Whom do I want to serve? The Lord in His miserable and poor. And what is my reward? I do not serve for reward or thanks, but out of thankfulness and love. My reward is that I am permitted to serve. And what if I perish in doing this? If I perish, I perish, said Esther, who did not know Him for whose sake I would gladly perish, and who will not let me perish. And what if I grow old in doing this? My heart will be green like a palm tree and the Lord will satisfy me with grace and mercy. I go in peace and without cares.[5]

Loehe thought to achieve this total, selfless serving, without asking for thanks or reward with his deaconesses, this high, almost superhuman ideal. In practice this means the total dedication of one's life and strength to the service of the weak and sick that have been entrusted to one. It means to obey every call of the motherhouse to another place of work and to give up any pay except for a little spending money every month. On the other hand, it also means to live in a sisterly community, to receive support from and regular visits to the motherhouse, and to be assured of security in case of sickness and in old age.

When the situation of women in the society changed so drastically during the second half of the 20th century, when values like equal rights for women, partnering and democracy became ascendant in the Church as well, the appreciation for the kind of life described above was lost. Since the sixties the number of deaconesses which once had reached 1,300 has steadily declined.

Few new young sisters are joining today. About 200 sisters remain in the Neuendettelsau deaconess community, but only 35 are still in active service; the others are retired. The Neuendettelsau motherhouse shares this fate with the other motherhouses in Germany. It appears the time of the motherhouse deaconate has come to an end.

As early as the tenth anniversary of the Deaconess Institute in 1864 Loehe foresaw that this end would come some day. He was astonished that it had lasted ten years. "One day," he thought at that time, "the Deaconess Institute also will perish, since nothing temporal is of eternal duration."[6]

That's how soberly Loehe saw the future of his work. He had hesitated to undertake the motherhouse deaconate. His ideal was a *Diakonie* that would be based in the local congregation. These thoughts of Loehe are becoming timely again as the *Diakonie* is looking for new ways. One has the impression that many suggestions of Loehe are being revived when reading the 2001/2002 Annual Report which lists the *Diakonie* stations in congregations, like the "diaconal sister- and brotherhood" and the "deaconate group." Since 1954 there is the "diaconal year" for young women above 16. All these co-workers of the *Diakonie Neuendettelsau* accept the charge of the Church for *Diakonie* and for living in community, even though they no longer wear the official garb and do not belong to a motherhouse.

THE MISSION

The direction of the mission institute after Loehe's death, as it had been for many years before then, was in the proven hands of Friedrich Bauer. He died in December 1874, not quite three years after his friend Loehe. His successor was Johannes Deinzer, Loehe's former vicar, who led the mission institute from 1875 to 1897.

NORTH AMERICA

The Indian mission in North America had become impossible during the time of the Indian wars. However, the Iowa Synod, founded by disciples of Loehe, continued to exist until 1930 when it merged with the Ohio, Buffalo and Texas Synod to form the American Lutheran Church. In 1987 it joined the ELCA (Evangelical Lutheran Church in America), the "largest merger of Lutheran Synods and Churches in the USA."[7] It has eight theological seminaries, including the "Wartburg Theological Seminary" founded by Loehe. The Missouri Synod, although it separated itself from Loehe in 1853, today eagerly honors his heritage and memory.[8]

The "Franconian colonies" to whom Loehe bade such a painful farewell, have become "flourishing congregations." Older people speak "a pure Franconian dialect" there. The "City of Frankenmuth" is especially eager to keep up the connection with the homeland and is in partnership with the Franconian city of Gunzenhausen. The "Bavarian Festival" in Frankenmuth, which is held annually, is an important tourist attraction with the "running of the little men"—a popular animated glockenspiel in the tower of the "Bavarian Inn"—and countless Christmas souvenirs in the "Christmas Wonderland."[9]

NEW GUINEA

A new field opened up for the Neuendettelsau Mission during the administration of Johannes Deinzer. It was at the other end of the world in Australia. As before Neuendettelsau missionaries started their work there among German emigrants.

From there, missionary Johann Flierls asked Neuendettelsau in 1885 whether he should start mission work among the Papuas in New Guinea. This mission among pagans was his great desire, but the Australian authorities were hesitating to grant him permission. The answer of Mission Inspector Deinzer—acting for the "Society"—was short and to the point: "Forward to New Guinea, quietly and quickly!"[10]

After initial obstacles and many setbacks, some small Christian congregations were gradually started. Missionary Christian Keysser, who was working in New Guinea from 1899 to 1920, had studied the language and the mentality of the Papuas. He understood that he could not approach them as individuals but that he had to reach the whole tribe and the families if he was to win them for Christianity.

The newly founded congregations "from the beginning make mission their own goal."[11] Native "helpers," together with the missionaries, brought the gospel to tribes that had not yet been converted. Here another one of Loehe's hopes was realized, namely that mission becomes the task of the congregation. Newly founded Christian congregations had the task of "border mission"[12] to adjacent pagan territories.

From these beginnings an independent native Church developed in Papua-New Guinea. Today it has 800,000 members and is in close partner relationship with the Neuendettelsau Mission. The bearer of this mission until 1972 was the "Society" that was founded by Loehe. In 1888 it added the term "*Aeussere Mission*" (foreign mission) to the already lengthy name, so that it is called "Society for Inner and Outer (foreign) Mission in the Understanding of the Lutheran Church." The Neuendettelsau Mission also developed a brisk activity among German emigrants in Brazil. An independent Church developed there in which many pastors sent from Neuendettelsau are currently working.

Society for Inner and Outer Mission In the Understanding of the Lutheran Church and Its Mission Work

In 1972 the Bavarian *Landeskirche* took over responsibility for Foreign Missions from the "Society." It calls itself today "Mission work of the Evangelical Lutheran Church in Bavaria." The Mission Work sees its purpose as supporting Bavarian congregations in "their participation in world-wide mission"[13] and to work as partners with the independent overseas Lutheran churches. Church and Mission more and more are united and cannot be separated from each other, especially since there is new spiritual life erupting in the young churches, which in turn influences the European congregations.

From Loehe's point of view, the Church can never be the Church unless it is a missionary Church. Neither could Loehe imagine being a Christian without giving witness to Christ. His great concern was the "integration of Church and Mission."[14] He thought that Church and Mission belonged closely together, because Mission is nothing but "the Church of God in motion."[15]

The "Society" still has its seat in Neuendettelsau. It has taken over new and different tasks. For Loehe, "Inner Mission" meant the mission of evangelization among the baptized. "Outer Mission" aimed to bring the unbaptized in touch with the Word of God. Both tasks today are the responsibility of the "Society" in its own country, where many people live without any religion at all, and many who do not confess any Christian religion. And those who earnestly want to follow Christ need help on their way to discipleship and help to enable them to witness to their faith in their every day Christian life.

After the "Society for Inner and Outer Mission" had given up the mission overseas, it had to find a new direction. There had been a generational change. New members joined the "Society." In cooperation with prominent persons from Church and Society it now publishes a magazine, whose name tells much about its contents: "CA

—Confessio Augustana. The Lutheran magazine for religion, society and culture." At the present time the "Society" has some 550 members. What has not changed is the endeavor of the "Society for Inner and Outer Mission in the Understanding of the Lutheran Church" to translate Loehe's spiritual impulses into our time, and to make them fruitful. The Society sees its task as "awakening faith in the Bible and hunger for the Lord's Supper."[16] The Society tries to reach people through Bible Weeks and lectures in many places far beyond the borders of Bavaria. It also supports, to the best of its abilities, Lutheran minority churches in East Europe in their missionary endeavors. Seminars and retreats for coworkers and congregations are held in a special retreat house ("*Haus Lutherrose*"). The house intends to be a place where faith can be found, deepened, and practiced. Beyond that, the "Society" is busy publishing, with the help of the Freimund publishing house which belongs to it, literature, tracts and other helpful writings to promote the faith.

The emblem of the "Society" shows what its members consider most important: the globe, the cross, and the chalice stand for passing on the gospel of Jesus Christ and the joy over the message of redemption and the Holy Communion, the source of all strength.

THE WORK OF PUBLISHING

For the Church, Loehe is "one of the most important authors of the 19th century."[17] He left behind a huge number of published and unpublished writings. The "Collected Writings of Loehe"[18] were issued in seven volumes from 1952 to 1966. Some of them were subdivided into two or three sub-volumes, so that a total of ten volumes were printed. Then followed two volumes with letters and diaries from his youth published in 1985–1986. The first volume of a supplementary series appeared in 1991.

Loehe's works contain, among others, his tracts, writings about Mission and *Diakonie*, about the Church and the office of ministry, and large collections of sermons, like the "Winter- and Summer Postille" and the "Epistle Postille" . Besides that there are works of liturgy like the "Agenda for Christian Congregations of the Lutheran Confession," collections of prayers, papers about the liturgy, hymnbook, and altar hangings. As in Loehe's life, one can find in his written works the "Triad of life and work of the Church," namely

"*Martyria*" (witness, proclamation), "*Leiturgia*," (divine service) and "*Diakonia*" (serving one's neighbor) in a "lively interconnection."[19]

Loehe has an "unusual power of language"[20] both as a preacher and as a writer. Powerful expression, richness of images, a passion stemming from innermost conviction, and precision mark his style. This is shown in the only hymn Loehe ever wrote. It is no longer printed in the new Evangelical Hymnbook of 1994, but until then it could be found in the Bavarian appendix to the Evangelical hymnbook:

O Son of God, Full of Eternal Power.

O Son of God, full of eternal power,/ O son of man in divine form,/ who has received God's power and honor,/ you highly praised Lord and Christ,/ the desire of all who are yours: / to you, o Lord, up to you/ to seeing you my spirit within is crying.

Thank God that I was born/ in the New Testament, my greatest gain!/ What is the temple of king Solomon,/ what is his altar, his sanctuary? / The poorest little church has the certain glory,/ that in it is united the body and the blood/ of the One who only in the next world will appear even more gloriously.

Therefore, until I can go to eternity,/ my home should stand by the altar:/ the bird has found his homey nest./ I am infused into Jesus,/ eternal life is given to me here./ Here even my flesh and bone is being renewed,/ my body and soul is given joy for eternity.

Yes, highly lauded and praised/ be our God's great friendliness./ For earth and heaven are now completely one/ in Christ's body and blood:/ what unites both is the same good./ Thus our time of waiting is comforted,/ this meal swallows up all bitterness.[21]

ENDNOTES

FOREWORD TO THE GERMAN EDITION

1. Wilhelm Löhe, *Gesammelte Werke*, 12 vols. and supplemental series v.1, *Abendmahlspredigten*. (Neuendettelsau: Freimund-Verlag, 1951–91).

INTRODUCTION

1. Lotze, 11–12.

1. CHILDHOOD

1. Schwammberger Adolf, *Der junge Löhe,* in: Katzenbach (ed.) *Anstoesse*, 19.
2. Deinzer I, 2: Löhe, *Jugenderinnerungen,* Deiner I, 2–36.
3. ibid., 13.
4. ibid., 18.
5. ibid., 12.
6. ibid., 13.
7. ibid., 5.
8. ibid., 16.
9. ibid., 4.
10. ibid., 17.
11. ibid., 18.
12. Kantzenbach, *Erweckungsbewegung,* 20.
13. Schwammberger, in: Kantzenbach (ed.) *Anstoesse*, 26.
14. Johann Arnd, *Sechs Buecher vom wahren Christentum,* also his *Paradiesgaertlein;* Johann Friedrich Starck, *Taegliches Handbuch in guten und boesen Tagen.*
15. Deinzer I, 14.
16. Löhe, *Abendmahlspredigten*, GWE 1, 33/34; cf. Wittenberg, 10–14.
17. Deinzer I, 20, cf. GW 4, 718.
18. Deinzer I, 23.
19. ibid., 22.
20. ibid., 20/21, note.
21. ibid., 24.
22. ibid., 27.
23. ibid., 26, note.
24. ibid., 28.

2. Time in the Gymnasium

1. Schwammberger, in: Kantzenbach (ed.) *Anstoesse,* 16.
2. ibid., 21.
3. Deinzer I, 34.
4. ibid., 5.
5. GW 1, 243.
6. Deinzer I, 29.
7. ibid., 30–31.
8. ibid., 33.
9. ibid., 20.
10. ibid., 32, note.
11. ibid., 34.
12. GW 2, 535.
13. Deinzer I, 44.
14. ibid., 35.
15. GW 1, 248.
16. Deinzer I, 7.
17. ibid., 9.
18. GW 2, 537; *Tagebuch vom 5. – 9. September 1825.*
19. ibid., 539.
20. ibid., 544.
21. ibid., 545.
22. ibid., 549.
23. ibid., 550.
24. ibid., 551–552.
25. GW 2, 558; *Tagebuecher 1826/1827.*
26. ibid., 565.
27. ibid., 575.
28. ibid., 591.
29. ibid., 607.
30. ibid., 586/7.
31. ibid., 555.
32. ibid., 556.
33. ibid., 557.
34. ibid., 560.
35. ibid., 558.
36. ibid., 565.
37. ibid., 566.
38. ibid., 576.
39. ibid., 569.
40. ibid., 617.
41. ibid., 577.
42. quoted from Deinzer I, 43.
43. GW 2, 562.
44. ibid., 601.

3. Study of Theology

1. Webcr, 51.
2. GW 1, 259.
3. ibid., 252.
4. quoted ibid., 174, from the *Lebenslauf zum 1. theologischen Examen.*
5. ibid., 256.
6. ibid., 261.
7. cf. Kantzenbach, *Erweckungsbewegung, 47–82.*
8. quoted from Stempel-De Fallois, 63.
9. Löhe, *Tagebuch des Missionsvereins,* GW 4, 9; about *Missionsverein* cf. Weber, 50–58.
10. GW 4, 10.
11. GW 1, 253.
12. ibid., 258.
13. ibid., 260.
14. ibid., 254.
15. ibid.,264.
16. ibid., 265.
17. quoted from Deinzer I, 71.
18. GW 1, 267.
19. quoted from Weber, 61, note 238.
20. GW 1, 271.
21. Stempel-De Fallois, 76.
22. GW 1, 273.
23. ibid., 275.
24. ibid., 276.
25. ibid., 282.
26. ibid., 296.
27. ibid., 294.
28. quoted GW 1, 169 from Löhe's *Tagebuch.*
29. GW 1, 292. (the quote is from a hymn by Zinzendorf, "*Christi Blut und Gerechtigkeit" (Albert Knapps Evang. Liederschatz, 4th ed. 1891, 1379, 8).*
30. ibid., 293.
31. ibid., 289.
32. ibid., 292.
33. quoted from Deinzer I, 83.
34. ibid., 84.
35. GW 1, 310.
36. Simon, 522.

4. Years of Wandering as a Vicar

1. GW 1, 65.
2. ibid., 308.

3. ibid., 312.
4. ibid., 316.
5. quoted from Deinzer I, 100.
6. ibid., 108, note.
7. ibid., 109.
8. ibid., 106.
9. ibid., 91.
10. ibid., 113.
11. ibid., 114.
12. ibid., 210.
13. GW 1, 329.
14. ibid., 330.
15. quoted from Stempel-De Fallois, 82, note 5.
16. GW 1, 337.
17. quoted from Stempel-De Fallois, 83.
18. GW 5/2, 1087.
19. ibid., 1076.
20. GW 3/1, 13–19, also 622–623.
21. quoted from Deinzer I, 144.
22. ibid., 130.
23. GWC1, 335.
24. ibid., 366.
25. ibid., 348, *Predigten in Kirchenlamitz,* see GW 6/1, 36–83, 794–796.
26. quoted from Stempel-De Fallois, 92.
27. quoted from Deinzer I, 124.
28. GW 5/2, 1075.
29. quoted from Deinzer I, 143; cf. GW 1, 368.
30. ibid., 151.
31. ibid., 154.
32. GW 5/2, 939; cf. Deinzer I, 156.
33. Deinzer I, 160.
34. For the protocol of this debate see GW 5/1, 20–23; cf. Deinzer I, 161–171.
35. GW 1, 390.
36. Deinzer I, 179.
37. quoted from Deinzer I, 177; cf. GW 5/2, 943.
38. GW 1, 382.
39. ibid., 384.
40. quoted from Deinzer I, 172.
41. GW 5/2, 1116.
42. Deinzer I, 186; cf. GW I, 77.
43. Deinzer I, 203.
44. ibid., 189, note.
45. ibid., 190.
46. GW 3/1, 20–33, together with 623–626.
47. GW 5/2, 1125.
48. ibid., 945.
49. GW 6/1, 280–376.

50. GW 3/1, 34–41, together with 626–631.
51. ibid., 38–39.
52. Weber, 116.
53. GW 6/1, 282.
54. quoted from Deinzer I, 204.
55. ibid., 207.
56. GW 1, 436.
57. ibid., 435.
58. Deinzer I, 224.
59. GW 1, 460.
60. ibid., 432.
61. Deinzer I, 217.
62. GW 1, 470.
63. Deinzer I, 229.
64. quoted from Stempel-De Fallois, 107, note.
65. GW 3/2, 356–357.
66. GW1, 479.
67. GW 3/2, 350.
68. GW 1, 464.
69. GW 3/2, 357.
70. GW 1, 477.
71. Schindler-Joppien, 223.
72. GW3/1, 249ff; cf. Schindler-Joppien 143ff.
73. GW 3/1, 250.
74. GW 3/2, 321–348, also 758; K. Ganzert in GW 3/1, 668–673 and Schindler-Joppien 300ff. (proof of more than 12 contributions by Löhe).
75. GW 1, 477.
76. quoted from Deinzer I, 237.
77. ibid., 238.
78. ibid., 239.
79. GW 1, 419.
80. Deinzer I, 212.

5. Neuendettelsau

1. GW 4, 403; cf. Rössler, *Unter Stroh- und Ziegeldaechern,* 139; cf. p. 186, note 2.
2. quoted from Deinzer I, 237.
3. GW I, 483.
4. Deinzer I, 232–233.
5. ibid., 234.
6. GW 1, 484.
7. ibid., 484–485. A *Florin* is the same as a *Gulden,* the equivalent of 60 *Kreuzer.* It is hard to determine its value. According to Weber, 199, not 17, 600 *fl.* were sufficient to support a small pastor's family in Franconia for a year.
8. ibid., 508.
9. Deinzer I, 184.
10. quoted from Stempel-De Fallois, 125.

11. GW 1, 488.
12. ibid., 348.
13. ibid., 489.
14. ibid., 497.
15. diary entry from January 29, 1836, quoted from Kressel, *Helene Löhe*, 10.
16. quoted from Deinzer II, 27.
17. diary entry from February 10, 1836, quoted from Kressel, *Helene Löhe,* 10.
18. GW 1, 491.
19. quoted from Deinzer I, 244–245.
20. GW 1, 494.
21. ibid., 501.
22. Deinzer I, 250.
23. ibid., 251.
24. GW 1, 499/500.
25. ibid., 511.
26. Lotze, 15.
27. quoted from Deinzer II, 9–10.
28. GW 1, 531.
29. ibid., 517.
30. diary entry of August 18, 1837, quoted from Kressel, *Helene Löhe,* 47, note 70.
31. GW 1, 514.
32. ibid., 538.
33. ibid., 514.
34. quoted from Deinzer II, 104.
35. ibid., 130.
36. ibid., 677.
37. quoted from Deinzer II, 115.
38. diary entry of Feb. 25, 1838, quoted from Kressel, *Helene Löhe,* 47, note 69.
39. quoted from Stempel-De Fallois, 165.
40. GW 1, 525.
41. ibid., 528.
42. ibid., 535.
43. quoted from Deinzer II, 32/33.
44. GW 1, 534, cf. Mark 5:13.
45. quoted from Deinzer, II, 31.
46. GW 1, 564.
47. quoted from Deinzer II, 17/18.
48. GW 1, 545.
49. quoted from Stempel-De Fallois, 142.
50. GW 1, 624.
51. quoted from Deinzer, II, 215.
52. Löhe, *Lebenslauf,* quoted by Deinzer II, 43.
53. GW 1, 636.
54. Löhe, *Lebenslauf,* 12.
55. ibid., 13.
56. ibid., 16.
57. GW 1, 646.

58. ibid., 648.
59. Hommel, 276.
60. GW 1, 647.
61. ibid., 652.
62. ibid., 653.
63. ibid., 654.
64. diary entry of Nov. 11, 1850, quoted from Kressel, *Helene Löhe,* 52, note 146.
65. GW 1, 683.
66. quoted from Deinzer II, 49.
67. ibid., 64.
68. ibid., 60.
69. ibid. 52.
70. Löhe, *Lebenslauf,* 16.
71. GW 1, 517.
72. ibid., 651.
73. quoted from Deinzer II, 53.

6. Mission in North America

1. quoted from Weber, 91.
2. GW 1, 487.
3. ibid., 481.
4. Thomasius, 144.
5. Löhe, *Von dem goettlichen Wort als dem Lichte, das zum Frieden fuehrt* (1835); GW 3/1, 39.
6. Löhe, *Drei Buecher von der Kirche* (1845); GW 5/1, 162.
7. ibid., 135.
8. BSLK, 797.
9. ibid., 801.
10. Löhe, *Drei Buecher von der Kirche* (1845); GW 5/1, 162.
11. GW 5/1, 85–179, and GW 5/2, 963–996. Now scholarly edited as *Wilhelm Löhe. Studienausgabe* 1; ed. D. Blaufuß. Neuendettelsau 2006 (with entry of pages from GW 5/1, 85–179!).
12. GW 5/1, 97.
13. ibid., 90.
14. ibid., 92.
15. ibid., 96.
16. ibid., 130.
17. ibid., 126.
18. ibid., 133.
19. ibid., 167, also D. Blaufuss, *Das Hohelied der Kirche.* Basic and pointing the way are Löhe's *Drei Buecher von der Kirche* in CA, nr. II, 1999, 17–20.
20. GW 1, 481.
21. ibid., 419.
22. ibid., 487.
23. quoted from Simon, 608; cf. Roepke, 354 and Heckel, 344ff.
24. quoted from Simon, 610.

25. Simon, 609; cf. Müller-Salget, 148.
26. GW 1, 670.
27. ibid., 666.
28. ibid., 661.
29. ibid., 660.
30. ibid., 661.
31. ibid., 670.
32. Löhe, *Die Mission unter den Heiden* (1843); GW 4, 35.
33. ibid., 50.
34. ibid., 43.
35. Weber, 176.
36. Löhe, *Bericht ueber seine Reise zum Dresdner Missionsfest* (1838); Weber, 521.
37. quoted from Weber, 182.
38. quoted from Löhe, *Die lutherischen Auswanderer in Nord Amerika* (1841); GW 4, 18.
39. ibid., 18.
40. quoted from Wcbcr, 199.
41. GW 1, 586.
42. ibid., 611.
43. ibid., 619.
44. ibid., 628.
45. Wittenberg, 23.
46. GW 4, 659; Löhe, *Rede bei deer Taufe eines juedischen Jueglings* (1836); GW 4, 236–246.
47. Wittenberg, 26 and 84.
48. GW 1, 626.
49. Löhe, *Rechtschaftsbericht* 1847; GW 4, 136.
50. ibid., 137.
51. GW 1, 659.
52. quoted from Weber, 236. GW 4, 655, Schadewitz's list of Löhe's contributions in *Kirchliche Mitteilungen*.

7. Between Work in the Congregation and among Emigrants

1. GW 1, 662.
2. Deinzer II, 132.
3. ibid., 159.
4. ibid.,162.
5. Lotze, 17.
6. GW 3/1, 718.
7. Löhe, Haus-, Schul- und Kirchenbuch, I, XI; cf. GW 3.1, 723, 32.
8. GW 1, 672.
9. GW 3/1, 142.
10. ibid., 144.
11. ibid., 137; cf. 613ff.

12. cf. Blaufuss, 344–351.
13. GW 1, 673.
14. ibid., 674.
15. ibid., 681.
16. ibid., 709.
17. ibid., 733.
18. ibid., 770.
19. ibid., 806–807.
20. ibid., 733.
21. ibid., 770.
22. ibid., 807.
23. ibid., 770.
24. ibid., 790.
25. GW 2, 11.
26. GW 1, 799.
27. ibid., 796.
28. ibid., 807–808.
29. ibid., 655.
30. ibid., 770.
31. ibid., 765.
32. ibid., 806.
33. GW 1, 95; cf. 1, 624.
34. ibid., 778.
35. Löhe, *Rechtschaftsbericht* (1847); GW 4, 143 and 645.
36. GW 4, 68–85 and 642–644.
37. GW 2, 42.
38. quoted from Weber, 346 with note 704.
39. Löhe, *Rechtschaftsbericht* (1847), GW 4, 142.
40. GW 1, 683; cf. Rössler, *Wilhelm Löhe und die Amerikaauswanderung*
41. Löhe, *Etwas ueber die deutsch-lutherischen Niederlassungen in der Grafschaft Saginaw, Staat Michigan* (1849); GW 4, 162.
42. ibid., 167.
43. ibid., 169.
44. ibid., 162.
45. Löhe, *Wirksamkeit der Gesellschaft durch Kolonisation*; GW 4, 192.
46. Deinzer III, 52.
47. GW 1, 802.
48. ibid., 695.
49. ibid., 805.

8. Struggle for a Lutheran Church

1. GW 2, 14.
2. ibid., 16.
3. ibid., 19.
4. GW 2/1, 155–156.
5. GW 2, 20.

6. ibid., 21.
7. Löhe, *Mitteilungen ueber eine Pastoralkonferenz* (March 27–28, 1848); GW 5/1, 205–212 together with GW 5/2, 969–971 and 1142–1147.
8. ibid., 214.
9. ibid., 216.
10. ibid., 213–252.
11. ibid., 218.
12. ibid., 220.
13. ibid., 221.
14. ibid., 229: Mt. 18:15–18.
15. ibid., 228.
16. ibid., 246.
17. ibid., 249.
18. ibid., 223.
19. GW 2, 43.
20. ibid., 44.
21. quoted from Deinzer II, 279.
22. GW 5/1, 406.
23. quoted from Simon, 614.
24. GW 5/1, 338–339.
25. GW 2, 59–60.
26. Deinzer II, 292.
27. GW 2, 60.
28. ibid., 57.
29. Deinzer II, 293.
30. GW 5/1, 341–362.
31. GW 2, 39.
32. quoted from Deinzer II, 324–325.
33. GW 5/1, 371–492.
34. GW 5/2, 1171f.
35. ibid., 998
36. ibid., 1184.
37. quoted from Deinzer II, 333.
38. Hebart, 199.
39. GW 5/1, 502.
40. GW 5/1, 390.
41. GW 2, 126.
42. GW 5/1, 605.
43. Deinzer II, 332.
44. GW 5/2, 1216.
45. GW 2, 128.
46. Deinzer II, 357.
47. GW 2, 115/116.
48. ibid., 82.
49. quoted from Stempel-De Fallois, 298.
50. GW 2, 137.
51. quoted from Deinzer II, 380.

52. GW 5/1, 612.
53. Hebart, 207.
54. GW 2, 141.
55. quoted from Stählin, Adolf von, 68.
56. ibid., 100.
57. quoted from Deinzer II, 328.
58. ibid., 418.
59. ibid., 424.

9. From the Missouri Synod to the Iowa Synod

1. GW 2, 205.
2. cf. Hebart, 228; Deinzer III, 80; Führer, 96–108.
3. GW 2, 43.
4. GW 1, 760.
5. GW 5/1, 255–330.
6. Löhe, *Zuruf aus der Heimat* (1845); GW 4, 78.
7. GW 5/1, 302.
8. GW 2, 103.
9. Löhe, *Neue Aphorismen* (1851); GW 5/1, 549.
10. Löhe, *Zugabe*; GW 5/1, 482.
11. ibid., 484.
12. quoted from Deinzer III, 88.
13. ibid., 90.
14. ibid., 94.
15. ibid., 89.
16. ibid., 92.
17. ibid., 95.
18. ibid., 101.
19. GW 2, 205–206.
20. ibid., 207–209.
21. ibid., 228.
22. quoted from Deinzer III, 130.
23. ibid., 136.
24. Löhe, *Ein Maertyrer der Mission am Deercreek* (1861); GW 4, 629–630.
25. GW 4, 650.
26. Schuster 131 and in sections XI, XIV and XVII, referring to Gesellschaft 1848–1945; cf. Stempel-De Fallois 256, note 223.
27. ibid., 106.
28. Beyreuther, 107.
29. Wichern, *Eine Denkschrift an die Deutsche Nation im Auftrage des Ceneralausschusses fuer die innere Mission* (1849) in Saemtliche Werke, vol. 1, 175–359.
30. GW 2, 76.
31. ibid., 78.
32. Löhe, *Innere Mission im allgemeinen* (1850); GW 4, 179–188.
33. GW 2, 78.

34. GW 4, 187.

10. The Deaconess Institute

1. ibid., 272–276.
2. ibid., 679.
3. ibid., 274.
4. ibid., 272. Löhe here refers to Spener's pietistic programmatic writing: "*PIA DESIDERIA oder Hertzliches Verlangen nach Gottgefaelliger Besserung der Wahren Evangelischen Kirchen,"* ed. Erich Beyreuther (revised by Albrecht Haismann) Giessen 1995. For other editions see Blaufuss, 26, note 25.
5. ibid., 273.
6. ibid., 260.
7. Rössler, *Unter Stroh- und Ziegeldaechern,* 173.
8. GW 4, 409.
9. ibid., 278.
10. ibid., 663.
11. Löhe, *Bruederliche Klage,* GW 5/2, 911.
12. GW 4, 276.
13. ibid., 271.
14. ibid., 278.
15. GW 2, 218.
16. GW 4, 409.
17. quoted from Deinzer III, 163.
18. GW 4, 289. The soup which was named after Count von Rumford (1743–1814) consisted of nourishing peas and beans, potatoes and pork.
19. ibid., 318.
20. quoted from Stempel-De Fallois, 290.
21. GW 4, 318–319.
22. GW 4, 402.
23. Sählin, *Therese I,* 95.
24. GW 4, 270.
25. Annual Report (*Jahresbericht*) (1856/57); GW 4, 669.
26. GW 4, 444.
27. ibid., 446.
28. Deinzer III, 228.

11. Neuendettelsau and the *Landeskirche*

1. GW 2, 218.
2. quoted after Roepke, 364.
3. GW 2, 255.
4. "Feimund": 1856, Nr. 47; quoted from GW 5/2, 1046.
5. quoted from Roepke, 364.
6. quoted from Hebart, 215; cf. Heckel, 82ff.
7. GW 5/2, 1298.

8. ibid. 1297–1316; cf. Heckel, 111–118.
9. GW 7/2, 731; cf. GW 5/2, 721–725, 1048f., 1317f.
10. GW 7/2, 539–542, also 730–731.
11. quoted from Deinzer II, 474.
12. GW 5/2, 724.
13. quoted from Deinzer II, 472; cf. GW 5/2, 1049.
14. GW 5/2, 727.
15. ibid., 741.
16. ibid., 742–743.
17. ibid., 729.
18. ibid., 831.
19. ibid., 822.
20. ibid., 825.
21. Deinzer II/ 493.
22. GW 5/2, 1325.
23. Löhe, *Meine Suspension im Jahre 1860* (1861); GW 5/2, 826–828, cf. GW 5/2, 1324.
24. ibid., 807.
25. GW 5/2, 1328; cf. Deinzer II, 509.
26. Deinzer II, 516.
27. ibid., 525; cf. GW 2, 497.
28. Stählin, *Therese* I, 113.
29. GW 2, 297.
30. ibid., 326.
31. ibid., 174.
32. ibid., 182.
33. ibid., 231.
34. ibid., 240.
35. ibid., 276.
36. ibid., 292.
37. Letter of Marianne Löhe to her father, Sep. 21, 1858. Löhe Archives, 7140.
38. GW 2, 299–300.
39. ibid., 302–303.
40. ibid., 324.
41. ibid., 330.
42. ibid., 315.
43. ibid., 341.
44. ibid., 347.
45. Letter of Marianne Löhe to her father, Sep. 18, 1858. Löhe Archives, 7139.
46. GW 2, 270
47. ibid., 228.
48. ibid., 328.
49. ibid., 316.
50. ibid., 360.

12. THE "DEACONESS FATHER"

1. GW 3/1, 449–494, also 705–713.
2. GW 2, 162. "*Einfalt*" (simplicity) is a central concept of Pietism; c. f. August Langen, *Der Wortschatz des Pietismus,* Tuebingen, 2nd Ed. 1968, 362.
3. GW 3/1, 451.
4. ibid., 455.
5. ibid., 458–459.
6. ibid., 461–462.
7. ibid., 467–468.
8. ibid., 476.
9. Stempel-De Fallois, 292.
10. Löhe, *Der evangelische Geistliche I* (1852); GW 3/2, 82.
11. Stählin, *Therese* I, 18.
12. ibid., 24.
13. Lotzc, 41.
14. Stählin, *Therese* I, 25–27.
15. ibid., 46.
16. ibid., 32f.
17. ibid., 30.
18. ibid., 69.
19. GW 3/2, 462.
20. Stählin, *Therese* I, 89.
21. GW 2, 333.
22. Stählin, *Therese* I, 74; cf. GW 7/2, 557–578, also 741–744.
23. GW 4, 419.
24. Stählin, *Therese* I, 55.
25. GW 4, 415.
26. Stählin, *Therese* I, 147–149.
27. ibid., 136–137.
28. ibid., 85.
29. ibid., 108.
30. ibid., 102.
31. ibid., 135.
32. ibid., 180.
33. ibid., 202.
34. ibid., 151f.
35. GW 5/2, 775.
36. Löhe, *Rede bei einer Schwester-Einsegnung*; GW 4, 548–554, also 715.
37. GW 4, 695.
38. GW 5/2, 776.
39. GW 4,695.
40. cf. Acts 10:10–16.
41. Pöschel, 17–22.
42. ibid., 27.
43. ibid., 50–51.

44 ibid., 46; *700 Jahre Neuendettelsau* (1998), 251.

13. Years of Sickness

1. quoted from Deinzer III, 314.
2. GW 2, 407; cf. p. 63.
3. ibid., 409.
4. Lotze, 52–55; *Musik in Geschichte und Gegenwart* 13 (1966–1989), 932f.
5. Stählin, *Therese* 1:140.
6. Deinzer II, 318.
7. GW 2, 429.
8. ibid., 428.
9. Lotze, 70.
10. Stählin, *Therese* I, 154.
11. GW 2, 446.
12. ibid., 420.
13. ibid., 426.
14. ibid., 427.
15. ibid., 419.
16. Hahn, 46.
17. GW 2, 432.
18. ibid., 445.
19. ibid., 449; cf. Hahn 48.
20. GW 2, 453.
21. ibid., 461.
22. ibid., 463.
23. ibid., 466.
24. ibid., 473.
25. ibid., 459.
26. ibid., 454.
27. ibid., 459.
28. ibid., 454.
29. ibid., 456.
30. ibid., 454.
31. ibid., 435.
32. ibid., 516.
33. ibid., 427.
34. ibid., 470.
35. ibid., 484.
36. Stählin, *Therese* I, 154.
37. Deinzer II, 202–203.
38. Lotze, 30.
39. Deinzer II, 207.
40. ibid., 204.
41. GW 2, 488.
42. Blumhardt, *Briefe,* series III, vol. 5, 269f.
43. ibid., 238.

44. quoted from Blumhardt, *Briefe*, series III, vol. 6, 208.
45. GW 2, 411.
46. Blumhardt, *Briefe,* series III, vol. 5, 358.
47. Löhe, *Das zehnte Jahr der Diakonissenanstalt Neuendettelsau* (1865); GW 4, 418.
48. GW 2, 475.
49. GW 4, 639; cf. Deinzer III, 142–144.
50. Deinzer III, 286.
51. GW 2, 489.
52. GW 2, 491.
53. ibid., 492.
54. Rössler, *Unter Stroh- und Ziegeldaechern,* 185.
55. quoted from Deinzer III, 319.
56. Stählin, *Therese* I, 196.
57. quoted from Deinzer III, 324.
58. Hahn, 61.
59. *Letzte Stunden, Tod und Begraebnis des hochwuerdigen Pfarrers Wilhelm Löhe,* Nuremberg, Gottfried Löhe-Buchhandlung (1872), 8–9.

14. In Retrospect: "A Cry for the Perfection of the Church"

1. GW 6/3, 842.
2. Löhe, *Drei Buecher von der Kirche*; GW 5/1, 117.
3. ibid., 127.
4. ibid., 134.
5. ibid., 160.
6. ibid., 161.
7. GW 4, 672.
8. Löhe, *Kirchliche Briefe*; GW 5/2, 846.
9. Löhe, *Drei Buecher von der Kirche*; GW 5/1, 159.
10. ibid., 160.
11. Löhe, *Ein Konferenzvortrag in Betreff der "Rosenmonate heiliger Frauen"*; GW 5/2, 763.
12. ibid., 773.
13. ibid., 771.
14. Löhe, *Kirchliche Briefe*; GW 5/2, 862.
15. ibid., 865.
16. GW 6/I, 695–706.
17. Confessio Augustana, Art. XVII, BSLK 72.
18. Deinzer III, 118.
19. GW 6/I, 833; cf. Deinzer III, 120.
20. Löhe, *Kirchliche Briefe*; GW 5/2, 857.
21. ibid., 858.
22. ibid., 859.
23. ibid., 860.

24. ibid., 854.
25. ibid., 861.
26. Löhe, *Meine Suspension im Jahre 1860*; GW 5/2, 834.
27. GW 2, 236.
28. Löhe, *Bruederliche Klage*; GW 5/2, 911.
29. Löhe, *Kirchliche Briefe*; GW 5/2, 848.
30. Löhe, *Eingabe an die Generalsynode 1861*; GW 5/2, 868.
31. GW 5/2, 1322.
32. quoted from Deinzer II, 526.
33. GW 5/2, 1322–1323.
34. Löhe, *Kirchliche Briefe*; GW 5/2, 848.
35. Löhe, *Bruederliche Klage*; GW 5/2, 911.
36. Deinzer II, 523.
37. Löhe, *Bruederliche Klage*; GW 5/2, 911.
38. quoted from Schober, 88.
39. Löhe, *Bruederliche Klage*; GW 5/2, 910.
40. ibid., 912.
41. GW 2, 415.
42. quoted from Deinzer III, 327.

15. LOEHE'S WORK AFTER HIS DEATH

1. Stählin, *Therese,* I, 211.
2. Lauerer, 53.
3. See also Lauerer, *100 Jahre Diakonissenanstalt Neuendettelsau, 1854–1954.*
4. Brochure *Leben gestalten – wir ueber uns – Diakonie Neuendettelsau,"* Neuendettelsau, 2000.
5. GW 4, 614 and 718.
6. GW 4, 418.
7. Weber, 554.
8. ibid., 556.
9. Rössler, *Wilhelm Löhe und die Amerikaauswanderung,* 397.
10. Wirth, 38; cf. Schuster, 174.
11. Weber, 412.
12. ibid., 415. For the influence of Löhe's thoughts on today's discussion about mission cf. Weber, 398–434: *"Wilhelm Löhe als Vordenker der Mission?"*
13. Tract of the *Missionswerk der Evang.-Luth. Kirche in Bayern: "Miteinander weltweit unterwegs."*
14. Weber, 433.
15. Löhe, *Drei Buecher von der Kirche*; GW 5/1, 96. See chapter 9, note 26 about the *"Gesellschaft"* 1848–1945.
16. Schlichting, Wolfhart, in: CA Confessio Augustana, 1999-nr. II, Information I.
17. Stählin, Adolf von, 29.
18. See Literatur.
19. Dietzfelbinger, Hermann, *Vorwort zu Kantzenbach (Hg., Anstoesse, 10).*
20. Stählin, Adolf von, 27.

21. Evangelisches Kirchengesangbuch, Ausgabe fuer die Evangelisch-Lutherische Kirche in Bayern, Muenchen o.J., Nr. 445. Cf. Weiss, Hans-Martin, *Löhe's Abendmahlslied,* in CA Confessio Augustana, 1999-nr. II, 63–66. More extensively in *Zeitschrift fuer bayerische Kirchengeschichte 58* (1939), 189–197.

APPENDIX

The following images appear in the German edition of *Wilhelm Loehe*. They have been reproduced here in the order in which they appear in the German edition.

1. House in Fuerth where Loehe was born

2. Loehe's mother around 1816

3. A commemorative stamp

4. Kirchenlamitz in Upper Franconia

5. Wilhelm Loehe in the year 1833

6. Loehe worked here briefly: Bertholdsdorf in Middle Franconia

Homiletisch- G.W.B.E. liturgisches

Correspondenzblatt.

Mittwoch den 7. September 1825. Nr. 1.

7. A publication that was used and appreciated by Loehe: The "Homiletic Liturgical Correspondence Paper". Here a facsimile of the first edition

Im Namen
Seiner Majestaet
KOENIGS

8. In March of 1837 the "Royal Protestant Supreme Consistory" with this writing to the "Royal Consistory in Ansbach" ordered that the wedding which Loehe refused to do should be performed by another member of the clergy.

9. Loehe's old village church and parsonage in Neuendettelsau (around 1840)

10. At one time Loehe's parsonage, today congregational center

11. Helene Loehe, nee Andreae
(1819 to 1843)

12. Loehe's children

Drei Bücher von der Kirche.

Den Freunden

der lutherischen Kirche

zur

Ueberlegung und Besprechung dargeboten

von

Wilhelm Löhe,

lutherischem Pfarrer.

Stuttgart,

Verlag von Sam. Gottl. Liesching.

1845.

Wilhelm Löhe-Archiv
Gesellschaft für Inn. u. Äuß. Mission
im Sinne der Lutherischen Kirche

13. Title page of "Three Books about the Church": An important instruction about the essence of the Church, even today

Agende

für

christliche Gemeinden

des

lutherischen Bekenntnisses.

Herausgegeben

von

Wilhelm Löhe.

Πάντα δὲ εὐσχημόνως καὶ κατὰ τάξιν γινέσθω!
1. Cor. 14, 40.

Nördlingen.
Druck und Verlag der C. H. Beck'schen Buchhandlung.
1844.

14. Facsimile of Loehe's Agenda of 1844

15. Dorothy Schroeder, nee Loehe (1804 to 1883)

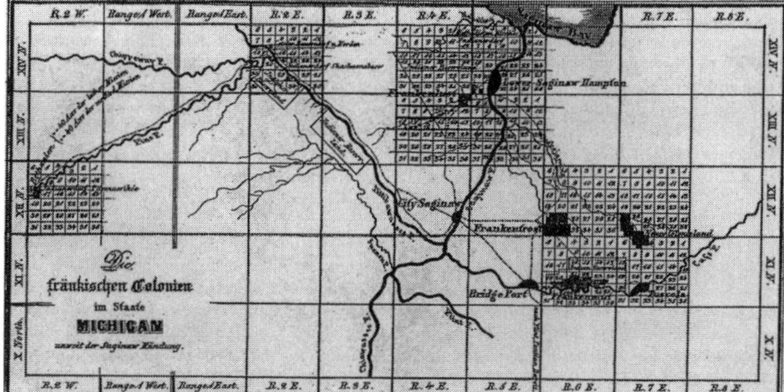

16. The Franconian "colonies" in the State of Michigan in North America

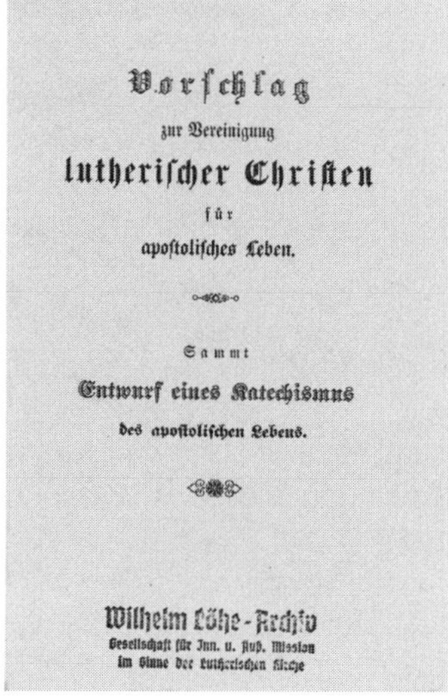

Vorschlag

zur Vereinigung

lutherischer Christen

für

apostolisches Leben.

Sammt

Entwurf eines Katechismus

des apostolischen Lebens.

Wilhelm Löhe-Archiv

Gesellschaft für Inn. u. Ausl. Mission

im Sinne der Lutherischen Kirche

17. Important for Loehe was not only doctrine, but "apostolic" living. Facsimile of his proposition of 1848

18. Wilhelm Loehe with his elderly Mother

19. Adolf from Harless (1806–1879)

Das älteste Bild des Missionshauses Hauptstraße Nr. 2
1853

20. The oldest picture of the Mission Institute from the year 1853

21. Artfully designed membership card

22. Loehe preaching from the lectern

23. An important date: May 9, 1854. The founding of the Deaconess Institute took place in the village inn

24. An enormous project: The Deaconess House arose on the green meadow in 1854

25. Amalie Rehm, the first mother superior (1815 to 1883)

26. Originally a place of worship, later workshop for paraments

27. Wilhelm Loehe (around 1850)

28. Wilhelm Loehe

29. Loehe instructing the first sisters in the service of Christian love. Detail from the Loehe monument in Fuerth

30. Konrecktor Ernst Lotze

31. Ferdinand Loehe (1838–1906)

32. Gottfried Loehe (1841–1916)

33. A facsimile of the death notice of Wilhelm Loehe

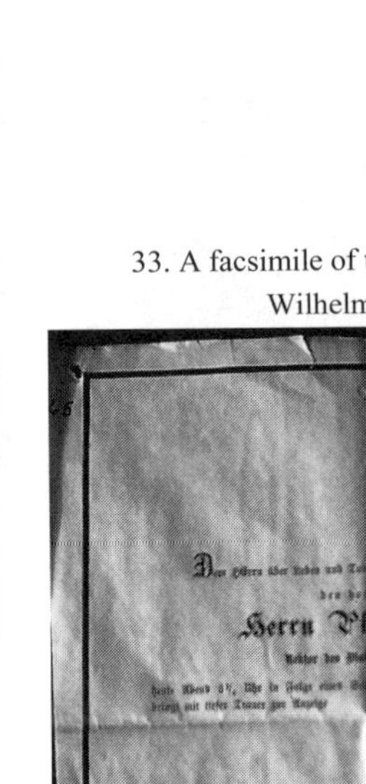

Herrn Pfarrer Löhe,

34. Loehe's modest grave in the village cemetery. Motto: "I believe in a communion of saints."

35. Wilhelm Loehe (around 1860)

36. Johannes Deinzer (1842–1897)

37. An impressive mission figure:
Johann Flierl (1858 to 1947)

38. Missionary, teacher, pastor:
Christian Keyßer (1878 to 1961)

39. Loehe gave impulses of far-reaching significance for liturgy, *Diakonie* and Mission. Until the sixties of the last century his monument stood in front of the Motherhouse in Neuendettelsau.

40. Loehe's deaconess motto expresses his thinking and his belief in regard to a life that is understood as a service for Christ. Many deaconesses adopted this motto as their very own. Even though the understanding expressed in these words was often maligned as outdated and unemancipated, it should be emphasized that it does correspond to the answering character of the Christian life. Serving—out of thankfulness for the redemption created through Christ and out of love for Him in following Him.

Was will ich? Dienen will ich!
Wem will ich dienen?
Dem HErrn in Seinen Elenden und Armen!
Und was ist mein Lohn?
Ich diene weder um Lohn noch um Dank, sondern aus Dank und Liebe;
mein Lohn ist, daß ich darf!
Und wenn ich dabei umkomme?
Komme ich um, so komme ich um, sprach Esther, die doch Ihn nicht kannte,
dem zuliebe ich umkäme und der mich nicht umkommen läßt!
Und wenn ich dabei alt werde?
So wird mein Herz grünen wie ein Palmbaum,
und der HErr wird mich sättigen mit Gnade und Erbarmen.
Ich gehe mit Frieden und sorge nichts!

679

I Cor. 13, 8.
Gal. 6, 10.
Röm. 10, 17.
I Tim. 4, 13.
Ebr. 11, 13-16.
I Cor. 16, 15. 16.

Irrenhausverwalter Hildebrandt,
Bayreuth,

Mitglied
der Gesellschaft für innere Mission
im Sinne der lutherischen Kirche.

Neuen Dettelsau
am 24. Merz
1860.

Obmann
Löhe, Pfr.

41. A membership card signed by Loehe on March 24, 1860. The dead wood comes alive and the Church rises like Phoenix out of the ashes. The card is framed by four wooden rods; around the rods a ribbon is wound which offered space for Bible words. Like a program, they represented the working areas of the Society that was founded by Loehe: For the area of Mission and Proclamation Romans 10:17; for the work of publicizing 1 Timothy 4:13, emphasizing Christian doctrine; for the accompanying of emigrants Hebrews 11:13–16, where there is mention of the seeking of an eternal home with God; and for the diaconal fighting against "local evils" (Loehe) 1 Corinthians 16:15–16. The Bible words on top stand for the entire enterprise: 1 Corinthians 13:8 and Galatians 6:10.

ILLUSTRATION CREDITS

Diakonie Neuendettelsau, Archiv: Cover artwork, 2, 4, 5, 6, 10, 12, 15, 18, 20, 22, 24, 25, 26, 27, 28, 30, 31, 32, 33, 35.

Löhe-Archiv der "Gesellschaft für Innere und Äußere Mission i.S. der lutherischen Kirche," Neuendettelsau: 7, 11, 13, 14, 16, 21, 23, 29, 36, 37, 40, 41.

Archiv Freimund-Verlag: 1, 3, 8, 9, 17, 19, 34, 38, 39.

TIMELINE

Important Dates for Contemporary and Cultural History

1804
Napoleon I Emperor of France (1804–1814).

1806
Bavaria emerges as kingdom under Maximillian I (formerly Elector Maximillian IV Joseph von Wittelsbach, 1806–1825).

1813
"Battle of Nations" (*Völkerschlacht*) at Leipzig: Collapse of Napoleonic rule in Germany.

1814–1815
Vienna Congress: Revision of borders in Europe.

1817
Union of the Lutheran and Reformed Church in Prussia under Frederick William III. (1797–1840).

Dates for Loehe's Life

1808
Feb. 21: Johann Konrad Wilhelm Loehe born in Fürth.

1816
Death of Loehe's father.

1821
Confirmation

Timeline

1825
Ludwig I King of Bavaria (1825–1848).

1826
Completion of university qualification exams, beginning of theological studies in Erlangen.

1828
Summer semester in Berlin, return to Erlangen for winter semester.

1830
July revolution in Paris: "Citizen King" Louis Philippe of Orleans (1830–1848).

1830
First theological exams in Ansbach.

1831
Begins work in Unterleinleiter and Aufseß. July 25: Ordination in Ansbach. Vicar first in Fürth, followed by Kirchenlamitz in October.

1834
February: Dismissal from Kirchenlamitz, return to Fürth. March: Journey to Munich to the High Consistory. May: Interim at the Reformed church of St. Martha in Nürnberg. By middle of June, Vicar at St. Aegidius in Nuremberg.

1835
First German railroad line from Nuremberg to Fürth is opened.

1835
April–June: Interim pastor in Behringersdorf. August: second theological exams in Ansbach. September: Interim pastor in Altdorf.

1836
April: Interim pastor in Bertholdsdorf. November: Interim pastor in Merkendorf.

Timeline

1837
July 25: Marriage to Helene Andreae in Frankfurt. Starting August 1, Pastor in Neuendettelsau.

1838
"Knee-bending Conflict"

1838
July 19: Birth of son Ferdinand.

1839
Dec. 12: Birth of daughter Marianne.

1840–1861
Frederick William IV King of Prussia.

1841
Beginning of work in North America. July 24: Birth of son Gottfried.

1842
July 11: Departure of the first "emergency helpers" (Adam Ernst and Georg Burger) to America.

1843
Jan. 1: Birth of son Philipp. Nov. 24: Death of wife Helene Loehe.

1844
Sept. 14: Death of son Philipp.

1845
Founding of mission colony Frankenmuth by August Crämer.

1848
February: Revolution in Paris. March: Revolutions in Vienna, Berlin, and Munich. Abdication of Ludwig I; successor Maximilian II (1848–1864). May 18: Opening of the German National Assembly in the Church of St. Paul in Frankfurt.

1848
Conference in Neuendettelsau. Journey to Bremen, Hamburg, Mecklenburg, Breslau.

1849
General Synod in Ansbach (Petition by Loehe and friends). Establishment of the "Society for Inner Mission in the Spirit of the Lutheran Church."

Timeline

1851
Visit from the “Americans” Walther and Wynecken in Neuendettelsau.

1852
Louis Napoleon becomes Emperor Napoleon III of France.

1852
“Missions Preparatory Institute” in Neuendettelsau under the leadership of Friedrich Bauer. Request by the High Consistory for the suspension of Loehe and his friends. Appointment of Adolf von Harless as President of the High Consistory.

1854
May 9: Founding of the Neuendettelsau Deaconess Institute.

1856
“Agendensturm” (Controversy over the *agenda*, the book of liturgy).

1858
Treatment in Karlsbad due to a kidney disease. Journey to Cannes with daughter Marianne.

1860
Suspension due to refusal to perform marriage ceremony of a divorcee.

1861
William I King of Prussia.

1861
Journey for recovery in Ragaz (Switzerland). Visit with Blumhardt in Bad Boll.

1863
June: Stroke. Recovery at Hohen Peißenberg and in Bad Schachen.

1864
Ludwig II King of Bavaria (1864–1886).

1864
10-year anniversary of the Deaconess Institute.

Timeline

1865
Purchase of the baronial estate Polsingen by Ferdinand Loehe. Opening of the first branch of the Deaconess Institute in Schloss Polsingen.

1866
Austro-Prussian war (Bavaria allied with Austria against Prussia).

1866
Gottfried Loehe's bookstore opens in Nuremberg. 25-year anniversary of North American mission work.

1867
Founding of the North German Confederation under the leadership of Prussia. Otto von Bismarck Chancellor and Prussian Prime Minister.

1867
Presented with the knight's cross of the order of St. Michael in Munich.

1870–1871
Franco-Prussian War

1871
Jan. 18: Wilhelm I of Prussia proclaimed German Emperor in Versailles (1871–1888).

1872
January 2: Death of Wilhelm Loehe
January 5: Burial

BIBLIOGRAPHIES

The following bibliography appears in the original German version of *Wilhelm Loehe*.

QUELLEN:

GW: Wilhelm Löhe, Gesammelte Werke, herausgegeben von Klaus Ganzert (collaborating Curt Schadewitz), Neuendettelsau 1951–1986:
Bd. 1 (1986): Briefe 1815–1847. (Mit einer Einleitung zum Gesamtwerk von Klaus Ganzert).
Bd. 2 (1985): Briefe 1848–1871, Tagebücher aus der Jugendzeit.
Bd. 3/1 (1951) und 3/2 (1958): Die Kirche in Gemeinde, Schule und Haus.
Bd. 4 (1962): Die Kirche in ihrer Bewegung: Mission, Diakonie.
Bd. 5/1 (1954) und 5/2 (1956): Die Kirche im Ringen um Wesen und Gestalt.
Bd. 6/1 (1957), 6/2 (1965) und 6/3 (1966): Die Kirche in ihrer Verkündigung.
Bd. 7/1 (1953) und 7/2 (1960): Die Kirche in der Anbetung.
GWE 1: Wilhelm Löhe, Gesammelte Werke, Ergänzungsreihe Bd. 1, Abendmahlspredigten (1866), herausgegeben von Martin Wittenberg, Neuendettelsau, 1991.
WLStA 1: Wilhelm Löhe. Studienausgabe, Bd. 1, Drei Bücher von der Kirche (1845), herausgegeben von Dietrich Blaufuß, Neuendettelsau 2006.
Löhe, Wilhelm, Lebenslauf einer heiligen Magd Gottes aus dem Pfarrstande, Manuskript für wenige (1844).
Löhe, Wilhelm, Haus-, Schul- und Kirchenbuch I. 4. Aufl., Gütersloh, 1877.

Archive in Neuendettelsau: Archiv der Gesellschaft für Innere und Äußere Mission im Sinne der lutherischen Kirche e.V. ("Löhe-Archiv"), Archiv des Evang.-Luth. Diakoniewerks (Diakonie Neuendettelsau), Archiv des Missionswerks der Evang.-Luth. Kirche in Bayern (Centrum Mission EineWelt).
Umfangreichste, den Zeitraum 1945 bis 1990 umfassende Literaturübersicht zu Löhe-Quellen und darüber hinaus:
Schmidt, Heiner, Quellenlexikon zur deutschen Literaturgeschichte, Bd. 19, Duisburg, 1999, 243–255.
86 Titel (Quellen, Literatur) 1991–2008 see Blaufuß (ed.), Wilhelm Löhe…, 2009, 347–350.

LITERATUR:

Beyreuther, Erich. Geschichte der Diakonie, 3. Aufl., Berlin, 1983.

Blaufuss, Dietrich. Wilhelm Löhe und die 'Alten Tröster' in: Ders., Korrespondierender Pietismus, Leipzig, 2003, 337–357.

———. (ed.) Wilhelm Löhe. Erbe und Vision. ILoeS | Loehe Theological Conference II Neuendettelsau 22. bis 26. Juli 2008, Gütersloh 2009.

———. Art. Löhe, Johann Conrad Wilhelm, in Killy Literatur Lexicon 7, 2010, 470-474.

Blumhardt, Johann Christoph. Briefe, hg. von Dieter Ising, Göttingen, 1999 Reihe III, Bd. 5 and 6.

Deinzer, Johannes. Wilhelm Löhes Leben. Aus seinem schriftlichen Nachlaß zusammengestellt: Bd. I, Neuendettelsau, (3.=) 4. Auflage, 1935; Bd. II, Gütersloh 1880; Bd. III, Gütersloh 1892.

Führer, Werner. Das Amt der Kirche, Neuendettelsau, 2001.

Hahn, Walter. Gottfried Löhe und sein Verlag in Nürnberg, in: Zeitschrift für Bayerische Kirchengeschichte 57, 1988, 27–62.

Hebart, Siegfried. Wilhelm Löhes Lehre von der Kirche, ihrem Amt und Regiment,Neuendettelsau, 1939.

Heckel, Theodor. Adolf von Harleß, München, 1933.

Hommel, Hildebrecht. Tagebücher des Friedrich Hommel, in: Bornkamm, Heinrich (Hg.) Pietismus in Gestalten und Wirkungen, Bielefeld, 1975.

Kantzenbach, Friedrich Wilhelm (Hg.). Wilhelm Löhe—Anstöße für die Zeit, Neuendettelsau, 2. Aufl., 1972.

Kantzenbach, Friedrich Wilhelm. Die Erweckungsbewegung, Neuendettelsau, 1957.

Keller, Rudolf. Von der Spätaufklärung und Erweckungsbewegung zum Neuluthertum, in: Handbuch der Geschichte der Evangelischen Kirche in Bayern, hg. von Gerhard Müller, Horst Weigelt, Wolfgang Zorn, Bd. II, St. Ottilien, 2000, 31–68.

Kressel, Hans. Helene Löhe: Ein Lebensbild, Neuendettelsau, 1956.

Kressel, Hans. Wilhelm Löhe: Der lutherische Christenmensch, Berlin, 1960.

Kressel, Hans. Wilhelm Löhe: Ein Lebensbild, 2. Aufl., Erlangen/Rothenburg o.d. Tauber, 1954.

Lauerer, Hans. 100 Jahre Diakonissenanstalt Neuendettelsau, Neuendettelsau, 1954.

Lotze, D. Ernst. Erinnerungen an Wilhelm Löhe, Neuendettelsau, 1956.

Müller-Salget, Klaus. Erzählungen für das Volk, Berlin, 1984.

Ost, Werner. Wilhelm Löhe, Neuendettelsau, 1992.

(Pöschel, Karoline). Er läßt mich nicht allein. Aus eigenhändigen Niederschriften zusammengestellt von A. Schuster, Neuendettelsau, 1954.

Roepke, Claus-Jürgen. Die Protestanten in Bayern, München, 1972.

Rössler, Hans. Unter Stroh- und Ziegeldächern, Aus der Neuendettelsauer Geschichte, Neuendettelsau, 1982.

Rössler, Hans. Wilhelm Löhe und die Amerikaauswanderung, in: Frankenland 44, 1992, 390–399.

Schindler-Joppien, Ulrich. Das Neuluthertum und die Macht, Stuttgart, 1998.

Schlichting, Wolfhart. Art.: Löhe, Konrad Wilhelm (1808–1872), in Theologische Realenzyklopädie 21 (1991), 410–414.

Schober, Theodor. Wilhelm Löhe. Ein Zeuge lebendiger lutherischer Kirche, Gießen, 1959.

Schuster, Adam. Aus tausend Jahren Neuendettelsauer Geschichte, Ansbach, 1963.

Simon, Matthias. Evangelische Kirchengeschichte Bayerns, 2. Aufl., Nürnberg, 1952.

Stählin, Adolf von. Löhe, Thomasius, Harleß, Abdruck aus der Realenzyklopädie für protestantische Theologie und Kirche, Leipzig, 1887.

Stählin, Therese. Briefe: Bd. I (1854–1883): Meine Seele erhebt den Herrn, Neuendettelsau, 1957.

Stempel-De Fallois. Anne, Das diakonische Wirken Wilhem Löhes, Stuttgart, 2001.

Thomasius, Gottfried. Das Wiedererwachen des evangelischen Lebens in der lutherischen Kirche Bayerns, Erlangen, 1867.

Weber, Christian. Missionstheologie bei Wilhelm Löhe: Aufbruch zur Kirche der Zukunft, Gütersloh, 1996.

Weigelt, Horst. Erweckungsbewegung und konfessionelles Luthertum im 19. Jahrhundert, Stuttgart, 1968.

Wichern, Johann Hinrich. Sämtliche Werke, Berlin/Hamburg, 1962 ff.

Wirth, Konrad. Das missionarische Erbe Wilhelm Löhes, Neuendettelsau, 1934.

Wittenberg, Martin. Wilhelm Löhe und die Juden, Neuendettelsau, 1954.

WILHELM LOEHE:

A BIBLIOGRAPHY OF LITERATURE IN ENGLISH

The following bibliography was compiled for the International Loehe Conference in 2008 by Craig L. Nessan and Lauren Tilley.

i. Primary Books

Loehe, Wilhelm. *Aphorisms on the New Testament Offices and their Relationship to the Congregation (1849)*. Translated by John Stephenson. Malone, TX: Repristination Press, 2008.

———. *Dialogue on Luther's Small Catechism*. Rajahmundry: Braun, 1908.

———. *Liturgy for Christian Congregations of the Lutheran Faith*.3d ed. Edited by J. Deinzer. Translated by F.C. Longaker with an introduction by Edward T. Horn. Newport, KY: n.p., 1902; reprint, Fort Wayne, IN: Repristination Press, 1995.

———. *Loehe on Mercy: Six Chapters for Everyone, the Seventh for the Servants of Mercy (1858–1860)*. Translation of *Von der Barmherzigkeit* by Holger Sonntag and with a Preface by Matthew C. Harrison. St. Louis: LCMS World Relief and Human Care, 2006.

———. *Of the Divine Word as the Light Which Leads to Peace*. Defiance, OH: Papenhagen & Deindoerfer, 1903.

———. *Questions and Answers to the Six Parts of the "Small Catechism" of Dr. Martin Luther*. 2d ed. Edited and translated by Edward T. Horn. Columbia, SC: W.J. Duffie, 1893; reprint, Fort Wayne, IN: Repristination Press, 1993.

———. *Seed-Grains of Prayer: A Manual for Evangelical Christians*. Chicago: Wartburg Publishing House, 1914.

———. *Three Books About the Church*. Translated and edited by James L. Schaaf. Philadelphia: Fortress, 1969.

———. *Three Books Concerning the Church, Offered to Friends of the Lutheran Church, for Consideration and Discussion*. Translated by Edward T. Horn. Reading, PA: Pilger Publishing House, 1908.

ii. Primary Articles

Loehe, Wilhelm. "A Sermon on the Lord's Supper (Exodus 12:1f; July 27, 1866)." Translated by Jason D. Lane, *Concordia Pulpit Resources* 18 (August 24–November 23, 2008): 3–6.

———. "A Sermon on the Sunday of the Holy Trinity." *Logia* 17, no. 3 (2008): 13–17.

———. "Lutheran Emigrants to North America: A Letter to the Readers of the *Sonntagsblatt*." Translated by Erika Bullmann Flores as transcribed by James L. Schaaf in his dissertation from *Noerdlingen Sonntagsblatt* 11 (January 10, 1841): 9–14.

———. "Of Confession to the Father Confessor." *Una Sancta* 31, no. 3, (Fall 1997): 11–12.

———. "Preface to the Agende Fuer Christiliche Gemeinden des Lutherischen Bekenntnisses." *Logia* 17, no. 3 (2008): 31–38.

———. "The Sacrament of Repentance." *Una Sancta* 10, no. 2, (1951): 1–11.

———. "The Sacrament of Repentance (Holy Absolution)." *Una Sancta* 10, no. 3, (1951): 10–23.

———. "Three Pieces on the Deaconess." Translated by Holger Sonntag, *Logia* 16, no. 2 (2007): 21–26.

———. "Why Do I Declare Myself for the Lutheran Church?" *Logia* 17, no. 3 (2008): 27–29.

iii. Secondary Books

Bickel, A.M., *Our Forgotten Founding Father: A Biography of Pastor William Loehe*. Napoleon, OH: A.M. Bickel, 1997.

Conser, Walter H. *Church and Confession: Conservative Theologians in Germany, England, and America, 1815–1866*. Macon, GA: Mercer UP, 1984, 57–72.

Forster, Walter O. *Zion on the Mississippi: The Settlement of the Saxon Lutherans in Missouri 1839–1841*. St Louis: Concordia, 1953.

Fry, George C. *Wilhelm Loehe in Perspective*. s.i.: s.n., 1977.

Heintzen, Erich H. *Love Leaves Home: Wilhelm Loehe and the Missouri Synod*. St. Louis: Concordia, 1973.

Hock, Albert Llewellyn. *The Pilgrim Colony: The History of Saint Sebald Congregation, The Two Wartburgs, and the Synods of Iowa and Missouri*. Minneapolis, MN: Lutheran University Press, 2004.

Hunnius, Nicolaus. *Epitome Credendorum.* With a preface by Wilhelm Loehe. Translated by Paul Edward Gottheil. Nuremberg: U.E. Sebald, 1847.

Keysser, Christian. *A People Reborn*. Translated by Alfred Allin and John Kuder. Pasadena: William Carey Library, 1980.

Lueking, F. Dean. *Mission in the Making. The Missionary Enterprise among Missouri Synod Lutherans 1846–1963*. St. Louis: Concordia, 1964.

Mauelshagen, Carl. *American Lutheranism Surrenders to Forces of Conservatism.* Athens, GA: University of Georgia Division of Publications, 1936.

Mayer, Herbert T. *A Reader in the History of Pastoral Care.* St. Louis: s.n., 1980.

Nessan, Craig L. *The Theology of Wartburg Theological Seminary: 1854–2004*. Dubuque, IA: 2005.

Ratke, David C. *Confession and Mission, Word and Sacrament: The Ecclesial Theology of Wilhelm Loehe*. St. Louis: Concordia, 2001.

Schober, Theodore. *Wilhelm Loehe Biography.* Translated by Bertha Mueller. 1959.

———. *Wilhelm Loehe: Witness of the Living Lutheran Church*. s.i.: s.n., s.d.

Schober, Theodore, Bertha Mueller, Frederick Sheely Weiser. *Treasure Houses of the Church: The Formation of the Diaconate Through the Lutherans Wilhelm Loehe, Hermann Bezzel and Hans Lauerer*. between 1961 and 1965.

Weiblen, William H. *Life Together at Wartburg Theological Seminary, 1854–2004.* Sesquicentennial Edition. Ed. Craig L. Nessan. Dubuque, IA: 2006.

Weiser, Frederick S. *Love's Response: A Story of Lutheran Deaconesses in America*. Philadelphia: United Lutheran Church, 1962.

Wiederaenders, Robert C. *Correspondence of Wilhelm Loehe in American Repositories.* Dubuque: Archives of the American Lutheran Church, Wartburg Theological Seminary, 1969.

iv. Chapters in Books

Chung, Paul S. "Wilhelm Loehe: Confession and a Public Diakonia." *Christian Mission and a Diakonia of Reconciliation: Reframing of Justification and Justice*, by Paul S. Chung, 100–116. Minneapolis: Lutheran University Press, 2008.

Mayer, Herbert T. "Wilhelm Loehe." *Pastoral Care: Its Roots and Renewal*, 195–212. (Atlanta: John Knox Press, 1979).

Old, Hughes Oliphant. "Wilhelm Loehe." *The Reading and Preaching of the Scriptures in the Worship of the Christian Church*. Vol. 6: The Modern Age, 121–123. (Grand Rapids: The Modern Age, 2007).

Schattauer, Thomas H. "The Reconstruction of Rite: The Liturgical Legacy of Wilhelm Loehe." *Rule of Prayer, Rule of Faith: Essays in Honor of Aidan Kavanagh, O.S.B.*, edited by Nathan Mitchell and John F. Baldovin, 243–277. Collegeville, MN: Liturgical Press, 1996.

Schmutterer, Gerhard M. and Charles P. Lutz. "Mission Martyr on the Western Frontier: Can Cross-Cultural Mission Be Achieved?" *Church Roots: Stories of Nine Immigrant Groups that Became the American Lutheran Church*, ed. Charles P. Lutz, 117–142. Minneapolis: Augsburg Publishing House, 1985.

Wittenberg, Martin. "Wilhelm Loehe and Confession: A Contribution to the History of *Seelsorge* and the Office of Ministry within Modern Lutheranism." *And Every Tongue Confess: Essays In Honor Of Norman Nagel On The Occasion Of His Sixty-fifth Birthday.* Edited by G. Krispin and J. Vieker, 113–50. Chelsea, MI: Book Crafters, 1990.

v. Dissertations

Bouman, Walter Richard. "The Unity of the Church in the 19th Century Confessional Lutheranism." Th.D. dissertation, University of Heidelberg, Heidelberg, 1962.

Carroll, Roy William. "Place, Praise and Faith: A Study of Architecture and Music in the Worship Life of the Lutheran Church." Ph.D. dissertation, University of Iowa, 1999.

Frank, Victor C. "The Work of Wilhelm Leohe in North America." Dissertation, Concordia Seminary, St. Louis, 1932.

Goebel, Hans Volkert. "An Analysis of Wilhelm Loehe's Theology of Worship with Special Emphasis Upon His Contribution to European and American Lutheranism." Thesis, Lutheran Theological Seminary at Gettysburg, Gettysburg, 1965.

Greenholt, Homer Reginald. "A Study of Wilhelm Loehe, His Colonies and the Lutheran Indian Missions in the Saginaw Valley of Michigan." Ph.D. dissertation, University of Chicago Divinity School, Chicago, 1937.

Heintzen, Erich Hugo. "Wilhelm Loehe and the Missouri Synod, 1841–1853." Ph.D. dissertation, University of Illinois, Urbana, 1964.

Hofrenning, James. "A Study of the Ecclesiology of the Newly Merged American Lutheran Church in Order to Determine to What Degree it Reflects the Theological Position of Wilhelm Loehe and Ole Hallesby Regarding the Doctrine of the church." Ph.D. Dissertation, New York University, New York, 1964.

Jahr, Arnold H. "Loehe's Contributions to Lutheranism in America." Dissertation, Wartburg Theological Seminary, Dubuque, 1939.

Korby, Kenneth Frederick. "The Theology of Pastoral Care in Wilhelm Loehe with Special Attention to the Function of the Liturgy and the Laity." Dissertation, Concordia Seminary, St. Louis, 1976.

Krueger, John W. "Discipline, Community, and Sacrifice in Wilhelm Loehe's Design for a Catechism of the Apostolic Life." S.T.M Thesis, Wartburg Theological Seminary, Dubuque, 1990.

Miesner, Willis. "Wilhelm Loehe and His Controversy with the Missouri Synod." Thesis, Concordia Theological Seminary, Springfield, 1968.

Ottersberg, Gerhard. "The Evangelical Lutheran Synod of Iowa and Other States 1854–1904." Dissertation, University of Nebraska, Lincoln, 1949.

Reents, John H. "Loehe's Works for the Lutheran Church in America Up to 1853." Thesis, Wartburg Theological Seminary, Dubuque, 1933.

Schaaf, James L. "Wilhelm Loehe's Relation to the American Church: A Study in the History of Lutheran Mission." D.Th. dissertation, Heidelberg, Heidelberg, 1961.

Schattauer, Thomas H. "Announcement, Confession, and Lord's Supper in the Pastoral-Liturgical Work of Wilhelm Loehe: A Study of Worship and Church Life in the Lutheran Parish at Neuendettelsau, Bavaria, 1837–1872." Ph.D. dissertation, University of Notre Dame, South Bend, 1990.

Schoenfuhs, Walter P. "An Indian Venture: The History of Missouri Synod Indian Missions in Michigan and Minnesota 1840–1868." Dissertation, Concordia Seminary, St. Louis, 1955.

Stuckwisch, Rick. "The Liturgical Theology of Johannes Konrad Wilhelm Loehe: Confessional Lutheran Liturgiologist." S.T.M. dissertation, Concordia Theological Seminary, 1994.

Tietjen, John H. "The Ecclesiology of Wilhelm Loehe." S.T.M. Thesis, Union Theological Seminary, New York, 1954.

Walker, Kevin G. "A Translation of Wilhelm Loehe's *Zugabe to Unsere Kirchliche Lage*: His Meditative Effort in the Church and Ministry

Controversy Between the Buffalo Synod and the Missouri Synod, with a Brief Intoduction and Historical Timeline." M. Div. Thesis, Concordia Theological Seminary, Fort Wayne, 2002.

vi. Secondary Articles

Blaufuss, Dietrich. "Loehe Preaches the Psalms." *Logia* 17, no. 3 (2008): 7–11.

———. "Saint and Heretic: Wilhelm Loehe in German Historiography since 1872." *Currents in Theology and Mission* 33.2 (April 2006): 105–112.

Briese, Russell John. "Wilhelm Loehe and the Rediscovery of the Sacrament of the Altar in Nineteenth-Century Lutheranism." *Lutheran Forum* 30 (1996): 31–34.

Conser, Walter H. "Wilhelm Loehe and the Revolution of 1848." *Logia* 17, no. 3 (2008): 39–43.

Fenton, John W. "Wilhelm Loehe's *Hauptgottesdienst* (1844) as Critique of Luther's *Deutsche Messe*." *Concordia Theological Quarterly* 64, no. 2 (April 2000): 127–148.

Gaiser, Frederick. "Witness and Worship: The Legacy of Loehe." *Word & World* 24, no. 2 (Spring 2004): 119–197.

Geiger, Erika. "The Biography of Wilhelm Loehe: Insights into His Life and Work." *Currents in Theology and Mission* 33, no. 2 (April 2006): 87–92.

Goebel, Hans. "Wilhelm Loehe and the Quest for Liturgical Principle." *Una Sancta* 22, no.4 (1965): 20–32.

Graebner, August L. "Johann Michael Gottlieb Schaller: A Biography." Translated by Walter R. Roehrs. *Concordia Historical Institute Quarterly* 54 (Spring 1981): 2–29.

Hopf, Friedrich Wilhelm. "Wilhelm Loehe as Witness for the Sacrament of the Altar." Translated by August J. Engelbrecht. *Wartburg Seminary Quarterly* 11, no. 3 (June 1948): 3–8, no. 4 (September 1948): 3–9.

Huggins, Marvin. "Help from the Homeland." *Lutheran Witness* 116 (1997): 11.

Kantzenbach, Friedrich Wilhelm. "Wilhelm Loehe—100 Years Later." *Springfielder* 35 (December 1971): 191–196.

Klein, Ralph W. "Wilhelm Loehe and His Legacy." *Currents in Theology and Mission* 33, no. 2 (April 2006): 82–86.

Kleinig, Vernon. "Lutheran Liturgies from Martin Luther to Wilhelm Loehe." *Concordia Theological Quarterly* 62 (April, 1998): 125–144.

Korby, Kenneth F. "Loehe's Seelsorge for His Fellow Lutherans in America." *Concordia Historical Institute Quaterly* 45 (November, 1972): 227–246.

———."Wilhelm Loehe and Liturgical Renewal." *Essays and Reports of the Lutheran Historical Conference* 5 (1974): 57–84.

Kraft, Karl. "Missionary Activity of Wilhelm Loehe Among German-Lutherans in North America." (1982). ELCA Region 5 Archives, Dubuque, IA.

Loehe, Max. "Wilhelm Loehe: Neuendettelsau Influence in the Lutheran Church of Australia." *Springfielder* 35 (December, 1971): 183–190.

Lohrmann, Martin J. "A Monument to American Intolerance: The 'Open Questions' of Loehe's Iowa Synod in Their American Context." Seminar Paper, Lutheran Theological Seminary at Philadelphia, 2007.

Ludwig, Frieder. "Mission and Migration: Reflections on the Missionary Concept of Wilhelm Loehe." *Word & World* 24, no. 2 (Spring 2004): 157–164.

Marzolf, Dennis. "Loehe in *Logia*." *Logia* 17, no. 3 (2008): 5.

Meyer, Carl S. "Johann Konrad Wilhelm Loehe—In Memorium." *Concordia Theological Monthly* 43 (July–August 1972): 442–445.

Mundinger, Gerhard H. "Wilhelm Loehe." *Concordia Historical Institute Quarterly* 70, no. 1 (Spring 1997): 2–20.

Nessan, Craig L. "Loehe and His Coworkers in the Iowa Synod." *Currents in Theology and Mission* 33, no. 2 (April 2006): 138–144.

———. "Loehe in America: Two Historical Trajectories in the Missouri and Iowa Synods." *Logia* 17, no. 3 (2008): 19–26.

———. "Missionary God, Missionary Congregations." *Dialog: A Journal of Theology* 40, no. 2 (Summer 2001): 112–117.

———. "Missionary Theology and Wartburg Theological Seminary." *Currents in Theology and Mission* 31, no. 2 (April 2004): 85–95.

Nichol, Todd W. "Wilhelm Loehe, the Iowa Synod and the Ordained Ministry." *Lutheran Quarterly* 4 (Spring 1990): 11–29.

Ottersberg, Gerhard. "Response to Dr. Schaaf's Paper ('Wilhelm Loehe and the Ohio Synod')." *Lutheran Historical Conference* 5 (1974): 102–107.

———. "Wilhelm Loehe." *Lutheran Quarterly* 4 (1952): 170–90.

Pless, John T. "Loehe as Pastoral Theologian: The Discipline of the Shepherd." *Lutheran Theological Journal* 43 (August 2009): 110–117.

———. "The Lively Use of Loehe: Kenneth Korby's Contribution to a Renewed Reception of His Pastoral Theology in the Lutheran Church-

Missouri Synod" in *Wilhelm Löhe: Erbe und Vision* edited by Dietrich Blaufuß. Gütersloh: Gütersloher Verlaghaus, 2009, pp. 110–126.

———. "The Missionary Who Never Left Home." *The Lutheran Witness* 127, no. 2 (February 2008): 11–13.

———. "Wilhelm Loehe and the Missouri Synod: Forgotten Paternity or Living Legacy?" *Currents in Theology and Mission* 33, no. 2 (April 2006): 122–137.

Ratke, David C. "The Church in Motion: Wilhelm Loehe, Mission, and the Church Today." *Currents in Theology and Mission* 33, no. 2 (April 2006): 145–156.

———. "The Ecclesial Vision of Wilhelm Loehe." *Lutheran Forum* 33 (Fall 1999): 29–33.

———. "Wilhelm Loehe and His Significance for Mission and Ministry." *Word & World* 24, no. 2 (Summer 2004): 136–144.

———. "Wilhelm Loehe and the Catholicity of the Church." *Pro Ecclesia* 9, no. 3 (Summer 2000): 261–284.

———. "Wilhelm Loehe and Worship, Mission, and Renewal." *Cross Accent* 14, no. 3 (2006): 32–37.

Sasse, Hermann. "Walther and Loehe: On the Church." *Springfielder* 35 (December 1971): 176–182.

Schaaf, James L. "Father from Afar: Wilhelm Loehe and Concordia Theological Seminary in Fort Wayne." *Concordia Theological Quarterly* 60, no. 1–2 (January-April 1996): 47–73.

———. "Loehe und die Missouri-Synod." *Concordia Historical Institute* 45 (1972): 53–67.

———. "Loehe's Influence on Lutheran Mission in America." *Lutheran Theological Journal* 22 (1988): 120–134.

———. "Paul August Baugmart: Loehe's Third Sendling." *Lutheran Historical Conference* 15 (1994): 92–112.

———. "Wilhelm Loehe and the Missouri Synod". *Concordia Historical Institute Quarterly* 45 (1972): 53–67.

———. "Wilhelm Loehe and the Ohio Synod." *Essays and Reports of the Lutheran Historical Conference* 5 (1974): 85–101.

Schattauer, Thomas H. "The Löhe Alternative for Worship, Then and Now." *Word & World* 24, no. 2 (Spring 2004): 145–156.

———. "Sunday Worship at Neuendettelsau under Wilhelm Loehe." *Worship* 59 (1985): 370–84.

———. " 'Sung, Spoken, Lived': Worship as Communion and Mission in the Work of Wilhelm Loehe." *Currents in Theology and Mission* 33, no. 2 (April 2006): 113–121.

Schmalenberger, Jerry L. "Chasing Loehe's Ghost." *Lutheran Partners* 14, no. 2 (March-April 1998): 370–384.

Schmelder, William. "A Synod is Born." *Lutheran Witness* 116 (1997): 8–14.

Schwarz, Hans. "Wilhelm Loehe in the Context of the Nineteenth Century." *Currents in Theology and Mission* 33 no. 2 (April 2006): 93–104.

Steele, Elizabeth and Sally L. Kerr. "The Diaconate: Loehe's Legacy of Service to the Neighbor." *Word & World* 24, no. 2 (Spring 2004): 165–170.

Streng, William D. "Where Have All the Heroes Gone?" *The Lutheran Standard* 12, no. 7 (April 4, 1972): 11.

Suelflow, August R. "Centennial of the Neuendettelsau Deaconess Institute, 1845–1954." *Concordia Theological Monthly* 25 (Spring 1954): 672–674.

Sundberg, Walter. "Wilhelm Loehe on Pastoral Office and Liturgy." *Word & World* 24, no. 2 (Spring 2004): 190–197.

Trachte, Larry. "Wilhelm Loehe, Disciple." *Currents in Theology and Mission* 33, no. 2 (April 2006): 157–159.

von der Hoek, Stephen. "The Unique Contribution of Wilhelm Löhe to the Renewal of the Practice of Private Confession." *Lutheran Theological Journal* 42 (August 2008): 100–108.

Weber, Christian. "The Future of Loehe's Legacy." *Currents in Theology and Mission* 31, no. 2 (April 2004): 96–102.

Weiser, Frederick S. "Wilhelm Loehe: Lutheran Pioneer in Communal Ministry." *Una Sancta* 21 (1964): 43–51.

Wenz, Armin. "Ministry and Pastoral Theology of Löhe and Vilmar." *Logia* XVI (Holy Trinity 2007): 15–24.

Wiederaenders, Robert C. "Correspondence of Wilhelm Loehe in American Repositories." Dubuque: Archives, American Lutheran Church, 1969.

Wilson, H. S. "Embracing Global Christianity: A Missiological Challenge." *Currents in Theology and Mission* 33, no. 2 (April 2006): 160–173.

Winger, Thomas M. "The Relationship of Wilhelm Löhe to C. F. W. Walther," *Lutheran Theological Review* 7 (1994/1995): 107–132.

vii. Reviews and Lectures

Korby, Kenneth F. "Pastoral Theology in Ecclesiology Perspective: A Review of *Three Books About the Church*." The Cresset (April 1970): 17–19.

Nessan, Craig L. Review of Wilhelm Loehe. *Drei Buecher von der Kirche. 1854. Studienausgabe*, edited by Dietrich Blaufuss. *Lutheran Quarterly* 22, no.1 (Spring 2008): 87–88.

Ottersberg, Gerhard. "Wilhelm Loehe and Wartburg Theological Seminary." *Lecture on 100th Anniversary of Loehe's Death*, Waverly: Wartburg College, 1972.

Pless, John T. "Review of *Confession and Mission, Word and Sacrament: The Ecclesial Theology of Wilhelm Loehe* by David Ratke." *Lutheran Quarterly* 17 (Winter 2003): 487–490.

Weber, Christian. "The Future of Loehe's Legacy." Address delivered at Wartburg Theological Seminary, October 30, 2001.

Authors, *editors*

i. Primary Books **ii.** Primary Articles **iii.** Secondary Books **iv.** Chapters in Books **v.** Dissertations
vi. Secondary Articles **vii.** Reviews and Lectures

8.7.2008/DB

Concordia Publishing House

Similar to the peer review or "refereed" process used to publish professional and academic journals, the Peer Review process is designed to enable authors to publish book manuscripts through Concordia Publishing House. The Peer Review process is well-suited for smaller projects and textbook publication.

We aim to provide quality resources for congregations, church workers, seminaries, universities, and colleges. Our books are faithful to the Holy Scriptures and the Lutheran Confessions, promoting the rich theological heritage of the historic, creedal Church. Concordia Publishing House (CPH) is the publishing arm of The Lutheran Church—Missouri Synod. We develop, produce, and distribute (1) resources that support pastoral and congregational ministry, and (2) scholarly and professional books in exegetical, historical, dogmatic, and practical theology.

For more information, visit:
www.cph.org/PeerReview.